COMICS AND ADAPTATION

COMICS AND ADAPTATION

EDITED BY Benoît Mitaine, David Roche,
and Isabelle Schmitt-Pitiot

TRANSLATED BY Aarnoud Rommens
and David Roche

UNIVERSITY PRESS OF MISSISSIPPI / JACKSON

www.upress.state.ms.us

Designed by Peter D. Halverson

The University Press of Mississippi is a member of the Association of University Presses.

Originally published in 2015 by Presses Universitaires Blaise Pascal as *Bande dessinée et adaptation*

First printing 2018
∞

Library of Congress Cataloging-in-Publication Data

Names: Mitaine, Benoît. editor. | Roche, David, 1976– editor. translator. | Schmitt-Pitiot, Isabelle. translator. | Rommens, Aarnoud. translator. | Translation of: Mitaine, Benoît. Bande dessinée et adaptation.
Title: Comics and adaptation / edited by Benoît Mitaine, David Roche, and Isabelle Schmitt-Pitiot ; translated by Aarnoud Rommens and David Roche.
Description: Jackson : University Press of Mississippi, [2018] | "Originally published in 2015 by Presses Universitaires Blaise Pascal as Bande dessinée et adaptation." | Includes bibliographical references and index.
Identifiers: LCCN 2018003404| ISBN 9781496803375 (hardcover) | ISBN 9781496815323 (epub single) | ISBN 9781496815330 (epub institutional) | ISBN 9781496815347 (pdf single) | ISBN 9781496815354 (pdf institutional)
Subjects: LCSH: Comic books, strips, etc.—Adaptations. | Motion pictures and comic books. | Literature—Comic books, strips, etc.—History and criticism. | Film adaptations. | Television adaptations.
Classification: LCC PN1995.9.C36 C665 2018 | DDC 741.436—dc23 LC record available at https://lccn.loc.gov/2018003404

British Library Cataloging-in-Publication Data available

CONTENTS

PART II: FROM PANEL TO SCREEN AND BACK AGAIN

ACKNOWLEDGMENTS

For the 2018 Edition

We are very grateful to University Press of Mississippi for giving this book a chance, to the anonymous reviewer for her/his support and feedback, and to PU Blaise Pascal for their backing. Thanks to Leila Salisbury for her initial interest, and especially to Vijay Shah and Lisa McMurtray for seeing the project to the end with diligence and enthusiasm, even in the heat of the summer! It was a pleasure to work with copyeditor Peter Tonguette again.

Translations of non-English quotes are our own, unless the works cited include the authorized translation. More thanks than we can ever possibly muster are due to Aarnoud Rommens, whose painstaking work was precious, and warm thanks also to Jan Baetens for recommending Aarnoud! We'd also like to thank Jean-Paul Gabilliet, Christophe Gelly, Nicolas Labarre, and Shannon Wells-Lassagne (twice!) for their input on the translation, and the American publishers (Fantagraphics and IBooks Graphic Novel) for image reprint authorization.

As always, love to our families and friends.

For the 2015 Edition

We would like to thank the Presses Universitaires Blaise Pascal, especially Aurélie Boucheret, Sylviane Coyault, and Alain Montandon, who backed up this project early on, as well as Sylvie Crinquand and Myriam Segura-Pineiro from the Centre Interlangues (EA 4182) of the Université de Bourgogne. Thanks to Odile Wavresky, our wonderful librarian in Dijon, and to Sandra Eva Boschenhoff, who generously sent us the useful article she wrote with Frank Erik Pointer. This book, as well as the two symposiums in which it originated, received funding from the Conseil Régional de Bourgogne through the PARI "Les discours visuels," a project administered by the Centre Interlangues. We are grateful to all the speakers who attended the symposia, the authors who put in a lot of hard work in their chapters and abided by the deadlines. Finally, warm thanks are due to the artists (Robert Crumb and Lorenzo Mattoti) and publishers (Casterman, Edicions de Ponent, Ikusager), who graciously authorized us to reproduce certain images, and thanks to Jean-Paul, who knows why.

Comics and Adaptation

Introduction: Adapting Adaptation Studies to Comics Studies

DAVID ROCHE, ISABELLE SCHMITT-PITIOT, AND BENOÎT MITAINE

Many critical, historical, and theoretical studies devoted to comics state their intention to defend the medium as soon as the opening lines. This book abides by that tradition: studying comics remains, today, an act of aesthetic and political legitimatization, of which the insistent usage of the term "ninth art" by fans and scholars is just one of the many symptoms. It is only proper to acknowledge it.

If film studies gained recognition in the 1960s, with film departments opening in North American and British universities (Sklar 300; Leitch 244), research on comics and graphic novels really took off in the 1990s. By proving that comics, like paraliterature, should be considered as an aesthetic form with cultural import, Umberto Eco's 1962 essay "The Myth of Superman"[1] no doubt contributed to arousing interest in the medium. That same year, the Club des bandes dessinées (i.e., the Comics Club) was founded and the first issue of their journal, *Giff-Wiff*, was published; the association's board included Pierre Couperie, Jean-Claude Forest, Francis Lacassin, and filmmaker Alain Resnais, and counted Eco among its sympathizers (Groensteen, *Un Objet* 110–29). Books and articles by Pierre Fresnault-Deruelle (1982), Luc Boltanski (1975), Alain Rey (1978), and Francis Lacassin (1982) were published in the 1970s. In North America, some of the first texts on comics included how-to books by Stan Lee (1984), famous for writing for Marvel in the 1960s, and by Will Eisner (1985), author of *The Spirit* (1940–52) and *A Contract with God* (1978), which is often considered to be the first graphic novel. If Eisner's aim was, above all, pedagogical, his books do make an effort to conceptualize comics art despite a lack of theoretical framework; theorists of the 1990s and 2000s have often taken Eisner's ideas as a starting point. The huge success of several graphic novels in the 1980s and 1990s further encouraged the development of comics studies. Works like Alan Moore and Dave Gibbons's *Watchmen* (1986–87), featured in the ALL-TIME 100 Novels of Time Entertainment,[2] Art Spielgeman's *Maus* (1973–91), which was awarded the Pulitzer Prize in 1992, Chris Ware's *Jimmy Corrigan: The Smartest Kid on*

Earth (1993–2000), which received the Guardian First Book Award in 2001, and Marjane Satrapi's *Persepolis* (2000–2003) managed to reach an audience that went beyond the usual comic book readership (Gabilliet 100–101). The proliferation of adaptations based on comics and graphic novels since the 2000s has, in all likelihood, drawn the attention of film scholars (Goggin and Hassler-Forrest 3), as well as that of theorists of adaptation, intermediality, and transmedia. Several academic journals emerged in the 2000s: the *International Journal of Comic Art* in 1999, *ImageText* in 2004, *European Comic Art* in 2008, *Studies in Comics* and *Journal of Graphic Novels and Comics* in 2010, and *Comicalités* in 2011.[3] Clearly, comics studies have gained ground,[4] and university libraries increasingly have sections exclusively devoted to them. Today, the field is dominated by two approaches that somewhat resemble those that characterize contemporary film studies: a formalist/semiological/semiotic and (mainly) European approach, represented by such scholars as Benoît Peeters, Thierry Groensteen, and Philippe Marion, and a more North American approach, drawing mainly on cultural studies, evidenced by the University Press of Mississippi's impressive catalogue.[5]

For a long time, the term "adaptation" has been synonymous with film adaptation. George Bluestone's 1957 book marked the birth of film adaptation as a central concern of both film and literary studies. This interest gave way to a full-fledged branch in the wake of Brian McFarlane's 1996 *Novel to Film*, which calls into question the idea of fidelity that had long been the thread of discussions on film adaptation. In 1993, André Gaudreault and Thierry Groensteen organized a conference in Cerisy, France, entitled "La Transécriture," i.e., "transwriting"; the proceedings, published in 1998, contain several articles on comics and adaptation.[6] The Austenmania phenomenon of the 1990s may also have contributed to the increasing interest in film adaptation; countless books, articles, and dissertations have been written on successful films and TV productions like *Sense and Sensibility* (Ang Lee, 1995), *Pride and Prejudice* (BBC, 1995), *Emma* (Douglas McGrath, 1996), *Mansfield Park* (Patricia Rozema, 1999), *Bridget Jones's Diary* (Sharon Maguire, 2001), *Bride and Prejudice* (Gurinder Chadha, 2004), and *Pride & Prejudice* (Joe Wright, 2005).[7] The Association of Adaptation Studies was founded in 2006, and in 2008 two academic journals, *Adaptation* and *Journal of Adaptation in Film & Performance*, were launched.

Although the edited volume *Film Adaptation* (2000) deals exclusively with film adaptations of literary texts (mainly novels), its editor, James Naremore, regretted that most studies of adaptation showed little interest in other media and popular culture (1, 12). The publication of Linda Hutcheon's *A Theory of Adaptation* in 2006 was, in this respect, a major turning point. Defining adaptation as an intersemiotic transposition from one system of signs to another (16), a new encoding that adapts the source to a different play on conventions and signs, Hutcheon analyzes all sorts of media—illustrations, video games, theme parks, opera, ballet, and comics (xiv)—proposing, for instance, case studies of the different avatars of Carmen in literature, theater, and opera (153). Adaptation, for Hutcheon, can even be conceived from a Darwinian perspective. Reprising the theory Richard Dawkins developed in *The Selfish Gene* (176), she compares "stories" to "memes"—i.e., ideas that are transmitted by mutating in order to adapt to changes in the environment. In so doing, adaptation, which associates both conservation and novelty, becomes the process by which a cultural heritage of stories, characters, and myths survive through evolution (167). Her very inclusive approach does not, however, lead to a boundless definition of adaptation that would entirely equate it to intertextuality, even though the two are closely linked. Moreover, Hutcheon clearly shifts the discussion away from comparative discussions that often boil down to establishing a hierarchy between the adapted work and its adaptations: an adaptation is "a work that is second without being secondary" (9). She nonetheless raises the question of legitimacy by underlining the paradox that adaptations are often looked down on, even though they are increasingly popular on the contemporary artistic scene (2). Economic motivations alone cannot explain this adaptation craze, as the pleasure of the viewer or reader aware that s/he is consuming an adaptation always depends on a tension between his/her memory of the adapted work and a taste for novelty (172). Hutcheon identifies three criteria necessary to define an adaptation:

> (1) an acknowledged transposition of one or several works into a similar or different medium;
> (2) an act of both creative *and* interpretative "appropriation/salvaging" (meaning that the adaptation is not a mere copy);
> (3) "[a]n extended intertextual engagement with the adapted work." (8)

For Hutcheon, adaptation should be taken both as a product and a process[8] of creation and reception; adaptations must systematically be studied as palimpsests haunted by the works they adapt, the creative process resembling a kind of variation (8, 173–76). Her search for common denominators between media and genres allows her to distinguish between media like literary texts that function in the "telling/narrating" mode; those like drama and film that function in the "showing/performing" mode; and those like video games that offer a form of interaction with the receiver, sometimes even an experience of actual immersion, as in a theme park (10–15, 38–52). Thus, questions of fidelity and legitimacy are cast aside, as analysis focuses largely on the receiver's modes of engagement, which vary from one medium to another, each medium engaging differently with the mind and imagination.

The relationship between comics and adaptation, either with comics as the source or the adaptation, has received little critical attention, and this book proposes to make up for that oversight. At first glance, comics adaptations of literary works would seem to be less frequent than film or TV adaptations of comics (Vanderbeke 104), a phenomenon which has gained ground in the 2000s. The practice of adapting films and TV shows into comics expanded in the 1980s, with the American publisher Dark Horse making it one of its specialities (Gabilliet 100). Publishers like Dark Horse, Tokyopop, Marvel, and Del Rey have been releasing more and more adaptations of successful contemporary writers like Stephen King and Dean Koontz, collaborating closely with them in order to assert that the adaptations have been blessed by the original authors (Price 23–26). In both cases, the process involves not so much adapting the text itself as exploring the diegetic universe through spinoffs. These forms of adaptation are central to the transmedia marketing strategies developed in the era of the new Hollywood blockbuster (Sklar 339–41; Cook 51), notably since George Lucas's *Star Wars* (1977), when the Marvel comic adaptation came out at the same time as the film.

And yet, according to Sandra Eva Boschenhoff and Frank Erik Pointner, the false impression that adaptation concerns film more than comics is simply due to the fact that the former enjoys more limelight. In fact, comics adaptations of literary texts far outnumber film adaptations of comics, but the phenomenon is less visible because the books are published in smaller numbers (Pointner and Boschenhoff 87) and the publicity power of film producers largely outweighs that of comics publishers. A cursory glance at the number of adaptations made and the number of publishers (Casterman, Delcourt, Vent d'Ouest, etc.) having started collections entirely dedicated to adaptations leaves no doubt that literature, what with the number of classics that are now in the public domain, represents a godsend for many publishers, authors, and cartoonists, who are able to pick and choose among the cultural heritage of the World Republic of Letters. This phenomenon is nothing new, though its proportions arguably represent a break from the past; from the 1940s to the 1960s, the Gilberton Company published over 160 titles in its famous comic book series Classics Illustrated, selling approximately 200 million books (Gabilliet 28). Although comics adaptations of literary classics became a quasi-industry from the 1950s on, the practice of adaptation dates back to the very origins of comics. 1840 saw the first adaptation of a comic into a novel (a fairly unique case of novelization in the history of adaptation) by the founding father and first theoretician of comics, Rodolphe Töppfer (Groensteen and Peeters vii), who presented his artistic exploit in his preface to *The Voyages and Adventures of Dr. Festus*[9] (1833):

> This extraordinary story was composed thanks to processes that were equally extraordinary. Initially represented graphically in a series of sketches, it was then translated from these sketches into the following text. Today, the text and sketches are being published both together and separately. The same story exists, then, in two forms, but, as the Abbot of Saint-Réal cleverly observed, the differences between two similar things largely change their similarities. (V–VI)

Comics had hardly been invented before the first comics self-adaptation had been created![10] So it should come as a no surprise that Winsor McCay, another of the medium's genius forefathers, was also at the origin of some of the first comics adaptations, first for the music hall, then on film (Thompson and Bordwell 41):

> In 1980, almost three years after its creation, *Little Nemo*[11] was performed on Broadway as a musical and went on tour across the United States. [. . .] In 1911, McCay enthusiastically set off on the cartoon adventure. Having taken comics to heights unsurpassed, he became one of the pioneers of animation film. (Peeters, "Une exploration transmédiatique" 250)

Töpffer and McCay are proof that the possibilities of adaptation—self-adaptation, novelization, transposition to the stage or screen, and thus from what Hutcheon calls narrating to performing arts (*A Theory of Adaptation* 10)—were quickly explored. The fact that these adaptations were contemporary to the original creations and that they were the work of the inventors of comics almost suggests that the practice is consubstantial to the medium.

Adaptation has thus been an integral part of the history of comics from the very beginning, facilitated, no doubt, by the polysemiotic nature of a medium that draws its capacity to tell stories both from images[12] and words. As early as 1845, Töppfer called it a "literature in prints"; Fresnault-Deruelle (1972) spoke of the alliance between an "iconic" and a "linguistic message" (58), Alain Rey (1978) of the co-presence of "textual and figural values" (104), McCloud (1994) of an art of "juxtaposed pictorial and other images in deliberate sequence" (9), Groensteen (1999) of the "simultaneous mobilization of the entirety of codes (visual and discursive)" (*The System* 6), and Ann

Miller (2007) of a "narrative and visual art" (75). The heterogeneity of comics endows them with the capacity of being both the source and recipient in the process of adaptation; whether adapted or adapter, comics can greatly benefit from this process.

Indeed, comics adaptations of literary texts were driven, early on, by a desire for legitimacy, as well as by the newborn industry's interest in multiplying potential profits—McCay's adaptations of *Little Nemo* are a good example of this. As Linda Hutcheon has noted, the question of why to adapt a work points both to economic motives—adaptation has commercial value (86–88)—and cultural motives that imply a hierarchy within the arts (91). This phenomenon has been noted by film historians and adaptation theorists, who have underlined that, in the 1910s, the American film industry, determined not to get bogged down in the carnival rut, turned to adapting novels as a strategy, on the one hand, to attract the middle and upper classes, who controlled the economic and cultural capital as well as the instruments of consecration, and, on the other, to guarantee commercial success by benefiting from the notoriety of the author being adapted (Sklar 30, 45; Thompson and Bordwell 2; Leitch, *Adaptation* 27; Carcaud-Macaire and Clerc 17–18). Needless to say, comics also partake in these survival strategies that invite the "weak" to parasitically feed on the strengths of the "strong"; a parallel may be made with what Pascale Casanova says of the translation of novels written in dominated languages into dominant languages, a relationship she presents not only as a "naturalization" (in terms of identity) but also as a form of "literarization" she describes as an "act of consecration which gives access to literary visibility and existence" (191). Of course, the quest for legitimacy is logically and simultaneously accompanied by a quest for economic capital, which contributes equally, in its own way, to an increase in symbolic capital. In short, adaptation is a sort of missing link in the comics genome, which can be thought in terms of the evolution of the species (whereby to adapt is to survive), of publishing and authorial strategies (obtaining economic and symbolic profits), and as a cultural symptom of a society experiencing a shift from *logos* (word) to *eikôn* (image).

However, reducing adaptation exclusively to economic gain could lead us to forget that, when it comes to comics—a medium in which the artist's autonomy remains central, if only because it is not a costly medium to work in—adaptation often originates in the personal choice of an artist or author (and not a publisher). Hutcheon insists that it is also necessary to take into account the adapter's personal and political motives (*A Theory of Adaptation* 92–95). An author's emotional response to a given work (bliss, fear, admiration, etc.) may have made him want to express it in another artistic form (Alberto Breccia adapting H. P. Lovecraft immediately comes to mind). Now and again, adaptation can be the fruit of love rather than commercial interest—love for a work of art from another medium and love for the medium the artist uses as a means of expression. Adapting becomes, then, a challenge.

Apart from Sandra Eva Boschenhoff's recent *Tall Tales in Comic Diction*, most articles on comics and adaptation are case studies of the many film adaptations of comics, or of comics adaptations of literary texts, such as Paul Karasik and David Mazzucchelli's *City of Glass* (1994),[13] adapted from Paul Auster's 1985 novel, Stéphane Heuet's *Remembrance of Things Past*[14] (1998), or the many adaptations of the tales of Edgar Allan Poe.[15] We have found few articles dealing with this issue in a general or theoretical manner, except for those of Gilles Ciment[16] (1998) and Pascal Lefèvre (2007) on film adaptations of comics, and those of Dirk Vanderbeke (2010) and Frank Erik Pointer and Sandra Eva Boschenhoff (2010) on comics adaptations of literary texts. Gaudreault and Groensteen (1998), Jan Baetens (2009), Thomas Leitch (*Adaptation* 192–201), and Hutcheon (*A Theory of Adaptation* 88) briefly discuss comics as both adaptation and adapted.

For Lefèvre, who only deals with live-action cinema, the distinction between comics and cinema has to do, above all, with the ontologies of drawn and photographic images (2). Focusing on adaptation as a practice, he identifies four problems adapters are faced with (12):

(1) the length of the story. As comics are usually too long, the adaptation process involves elisions as well as additions (3–4);
(2) the specific characteristics of the layout of a comic book and of the composition of the film image. Comics are a "more spatial" medium that enables the reader to move back and forth from one panel to another, while cinema is a more linear form (5–6). Some adaptations, like *Hulk* (Ang Lee, 2003), thus resort to the split screen in order to imitate panels (Lefèvre 6; Boillat 47);
(3) the translation from drawn to photographic image. For Lefèvre, photography is deemed more "realistic," while drawn images are always, from the start, a "visual interpretation of the world" (8–9). Some adapters choose to emphasize the artificiality of the sets to evoke a comic book world (10). In this respect, *Dick Tracy* (Warren Beatty, 1990) represents, for Michael Cohen, the first attempt to reproduce a comics aesthetics in film (13); Alain Resnais's *I Want to Go Home* (1989) also comes to mind;
(4) sound. Comics is a "silent" medium (4) and is, in this respect, closer to silent cinema (11).

If points (1) and (4) equally concern film adaptations of literary texts, points (2) and (3) are more specific to film adaptations of comics. That said, Lefèvre seems to confuse the process of adaptation and a work which foregrounds its own status as an adaptation when he implies that it is desirable for the adapted work to transpire in the adaptation. Yet an adaptation has no obligation to visually resemble the adapted work. Moreover, what Alain Boillat, in a chapter in this volume, calls a "comics effect" can be produced in a film that is not an adaptation. What Lefèvre's article rightly draws attention to is that, when dealing with a film adaptation of a comic book or a graphic novel, the question of fidelity involves not only the story and the characters but also the "visual fidelity" of the adaptation (Hassler-Forest 120), since the comic book can practically serve as a storyboard.

Vanderbeke is also interested in the specificities of literary fiction and comics, but he reflects mainly on the way certain key aspects are dealt with in both media:

(1) the relationship between text and image. The fidelity to the source text sometimes leads to a lack of balance that is detrimental to the image, suggesting that the artist does not sufficiently trust the specificities of his/her own medium (108). Vanderbeke's analysis of *City of Glass* largely recalls Eisner's contention that the text should never be redundant, making the image a mere "illustration," but must aim at producing effects of contrast (*Comics and Sequential Art* 132);

(2) subjectivity. Comics are very much capable of evoking the inner life of characters, notably through the usage of color (112). In this respect, they are closer to literary fiction than to film;

(3) time. Sequentiality enables comics to both expand and compress time (113), in a similar manner as literary fiction;

(4) intertextuality. Pictural references can largely compensate for the medium's "lack of linguistic depth" (114);

(5) the implicit. The gutter, which many critics see as comics' discrete element *par excellence* (McCloud 60–93; Peeters, *Case* 31; Groensteen, *The System* 114–15; Goggin and Hassler-Forest 1), produces ellipses and forms of "unseen" equivalent, to some extent, to the unsaid in a literary text (Vanderbeke 116). This ties in with Groensteen's considerations regarding the intericonic "blank," whose function is to guarantee iconic interdependence, and which he compares to the "blanks"[17] Wolfgang Iser argues the reader fills in the act of reading (*The System* 114); Leitch has recently made a similar parallel (195).

Vanderbeke's approach is laudable insofar as he does attempt to offer a more theoretical and aesthetic perspective. Clearly, studying adaptation allows us, here, to compare two media and foreground their specificities. However, it is, no doubt, possible to draw the same conclusions without resorting to a corpus of adaptations. Moreover, Vanderbeke's selection of five key points raises further questions concerning the handling of space, narration, or narrative structure in both media.

Like Seymour Chatman in "What Novels Can Do That Films Can't (and Vice Versa)" (1981), Boeschenhoff and Pointner attempt to identify what comics do better than literature by exploring the specificity of each medium. Referring to Gotthold Ephraim Lessing's 1776 thesis according to which painting is a spatial art and literary fiction a temporal one (89), they posit that, like any image, comics are better suited to evoking both wide spaces or claustrophobic settings than literature (90–91), but perhaps less suited to translating allegory (104–5). The drawn image can, in effect, express inner states through objects, situations, or actions in a form of "objective correlative" (92). In comics, focalization is therefore not restricted to the text but equally involves the image (95).[18]

Considering how little has been written on the relationship between comics and adaptation, it seems necessary to take up Jan Baetens's (2009) suggestion to turn to the theory and practice of film adaptation in order to assess how some issues and methodologies can be adapted to comics studies. True, critical and theoretical writings on comics have found it difficult to free themselves from film studies. Even though the origins of sequential art go back to the eighteenth and nineteenth centuries, the literature on comics has often borrowed terms like "framing," "montage, " and "sequence" from film studies, claiming a sense of legitimacy from its filiation to film at the risk of ignoring the medium's specificities (Boillat 13, 18, 20)—Matteo Stefanelli goes so far as to conclude that "comics became a medium thanks to cinema" (299). It is certainly not out of a desire to legitimatize comics that we will draw on film adaptation studies, but only in order to identify the stakes common to adaptations in both media. The points of discussion that follow thus draw on some of the major writings on film adaptations that have proposed varying and complementary approaches: Linda Coremans (1990), Brian McFarlane (1996), James Naremore (2000), Robert Stam (2000 and 2005),[19] Michel Serceau (2007), Thomas Leitch (2009), and Francis Vanoye (2011).

The Criterion of Fidelity

Studies of comics adaptations have yet to free themselves from it, as Baetens (2009) and Boschenhoff and Pointner (88) have noted. If fidelity has, since McFarlane, repeatedly been called into question in film adaptation studies, in practice it still underlies many studies, even in books edited by critics who deplore it (Naremore 2; Leitch 4). This may be due to the fact that, historically, interest in film adaptation first arose within the field of literary studies and not film studies (Leitch 1). The notion of fidelity raises several questions, including the matter of what the adapter is supposed to be faithful to. Is it to the story, the characters, or the original author's intentions, if it is even possible to know what they were in the first place (Stam 15)? The canonical text is, then, upheld as a sort of transcendent benchmark (Leitch 3), instead of the many criteria that could enable an assessment of whether or not the adaptation is a "good" film, a "good" comic book or a "good" novel. In the end, analyzing an adaptation with this criterion in mind often leads to confirming the superiority of the literary work over the adaptation—and even that of literature over cinema (Stam 4); Leitch stresses that the opposite situation also exists, for instance when a filmmaker like Alfred Hitchcock deliberately adapts little-valued works in order to reinforce his own status as an auteur (5, 239). The concern with fidelity is, moreover, deeply rooted in the reader's psyche when it involves the adaptation of a literary work into a visual art because, as Stam has remarked, the adaptation then competes with the reader's "phantasmatic relation to the source text" (15). This is why fidelity also preoccupies artists and producers, who seek the approval of fans of the original, often for financial reasons. The "visual fidelity," which the transposition from one visual art to another seems to demand, can, as Leitch has noted, become outright "fetishism" in a film like *Sin City* (Robert Rodriguez and Frank Miller, 2005) (201). In the end, "fidelity to the medium" may be more important than fidelity to the source (Gaudreault and Marion, "Transécriture" 269).

Comparative Analysis

Stam describes it more precisely as a "comparative narratology." It raises the following question: "What events from the novel's story have been eliminated, added, or changed in the adaptation, and, more important, why?" (34). Additions, elisions and modifications,[20] including amplifications and condensations, must then be examined in order to determine "[w]hat principles orient the choices" (Stam 34). These principles can be grounded in financial economy (filming such and such a scene is too costly; Stam 43), narrative economy (expanding a short story, cutting a novel; Leitch 99)), or censorship and, more generally, surrounding ideological discourses (Stam 42). All these aspects may concern comics, which are subject to both length and censorship constraints (in the US, for instance, the Comics Code Authority was implemented in 1954). The problem with the comparative approach is that it is often haunted by the notion of fidelity when the source is considered to be an "unsurpassable model" (Baetens 2009). This is why Baetens (2009) advocates, rather, that its status as an adaptation be taken into account, which is what Leitch brilliantly does in *Film Adaptation and Its Discontents*. By relying on the writings of the narratologists and semiologists of each medium (for instance, Roland Barthes and Gérard Genette for literature; Christian Metz, David Bordwell, Kristin Thompson, Edward Branigan, and François Jost for film; Groensteen and Ann Miller for comics), comparative narratology could feed theoretical debates both on the specificities of each medium and on the history of research fields that have often developed concepts and terms borrowed from one another.

Analyzing "Media Specificity"

This has long been the approach favored in adaptation studies—namely, in the book edited by Gaudreault and Groensteen (Groensteen, "Fictions" 11). Its aim is to determine the possibilities of such and such medium. It tends to describe the process of adaptation as a form of "translation" or "transposition." The story is viewed as potentially stable, and the questions raised are thus: "Can stories 'migrate' from a less to a more appropriate medium? Do stories pre-exist their mediation?" (Stam 16); these questions recall Philippe Marion's notion of a story's "mediagenia"[21] or of a media's "adaptagenia" (Gaudreault, "Variations" 270–71; Groensteen, "Le processus" 276). It is with these questions in mind that assessing to what extent comics really represent an "intermediate form" between text and film acquires particular relevance (Vanderbeke 107). For Stam (2000), this approach is particularly fruitful when studying an adaptation that is very close to its source, like *The Grapes of Wrath* (20th Century Fox, John Ford, 1940), based on John Steinbeck's 1939 novel, because it is then possible to highlight that the change in media "generates an inevitable supplement" (55). However, this often leads full circle to one of the problems underscored above: this approach, especially when grounded in a comparative analysis of a canonical source and its adaptation, all too often leads to the conclusion that the original work is superior to the adaptation, and that literature is superior to cinema. For Leitch, "no matter how clever or audacious an adaptation is, the book will always be better than any adaptation because it is always *better at being itself*." Conversely, the opposite is equally true: the film is also better at being itself (16). Studying media specificity presents the additional danger of adopting an essentialist view of both media, as Baetens (2009) has emphasized:

> Without losing any of its relevance—because, whether we like it or not, we always need to know what various media "are," even if we have abandoned any essentialist ambition in the matter—the debate is now viewed in historical terms: any discussion of media specificity is seen as the symptom of a change in context, whereby the medium in question is required to reposition itself in the media ecology of the moment.

It is thus indispensable to consider the various media in context. When Francis Ford Coppola adapted *Dracula* in 1992, cinema was no longer what it was in 1922, the year that F. W. Murnau released *Nosferatu*. Comics have likewise evolved in the time between *Shermlock Shomes in the Hound of the Basketballs*, published in *Mad Magazine* in October 1954, and the many Arthur Conan Doyle adaptations that have proliferated since his stories became public domain in the 1980s (Levet 136). The study of the "ontology" of a medium is problematic insofar as any medium is constantly evolving. The question of media specificity cannot, therefore, ignore the medium's history.

The "Mythical" Dimension of the Story and/or Its Hero(es)

Michel Serceau posits that the power of the myth on which the source text is founded may be what justifies the numerous adaptations and re-adaptations (64). He then raises the question of what makes a character more or less mythical, and thus more or less adaptable. He remarks that Carmen, Tarzan, Frankenstein, and Dracula have often been adapted directly, whereas the shadow of Don Juan merely transpires through the motif of Don Juanism (84–86): "the recurrence—or even the resonance—of a myth's actantial schema must therefore be opposed to its not being embodied through its character(s)" (89). Indeed, an adaptation can also subject itself "to the mythical energy of another text or adaptation" (91). Serceau's thesis relies, then, on the essentialist assumption, identified by Stam, that the source narrative is a "kernel" that can be extracted (10), a topic endowed with an intrinsic configuration (Gaudreault and Marion 31), but it may partly explain why authors like Lovecraft who have invented a cosmogony, characters like Dracula, or superheroes from comics[22] are so frequently adapted. The question of a character's mythical potential is explored by Thomas Faye in his chapter on *El Cid* and is raised by Philippe Bourdier in the conclusion to his article on *Corto Maltese.*

Adaptation as Intertextuality

Adaptation critics and theorists (notably Coremans, Stam, Naremore, Hutcheon, Leitch, and Vanoye) now consider adaptation to be an aspect of the broader phenomenon of intertextuality. Relying on the writings of Mikhaïl Bakhtin and Genette (26–27), Stam describes adaptation as a "hypertext"[23] derived from a "hypotext" that precedes it, and posits that adaptations are caught up "in an endless process of recycling, transformation, and transmutation, with no clear point of origin" (31); movie tie-ins can even be seen as elements of the "paratext" (Stam 28), as Dick Tomasovic's chapter on film adaptations of Marvel comics evidences. Leitch calls into question the hierarchy implied in the hypotext/hypertext model;[24] for him, adaptation doesn't so much presuppose a relationship between the intertext and the source text, but rather a relationship between two intertexts, since all texts rely on intertextuality (17). Leitch's study of Biblical adaptations, for instance, aims at revealing how the Scriptures, though they position themselves as a "prototext," equally participate in intertexuality (66). However, in order to avoid a sort of leveling of all texts, he proposes a typology from adaptation to allusion, defining ten postures that a "hypertext" can take in relation to a prior text:

(1) "celebration." It attempts to reproduce the source work according to four modes: "curatorial adaptation," e.g., many BBC adaptations of literary classics; "replication," e.g., the first version of *Greed* (MGM, Erich von Stroheim, 1924), an adaptation of Frank Norris's *McTeague* that lasted twenty-three hours; "homage," e.g., *Nosferatu* (Werner Herzog, 1979); and "heritage adaptation" evidencing nostalgia for the source's time-setting, e.g., *The Great Gatsby* (Jack Clayton, 1974) (96–97);

(2) "adjustment." Leitch contends that this is the most common posture. It implies the necessity to modify the work according to five strategies: "condensation," "amplification," "modification," "updating," i.e., transposing the story in a contemporary world, and the "superposition" of several sources, e.g., the reference to Shakespeare's play in *Cleopatra* (Joseph L. Mankiewicz, 1963) (98–103);

(3) "neoclassical imitation." It views history in terms of cycles and reprises an old model in order to offer a critique or even satire of contemporary culture. Examples: *Richard III* (Richard Loncraine, 1993), *Clueless* (Amy Heckerling, 1993), based on Austen's *Emma* (103–4), *Tamara Drewe* (2007), the graphic novel by Posy Simmonds and the movie by Stephen Frears (2010), which transpose Thomas Hardy's 1874 novel *Far from the Madding Crowd* to contemporary England;

(4) "revision." It evidences a desire to re-evaluate the past (106) and effects what Leitch called a "demystifying critique" (63). For instance, *Mansfield Park* (1999) brings to the fore the slave trade underlying the narrative of Austen's novel (Leitch 107 ; Wells-Lassange 193–97);

(5) "colonization." It involves appropriating the source work and modifying the cultural framework of the story in order to endow it with new meaning (109). On the one hand, these adaptations assert the universality of the story and even its topic, while, on the other, they highlight the cultural and historical specificities of the source and the adaptation. *Ran* (Akira Kurosawa, 1985) and *Bride and Prejudice* (2004) are prime examples (109–10);

(6) "(meta)commentary or deconstruction." The adaptation takes on a reflexive posture vis-à-vis its status as an adaptation (111). Examples: *The French Lieutenant's Woman* (Karel Reisz, 1981) and *Adaptation* (Spike Jonze, 2002) (112–13). Adaptations and remakes tend to limit this posture to their prologue or opening credits, underlining their relation to the source at least partly for economic reasons. This is the case in the remake *The Texas Chainsaw Massacre* (Marcus Nispel, 2003) (Roche 133–35) and in many adaptations of Marvel comics, as Alain Boillat demonstrates in his chapter;

(7) "analogy." A parallel is established between certain elements of two works (113). For example, the diegesis of *Bridget Jones's Diary* (Sharon Maguire, 2001) recalls Austen's *Pride and Prejudice*, but the heroine hardly resembles Elizabeth Bennet (133);

Leitch then refers to Genette's categories[25] of (8) "parody" and "pastiche" (116), (9) "imitation" (120), and (10) "allusion" (121). These ten postures can be combined in the same adaptation, as in *Romeo+Juliet* (Baz Lurhmann, 1996) (123–25). If Leitch seems to want to identify the various postures a work can take in relation to another, the fact that he calls them "strategies" (123) indicates that they can be wholly intentional on the part of the adapters. Analyzing them may then lead to determining whether or not they are deliberate, and thus assessing the adapters' degree of success, as well as the coherence of these postures when they are combined. As these "strategies" exist independently of media specificity, it is possible to resort to them to describe the relationship between two works in different media. Thus, in this book, Benoît Mitaine's analysis of *El hombre descuadernado* proves that the authors' strategy involves at least three postures: "adjustment," "colonization," and "(meta)commentary."

The relationship between adaptation and parody is paramount. The majority of French and Belgium comics and American comic strips tends to be humoristic. For Groensteen (2010), one of the main forms humor takes in comics is parody, a form of intertexuality that is closely related to adaptation.[26] Adaptation studies generally describe the practice of adaptation as a quasi-surgical transformation (removal, graft, transfusion), which introduces ideological modifications due to the choices made by the adapters, but does not necessarily constitute a deliberately subversive project endowed with a critical intent aiming at bringing about change and destabilizing the norm. Some even seem to view adaptation as bathing in a sort of baptismal grace, making it a neutral process in which works migrate from one medium to another. Conversely, parody, because it introduces a distance or gap, casts a critical light on the hypotext, even when it is considered "inoffensive." Parody always effects an effort to "demystify the 'sacrosanct name of the author' and 'to desacralize the origin of the text'" (Hutcheon, *Parody* 5). While adaptation is described as a mostly unaggressive[27] and evolutionary (in the Darwinian sense) cultural practice—"[a]daptation is how stories evolve and mutate to fit new times and different places" (Hutcheon, *Adaptation* 176)—parody, because of its transgressive[28] potential, is described as "transformative" (Hutcheon, *Parody* 101). Parody is not intent on patiently adapting itself to contemporary times, but, rather, on adapting modern times to new forms. If adaptation sometimes unintentionally makes way for pastiche, as Baetens argues in the first chapter of this book, parody remains a privileged means of producing a derivative work capable of expressing the tension between homage and critique; adaptation, however, would express, though often unintentionally, the tension between homage and disavowal, as Leitch has argued in his article on remakes ("Twice-Told" 55) and as Alain Boillat contends in his chapter. In the end, parody and adaptation can both be viewed as symptoms shedding new light on an era but they have divergent intentions. While parody is "a symptom of historical processes which invalidate the normal authenticity of primary forms" (Hutcheon, *Parody* 36), adaptation is a historical process which facilitates the access to a "better understanding of the literary values of a given moment," as Baetens concludes in the first chapter of this book.

Adaptation and Ideology

The politics of both adapted and adaptation must be taken into consideration in relation to their specific contexts (Stam 42). This approach is dominant in the numerous case studies based on a cultural studies methodology. Dan Hassler-Forest, for instance, argues that *300* (Zack Snyder, 2006) is more reactionary than Frank Miller's 1998 graphic novel because the film's Trojan warriors, torn between the threat of foreign tyranny and domestic political corruption (122), also embody the values of the American family (125), while the graphic novel mainly emphasizes "the power of mythological narratives and storytelling in cementing one's own immortality" (124). Danielle Chaperon deplores that Alan Moore's critique of Thatcherite Great Britain has entirely disappeared from *V for Vendetta* (James McTeigue, 2005), which offers a less ambiguous subtext in terms of ethics and politics (324). Nevertheless, the contemporary transposition operated by the film invites astute comparisons between the Thatcher administration of the 1980s and the Blair and Bush Jr. administrations of the 2000s, and shows how the figure of V can incarnate revolt against different forms of totalitarian regimes or societies perceived as such; the Anonymous movement's appropriation of V's apparel obviously comes to mind. Jean-Paul Gabilliet's chapter on *Fritz the Cat* (Ralph Bakshi, 1972) in this volume proves that a few years between adapted and adaptation suffice to provide differing political perspectives on a given context; in this case, the differences largely stem from the artists' divergent backgrounds. Thus, the subtext of the source text should not be considered as stable. Indeed, Stam (2000) insists on the fact that adaptations can sometimes allow one to re-evaluate the source by "shed[ding] a new cultural light on the novel"[29] (63); for instance, adaptations of *Robinson Crusoe* from *Man Friday* (Jack Gold, 1975) on have brought out the novel's latent homoeroticism, which was, no doubt, not at all obvious to Defoe's contemporaries (67).

Logophilia vs. Image Culture

Stam believes that a "fourth, related source of hostility to film and adaptations is the obverse form of iconophobia, to wit logophilia, or the valorization of the verbal, typical of cultures rooted in the sacred word of the 'religions of the book'" (6). It is highly likely that comics also suffer from logophilia coupled with iconophobia. Adaptations of text into image could, however, be seen as the sign of changing cultural practices that are both symptomatic and systemic, insofar as they could mark the beginning of a weakening of the very logocentrism upon which the Western world has constructed itself throughout the last millennium. The novel could be the first victim of these changing times, largely weakened by modernity's lack of time and the inexorable advance of multimedia devices designed for images more than words. True, the thesis of the death of the novel and the demise of reading already existed in the 1950s, therefore inviting us to consider with caution the contention according to which "the passage from written stories to image stories could actually be literature's salvation, a sort of sanctuary to survive in while waiting for better times to come" (Baetens,[30] "Roman graphique" 206). It is, however, less disputable that, in the minds of publishers and prescribers (notably the authors and designers of schoolbooks), adaptation serves as a sort of cultural transmitter meant to lead the young reader to the original work (Groensteen, "Fictions" 20). Viewed in this light, adaptation would be nothing more than a "go-between," an "agent" for literature (Baetens, "Roman graphique" 206). Such a view of adaptation is pernicious because it ultimately hierarchizes the arts and considers comics adaptations (and comics in general) as a functional sub-literature. If there is no doubt that "traditional literature" continues to exercise its influence on, and hold over, both comics and even cinema, it is equally true that the hierarchy between narrative arts (high culture vs. low culture) has clearly been following a process of effacement for several decades, as theorists of postmodernism have argued at length (Hutcheon, *The Politics* 18; Jameson 63; Stam 8–10). Although it is possible and even likely that, historically, adaptation has contributed to legitimatizing comics, comics adaptations do remain a minor category compared to the thousands of "original" works published every year, unlike the film industry where 40 percent of the films released in 1998 were, in Naremore's estimate, adaptations (10). Moreover, the multiplication of film adaptations based on comics and graphic novels is a form of consecration, making comics less an indebted, adapting medium than a creative, adapted medium.

■ ■ ■

The chapters that follow offer both theoretical essays and case studies that explore the questions raised by adaptation and intermediality. While they focus on European and American comics, we hope some of the theses developed here will also prove useful to studies of Japanese and South American comics. The authors have tried to avoid a binary approach that would involve assessing the gap between the source and its adaptation in terms of the quality or even the "dignity" of the adaptation compared with the original work, and have refrained from reasoning in terms of losses and benefits, or of a hierarchy between hypotext and hypertext. In any case, the adaptations are studied both as specific works and in their media specificity, with comics in the first part, cinema and TV shows in the second. Attention is paid to the forms they take when they betray their lineage and reveal themselves as adaptations, thereby encouraging the reader or viewer to reconsider the source.

The first part deals with comics adaptations of literary texts. The five case studies follow the lead of Baetens's theoretical chapter by systematically viewing adaptation as a process. Most chapters are grounded in Hucheon's definition of adaptation as "an extended, deliberate, announced revisitation of a particular work of art" (*A Theory of Adaptation* 170). However, they endeavor to build on Hutcheon's thesis by showing the extent to which the dynamics of adaptation turn out to be necessary, like the new performance of a musical score, insofar as they redefine the boundary between author and reader. By recalling that the enunciation of any work is always multiple (Baetens), the authors insist that the source is a voice among others in a polyphony that is common to both adaptations and comics, which are multimodal by nature (Faye, Labarre).

The form an adaptation takes is intimately bound to its purpose. In other words, the question "How to adapt?" largely depends on the question "Why adapt?" If didactic adaptations are meant to illustrate the classics and facilitate a young readership's access to them by utilizing as clear a line as possible, they nonetheless represent an intersemiotic enterprise, as they allow the work of fiction to develop through other means than the written word. Thus, because comics represent a multimodal discourse of their own through juxtaposed images and the visual co-presence of different sign systems (Faye, Labarre), they can, for instance, call into question and even undo the established representations of mythical characters (Faye), thereby participating in the work's inscription within a specific historical context of production and reception (Labarre). Likewise, displaying their own lineage through a network of references that go beyond the source work can enable adaptations to redefine a genre through appropriation, as Tardi has done with noir (Gelly).

Various levels of distance vis-à-vis the source are involved in comics adaptations. Sometimes the adaptation strives to produce a non-figurative image, undermining traditional narration, so that the act of reading is then torn between linearity, on the one hand, and the contemplation of images, on the other, in a process associating global and fragmented reading (Caraballo). In this case, adapting a text into comics leads to the production of a composite object that, because of the nature of the transposition and the dialogue between word and image inherent in the medium, offers the reader multiple points of entry. This hybridity is particularly appropriate for genres like detective fiction (Gelly) and the Fantastic (Mitaine), or for more personal works incorporating biographical and autobiographical elements (Caraballo, Mitaine); the freedom involved in producing such works allows for various hybrid strategies.

Most chapters also examine the author's stance by studying the choices made by the adapters, whether they attempt to efface themselves or assert their own personal style, both approaches occasionally merging in a pastiche (Baetens). Paradoxically, adaptation can sometimes allow an artist to "free" himself from the story and concentrate exclusively on his own style (Gelly). From an intermedial perspective, this is but one of the many challenges any medium presents other media with.

The second part devoted to film adaptations of comics shows that they, too, are palimpsests affected by the medium of the source. Sometimes they even offer particular effects that recall the source and introduce a reflexive dimension—for instance, by resorting to split screens or various avatars of the freeze-frame (Boillat). In many cases, the film attempts to display its composite nature by both referring to the source and relying on its own characteristics, thereby drawing attention to a process of visual creation that can evolve depending on the degree of visual continuity between the various modes of representation. Thus, animation films adapting comics employ specific strategies that distinguish them from live-action films; for instance, they expand the possibilities of the roughly sketched settings of the original comic book (Bourdier) or indulge in an experience of extreme hybridity wherein actors animate their own virtual bodies (Floquet).

Whether they are animation or live-action films, these adaptations enable an actualization of the features of the protagonists, who are given voices and bodies, by producing shifting combinations between character, persona and person, a phenomenon reinforced by the relationship established between drawn and embodied characters, especially when the character is imbued with an aura of celebrity, like Fritz the Cat (Gabilliet) or Corto Maltese (Bourdier). Moreover, technical advances can modify the actors' bodies in spectacular action scenes that recall cinema's carnival origins (Tomasovic), the film's special effects and comics source combining and conflicting to create a new filmic material where human actors, for example, are made less realistic in order to resemble the comic book characters they embody (Floquet).

Adapting a medium that plays on the tension between the autonomy of the individual panel and the juxtaposition of images creates a split in the viewing experience, as well as a tension between homage and disavowal vis-à-vis the source (Boillat). This division can be reinforced when an autobiographical graphic novel and the documentary that adapts it—the Spanish film *María y yo* (Félix Fernández de Castro, 2010) comes to mind—associate various modes of representation, such as drawing, text, or photography, because the didactic intent at its heart calls for the invention of an appropriate form of expression to depict a special individual and reverse the views that person is usually subjected to.

The duality of film adaptations of comics can also be considered from a historical perspective, when an adaptation mingles fidelity and deviation, introducing ideological changes due to a gap in time and underlying political divergences (Gabilliet). These adaptations are further marked by their respective economic and cultural contexts; indeed, film adaptations are usually required to make a substantial return, attracting different and larger audiences than comics. Films characterized by intermediality, especially superhero movies, have emerged since the beginning of the 2000s, due to this policy to expand and renew the audience. The significance of the upheaval of hierarchy and the upsetting of chronology is such that it is sometimes difficult to tell adapted and adaptation apart, all the more so as comics and cinema are no longer the only media involved in these economic and creative principles that involve many industry sectors (Tomasovic, Wells-Lassagne).

These increasingly interactive networks, boosted by mass culture's logic of horizontal integration, produce transmedia stories that integrate reflexive postures within mass audience products. Thus, even a TV show aimed at a wide audience can thematize adaptation by establishing a constant dialogue between the audiovisual source and the comics via the tie-ins present both within the diegesis and in bookshops (Wells-Lassagne). This evolution points to the *raison d'être* underlying any adaptation, a process that should always be analyzed in terms of desire, whether it be that of the author, publisher, or producer, or the reader/viewer's desire to reread, reprise, or rewatch works which, caught up in a nexus of several media and genres, never cease to be renewed.

Whether they deal with comics adaptations of literary texts or film and TV adaptations of comics, most of the authors insist on the loss of stable points of reference within what Henry Jenkins calls a convergence culture, where it is no longer possible to confine a work to one medium. Today, adaptation seems to be less about transposing a story, characters, or a diegesis from one medium to another, and more about adding to a universe, as in the case of spinoffs and tie-ins, following a practice in which the work seems to migrate in order to adapt and survive within changing production and reception contexts. If some may consider the effacement of the limits between media to be a loss resulting in the leveling of the hierarchy between more or less legitimate cultural products, the contributors to this book do not indulge in nostalgia, but insist, rather, on the inventiveness and vitality of these complex and bountiful works.

Notes

1. Eco's article was published in English in 1972 and in French in 1976. Therein, Eco examines the narrative and ideological incoherencies of the comic book character, stemming from the fact that the quasi-immortal superman's actions lead him to paradoxically consume himself anyway (16). "A Reading of Steve Canyon" (1964) was published in English in 1976 and in French in 1985.

2. http://entertainment.time.com/2005/10/16/all-time-100-novels/slide/watchmen-1986-by-alan-moore-dave-gibbons. Accessed on December 22, 2015.

3. The *Comics Journal*, founded in 1976, publishes interviews and book reviews.

4. See the bibliographies published by Norbert Spehner in 2005, by Jean-Paul Gabilliet in 2010, and by Matteo Stefanelli in 2012.

5. http://www.upress.state.ms.us/category/comics_popular_culture. Accessed on December 22, 2014.

6. The articles by Thierry Groensteen, André Gaudreault, and Philippe Marion, and by Gilles Ciment, Jacques Samson, and Benoît Peeters focus entirely or partly on comics.

7. For instance, *Jane Austen in Hollywood* (1998), edited by Linda Troost and Sayre Greenfield, Sue Parrill's *Jane Austen on Film and Television* (2002), and *The Cinematic Jane Austen* (2009), edited by David Monaghan, Ariane Hudelet, and John Wiltshire.

8. Gaudreault has suggested that "adaptation" is a "method [*procédé*]," whereas what he and Marion call "transwriting" is a "procedure [*processus*]" ("Variations" 268).

9. The novelization of *Dr. Festus* can be downloaded for free here: http://www.ebooks-bnr.com/nos-ebooks. Accessed on December 24, 2014.

10. It is difficult to pinpoint exactly the birth of comics. For Groensteen and Peters (1994), comics started in the 1830s with the Swiss artist Rodolphe Töpffer. Other scholars go even further back in time: Smolderen (2009) points to William Hogart's engravings (from 1732 on); David Kunzle (1973) to the beginning of the printing press and thus to Gutemberg; and others go as far back as the Bayeux tapestries or even rock paintings (Altarriba, "Introducción" 10–11). Though Groensteen and Peeters's view is widely shared in Europe, North American scholars tend to see Richard F. Outcault's Yellow Kid as the beginning of comics. If Töpffer had invented many comics techniques, comics became a part of popular culture and mass media in the US at the end of the nineteenth century.

11. The *Little Nemo in Slumberland* comic strip was first published in the *New York Herald* in 1905. Bud Fischer followed McCay's lead with his *Mutt and Jeff* comic strip, first published in 1911 and adapted in 1916 (Thompson and Bordwell 149).

12. Groensteen disagrees with this view, since he argues that comics have repeatedly proven to be capable of telling a story without words and are thus by no means subjected to their twofold semiotic nature. Thus, he considers comics to be a "predominantly visual narrative form" (*The System* 12).

13. See, for instance, David Coughlan's 2006 article or Martha Kuhlman's 2009 article.

14. See, for instance, Sjef Houppermans's 2008 article or Guillaume Perrier's 2012 article.

15. See, for instance, Jacques Samson's 1998 article, Derek Parker Royal's 2006 and 2007 articles, Mary J. Couzelis's 2012 article, and M. Thomas Inge's 2012 article.

16. Ciment notes that many contemporary "film adaptations of comics resort to a musical connotation" (207).

17. Groensteen seems to use Iser's term in a more restrictive sense. For Iser, the blank is not just a texual one: "It is an empty space which both provokes and guides the ideational activity. In this respect, it is a basic element of the interaction between text and reader" (194–95).

18. Boschenhoff and Pointner's usage of "focalization" recalls François Jost's redefinition of Genette, that is that focalization corresponds to "the cognitive point of view of the story" (Gaudreault and Jost 130). The distinction Jost makes between focalization and what he calls "ocularization"—i.e., the relationship between the image and the characters' vision (Gaudreault and Jost 130)—could be relevant to comics studies.

19. All references are to Stam's 2005 introduction to *Literature and Film*, which is a longer version of the 2000 article published in *Film Adaptation*, edited by Naremore, except if the 2000 text is indicated as the source.

20. Groensteen proposes four types of modifications: of dramatic situations, enunciative situations, characters, and time and place ("Le processus" 276).

21. For Marion, "mediagenia is, then, the evaluation of a 'range': that of the *reaction* indicating the more or less successful fusion of a narration and its mediatization, within the context—which also comes into play—of the horizon of expectations of a given genre. Assessing the mediagenia of a story, thus, implies attempting to observe and apprehend the dynamics of an interfertilization" (86). It could be said that Marion's notion is somewhat essentialist, but it is tempered in the following lines: "The *mediagenic treatment* thus designates how a media might have encountered the facet of that great story which best suited it. And vice versa" (87). We would like to insist on the word "facet," which implies not so much an adequateness between the story and its medium, but rather between the story and *the way* that story *is approached* through this medium. Creative possibilities are, then, freed from the threat of essentialism.

22. For Eco, Superman has, from the start and by definition, all the characteristics of the mythic character ("The Myth" 15).

23. These terms are defined by Genette in *Palimpsests* (5).

24. Stam actually agrees with Leitch, as he insists that the writings of Jacques Derrida invite us to call into question the notions of "original" and "copy" (8), but he does not carry the idea to its logical conclusion.

25. See chapters I to VII of *Palimpsests*.

26. It seems that a work's status as an adaptation is, above all, determined on a pragmatic level. Saying that a parody is a parodic adaptation would, then, be a question of quantity; parodying just a sentence or a scene would not necessarily be considered an adaptation.

27. This view should be qualified when an adaptation aims at denying or entirely supplanting its source.

28. Parody is only partially transgressive because, as Hutcheon notes (*Parody* 101), it is always at the same time transgressive and conservative insofar as it repeats (and respects) a part of the adapted work. Parody would, therefore, have more to do with subversion.

29. This idea can be related to Arthur C. Danto's contention that the art world is characterized by "the retroactive enrichment of entities" (583). Jean-Marie Schaeffer furthers this idea when he argues that, "as soon as an innovative work introduces a new artistic predicate, all prior existing works are automatically attributed the opposite predicate" (142–43). Both Marie-Claire Ropars-Wuilleumier (135) and Groensteen ("Le Processus" 277) develop this idea in *La Transécriture*.

30. Note that Baetens is merely evoking this theory which he distances himself from by cautiously resorting to the conditional mode.

Works Cited

Baetens, Jan. "Littérature et bande dessinée : Enjeux et limites." *Cahiers de Narratologie* 16 (2009). http://narratologie.revues.org/974. Accessed on December 27, 2014.

Baetens, Jan. "Le Roman graphique." *La Bande dessinée : une médiaculture*. Eds. Éric Maigret and Matteo Stefanelli. Paris: Armand Colin, 2012. 200–216.

Bluestone, George. *Novels into Film*. Baltimore: Johns Hopkins University Press, 2003 [1957].

Boillat, Alain, ed. "Prolégomènes à une réflexion sur les formes et les enjeux d'un dialogue intermédial : Essai sur quelques rencontres entre la bande dessinée et le cinéma." *Les Cases à l'écran : Bande dessinée et cinéma en dialogue*. Genève: Georg, 2010. 25–121.

Boltanski, Luc. "La constitution du champ de la bande dessinée." *Actes de la recherche en sciences sociales* 1 (January 1975): 37–59.

Bordwell, David. *Narration in the Fiction Film*. Madison: University of Wisconsin Press, 1985.

Boschenhoff, Sandra Eva. *Tall Tales in Comic Diction: From Literature to Graphic Fiction; an Intermedial Analysis of Comic Adaptations of Literary Texts*. Trier: WVT Wiss. Verlag, 2013.

Casanova, Pascale. *La République mondiale des lettres*. Paris: Seuil, 1999.

Chaperon, Danielle. "Maladaptation ! (autour de *V pour Vendetta* de David Lloyd et Alan Moore)." *Les Cases à l'écran*. Ed. Alain Boillat. Genève: Georg, 2010. 303–28.

Ciment, Gilles. "Des *comics* au *musical*: un genre translatif." *La Transécriture*. Eds. André Gaudreault and Thierry Groensteen. Québec and Angoulême: Editions Nota Bene / CNBDI, 1998. 187–214.

Cook, David A. *Lost Illusions: American Cinema in the Shadow of Watergate and Vietnam, 1970–1979*. Berkeley, Los Angeles, and London: University of California Press, 2000.

Coremans, Linda. *La Transformation filmique : Du* Contesto *à* Cadaveri Eccelenti. Bern, Frankfurt, and New York: Peter Lang, 1990.

Coughlan, David. "*Paul Auster's* City of Glass: The Graphic Novel." *MFS* 52.4 (Winter 2006): 832–54.

Couzelis, Mary J. "What Can 'The Tell-Tale Heart' Tell about Gender?" *Adapting Poe: Re-Imaginings in Popular Culture*. Eds. Dennis R. Perry and Carl H. Sederholm. New York: Palgrave Macmillan, 2012. 217–29.

Danto, Arthur C. "The Artworld." *Journal of Philosophy* 61.19 (October 1964): 571–84.

Dawkins, Richard. *The Selfish Gene*. New York and Oxford: Oxford University Press, 1976, 1989.

Eco, Umberto. "The Myth of Superhuman" (1962). Trans. Natalie Chilton. *Diacritics* 2.1 (Spring 1972): 14–22.

Eco, Umberto. "A Reading of Steve Canyon" (1964). Trans. Bruce Merry. *Comic Iconoclasm*. Ed. Shenna Wagstaff. London: Institute of Contemporary Arts, 1988. 20–25.

Eisner, Will. *Comics and Sequential Art: Principles and Practices from the Legendary Cartoonist*. New York and London: Norton, 2008 [1985].

Eisner, Will. *Expressive Anatomy for Comics and Narrative: Principles and Practices from the Legendary Cartoonist*. New York and London: Norton, 2008.

Eisner, Will. *Graphic Storytelling and Visual Narrative: Principles and Practices from the Legendary Cartoonist*. New York and London: Norton, 2008 [1996].

Fresnault-Deruelle, Pierre. *La Bande dessinée : Essai d'analyse sémiotique*. Paris: Hachette, 1972.

Gabilliet, Jean-Paul. "Essai bibliographique." *Transatlantica* 9.1 (2010). http://transatlantica.revues.org/4934. Accessed on January 13, 2015.

Gabilliet, Jean-Paul. *Of Comics and Men: A Cultural History of American Comic Books*. Jackson: University Press of Mississippi, 2009 [2005].

Gaudreault, André. "Variations sur une problématique." *La Transécriture*. Eds. André Gaudreault and Thierry Groensteen. Québec and Angoulême: Editions Nota Bene / CNBDI, 1998. 267–71.

Gaudreault, André, and Thierry Groensteen, eds. *La Transécriture : Pour une théorie de l'adaptation*. Québec and Angoulême: Editions Nota Bene / CNBDI, 1998.

Gaudreault, André, and François Jost. *Le Récit filmique : Cinéma et récit II*. Paris: Nathan, 1990.

Gaudreault, André, and Philippe Marion. "Transécriture et médiatique narrative : l'enjeu de l'intermédialité." *La Transécriture*. Eds. André Gaudreault and Thierry Groensteen. Québec and Angoulême: Editions Nota Bene / CNBDI, 1998. 31–52.

Genette, Gérard. *Figures III*. Paris: Seuil, 1972.

Genette, Gérard. *Palimpsests: Literature in the Second Degree*. Trans. Channa Newman and Claude Doubinsky. Lincoln: University of Nebraska Press, 1997 [1982].

Goggin, Joyce, and Dan Hassler-Forest, eds. *The Rise and Reason of Comics and Graphic Literature*. Jefferson, NC, and London: McFarland, 2010.

Groensteen, Thierry. *Comics and Narration*. Trans. Ann Miller. Jackson: University Press of Mississippi, 2013 [2011].

Groensteen, Thierry. "Fictions sans frontières." *La Transécriture*. Eds. André Gaudreault and Thierry Groensteen. Québec and Angoulême: Editions Nota Bene / CNBDI, 1998. 9–29.

Groensteen, Thierry. *Un Objet culturel non identifié*. Angoulême: Les Éditions de l'An 2, 2006.

Groensteen, Thierry. *Parodies : La bande dessinée au second degré*. Paris: Skira-Flammarion, 2010.

Groensteen, Thierry. "Le Processus adaptatif (Tentative de récapitulation raisonnée)." *La Transécriture*. Eds. André Gaudreault and Thierry Groensteen. Québec and Angoulême: Editions Nota Bene / CNBDI, 1998. 273–77.

Groensteen, Thierry. *The System of Comics*. Trans. Bart Beaty and Nick Nguyen. Jackson: University Press of Mississippi, 2007 [1999].

Groensteen, Thierry, and Benoît Peeters, eds. *Töpffer : L'invention de la bande dessinée*. Paris: Hermann, 1994.

Hassler-Forest, Dan. "The *300* Controversy: A Case Study in the Politics of Adaptation." *The Rise and Reason of Comics and Graphic Literature*. Eds. Joyce Goggin and Dan Hassler-Forest. Jefferson, NC, and London: McFarland, 2010. 119–27.

Houppermans, Sjef. "À la recherche des images perdues : Proust et Heuet." *RELIEF* 2.3 (2008): 398–423.

Hutcheon, Linda. *The Politics of Postmodernism*. London and New York: Routledge, 1989, 2002.

Hutcheon, Linda. *A Theory of Adaptation*. New York and London: Routledge, 2006.

Hutcheon, Linda. *A Theory of Parody: The Teachings of Twentieth-Century Art Forms*. Chicago: University of Illinois Press, 1985, 2000.

Inge, M. Thomas. "Comic Book and Graphic Novel Adaptations of the Works of Edgar Allan Poe: A Chronology." *Adapting Poe: Re-Imaginings in Popular Culture*. Eds. Dennis R. Perry and Carl H. Sederholm. Basingstoke, UK, and New York: Palgrave Macmillan, 2012. 231–47.

Iser, Wolfgang. *The Act of Reading: A Theory of Aesthetic Response*. Baltimore and London: Johns Hopkins University Press, 1978.

Jameson, Frederic. *Postmodernism or The Cultural Logic of Late Capitalism*. London and New York: Verso, 1991.

Jenkins, Henry. *Convergence Culture: Where Old and New Media Collide*. New York and London: New York University Press, 2006.

Kuhlman, Martha. "Teaching Paul Karasik and David Mazzucchelli's Graphic Novel Adaptation of Paul Auster's *City of Glass*." *Teaching the Graphic Novel*. Ed. Stephen E. Tabachnik. New York: Modern Language Association of America, 2009. 120–28.

Lacassin, Francis. *Pour un neuvième art : La bande dessinée*. Paris and Geneva: Slatkine, 1982.

Lee, Stan. *Stan Lee's How to Draw Comics the Marvel Way*. New York: Watson-Guptill, 2011 [1984].

Lefèvre, Pascal. "Incompatible Visual Ontologies? The Problematic Adaptation of Drawn Images." *Film and Comic Books*. Eds. Ian Gordon, Mark Jancovich, and Matthew P. McAllister. Jackson: University Press of Mississippi, 2007. 1–12.

Leitch, Thomas. *Film Adaptation and Its Discontents: From* Gone with the Wind *to* The Passion of the Christ. Baltimore: Johns Hopkins University Press, 2009.

Leitch, Thomas. "Twice-Told Tales: Disavowal and the Rhetoric of the Remake" [expanded version of 1990 essay]. *Dead Ringers: The Remake in Theory and Practice*. Eds. Jennifer Forrest and Leonard R. Koos. Albany, NY: SUNY Press, 2002. 37–62.

Lessing, Gotthold Ephraim. "*Laocoön*." (1766) *Critical Theory Since Plato*. Ed. Hazard Adams. Fort Worth: Harcourt, 1971. 338–41.

Levet, Natacha. *Sherlock Holmes : De Baker Street au grand écran*. Paris: Autrement, 2011.

Marion, Philippe. "Narratologie médiatique et médiagénie des récits." *Recherches en communication* 7 (1997): 61–87.

McCloud, Scott. *Understanding Comics: The Invisible Art*. New York: William Morrow, 1994.

McFarlane, Brian. *Novel to Film: an Introduction to the Theory of Adaptation*. Oxford: Clarendon Press, 1996.

Monaghan, David, Ariane Hudelet, and John Wiltshire, eds. *The Cinematic Jane Austen: Essays on the Filmic Sensibility of the Novels*. Jefferson, NC, and London: McFarland, 2009.

Naremore, James, ed. *Film Adaptation*. New Brunswick: Rutgers University Press, 2000.

Parrill, Sue. *Jane Austen on Film and Television*. Jefferson, NC: McFarland, 2002.

Peeters, Benoît. *La Bande-dessinée : Un exposé pour comprendre, un essai pour réfléchir*. Paris: Flammarion, 1993.

Peeters, Benoît. *Case, planche, récit : Lire la bande dessinée*. Paris: Flammarion, 2010 [1998].

Peeters, Benoît. "Une exploration transmédiatique : *Les Cités obscures*." Eds. André Gaudreault and Thierry Groensteen. *La Transécriture*. Québec and Angoulême: Editions Nota Bene / CNBDI, 1998. 249–63.

Pointer, Frank Erik, and Sandra Eva Boschenhoff. "Classics Emulated: Comic Adaptations of Literary Texts." *CEA Critic* 72.3 (Spring–Summer 2010): 86–106.

Price, Ada. "Novel to Graphic Novel: Turning Popular Prose into Comics." *Publishers Weekly* 257.14 (April 2010): 23–26.

Rey, Alain. *Les Spectres de la bande*. Paris: Les Éditions de Minuit, 1978.

Roche, David. *Making and Remaking Horror in the 1970s and 2000s: Why Don't They Do It Like They Used To?* Jackson: University Press of Mississippi, 2014.

Ropars-Wuilleumier, Marie-Claire. "L'Œuvre au double : sur les paradoxes de l'adaptation." *La Transécriture*. Eds. André Gaudreault and Thierry Groensteen. Québec and Angoulême: Editions Nota Bene / CNBDI, 1998. 31–49.

Royal, Derek Parker. "Sequential Poe-try: Recent Graphic Narrative Adapations of Poe." *Poe Studies/Dark Romanticism* 39–40 (2006–2007): 55–67.

Samson, Jacques. "L'Autre texte." *La Transécriture*. Eds. André Gaudreault and Thierry Groensteen. Québec and Angoulême: Editions Nota Bene / CNBDI, 1998. 233–48.

Schaeffer, Jean-Marie. *Qu'est-ce qu'un genre littéraire ?* Paris: Seuil, 1989.

Sklar, Robert. *Movie-Made America: A Cultural History of American Movies*. New York: Vintage, 1994 [1975].

Smolderen, Thierry. *Naissances de la bande dessinée: de William Hogarth à Winsor McCay*. Bruxelles: Impressions Nouvelles, 2009.

Spehner, Norbert. "Bibliobulles : Bibliographie internationale sélective des études sur la bande dessinée." *Belphegor* 5.1 (December 2005). http://etc.dal.ca/belphegor/vol5_no1/articles/05_01_spehne_bibliobd_fr.html. Accessed on July 1, 2013.

Stam, Robert. "Introduction: The Theory and Practice of Adaptation." *Literature and Film: A Guide to the Theory and Practice of Film Adaptation*. Eds. Robert Stam and Alessandra Raengo. Malden, MA, Oxford, and Carlton, Australia: Blackwell, 2005. 1–52.

Stefanelli, Matteo. "Du cinéma-centrisme dans la bande dessinée : L'influence du cinéma sur la théorie et la pratique du « 9e art »." *Les Cases à l'écran*. Ed. Alain Boillat. Genève: Georg, 2010. 283–301.

Stefanelli, Matteo. "Un siècle de recherches sur la bande dessinée." *La Bande dessinée : Une médiaculture*. Eds. Éric Maigret and Matteo Stefanelli. Paris: Armand Colin, 2012. 17–19.

Thompson, Kristin. *Storytelling in the New Hollywood: Understanding Classical Narrative Technique*. Cambridge: Harvard University Press, 1999.

Thompson, Kristin, and David Bordwell. *Film History: An Introduction*. 3rd edition. New York: McGraw Hill International Edition, 2010 [1994].

Töpffer, Rodolphe. *Voyages et aventures du Dr Festus*. Paris: Slatkine, 1986 [1840].

Troost, Linda, and Sayre Greenfield, eds. *Jane Austen in Hollywood*. Lexington: University Press of Kentucky, 1998.

Vanderbeke, Dirk. "It was the Best of Two Worlds, It was the Worst of Two Worlds: The Adaptation of Novels and Graphic Novels." *The Rise and Reason of Comics and Graphic Literature*. Eds. Joyce Goggin and Dan Hassler-Forest. Jefferson, NC, and London: McFarland, 2010. 104–18.

Vanoye, Francis. *L'Adaptation littéraire au cinéma : Formes, usages, problèmes*. Paris: Armand Colin, 2011.

Wells-Lassagne, Shannon. "Filming Theory in Patricia Rozema's *Mansfield Park* (1999)." *Approaches to Film and Reception Theories*. Eds. Christophe Gelly and David Roche. Clermont-Ferrand: Presses Universitaires Blaise Pascal, 2012. 191–205.

PART I

From Page to Panel

Adaptation: A Writerly Strategy?

JAN BAETENS

We are all well aware of the great pitfall of classic studies on adaptation. It is not so much their attachment to the principle of *fidelity* that several recent studies have foregrounded,[1] but rather their inability to break free from a certain binary approach. Adaptation implies a *here* and an *elsewhere*, as well as a *before* and an *after*, and the insistence on maintaining a similar gap between *adapted* and *adapting* remains one of the main elements hampering the development of adaptation studies. This issue is at the heart of contemporary debates. By expanding the theoretical model of adaptation to the field of cultural studies and the cultural history of the contemporary on the one hand, and trying to complement the more conventional paradigms of semiotics or translation studies on the other, current studies of adaptation attempt to offer an approach to the phenomenon in less binary terms.[2] All of them highlight the need for adaptation as one of the basic practices of media culture, including notably innovation and serialization,[3] or of the centrality of adaptation in a so-called "convergence culture" where it is no longer possible to confine a work to the form of its medium.[4] Today, adaptation truly is everywhere, and the works themselves can only survive if they constantly migrate from one medium to another.

Oeuvre as Adaptation, Adaptation as Oeuvre

In this analysis, I begin by tackling the question of adaptation obliquely, casting it in a transdisciplinary[5] mold by reading it through a wholly different field, i.e., music studies. More specifically, my starting point is Peter Szendy's book *Écoute : Une histoire de nos oreilles*, whose importance to a new approach to adaptation I deem fundamental. What is Szendy's argument? First, that music only exists by virtue of listening, which produces it—and, of course, we readily say as much about texts or comics, where reading is not a secondary operation (which is, of course, a truism). The text must be read, as actively as possible, much in the same way as music should be listened to and not merely heard. Secondly, that listening to music seems, at first, to be an immaterial process.

Nonetheless, it is possible to grasp it indirectly through its adaptations. These are manifold, and Szendy gives varied examples: the arrangements, transcriptions, performances (private or public), recordings, or reproductions, notably with the help of all kinds of machines, ranging from the overly crude to those of unprecedented sophistication. Again, the analogies with textual practices are obvious, even trivial, yet it is evident that such observations have considerable impact on the theory of adaptation, warranting our attention.

Szendy's ideas on listening to music radically transform the status of adaptation. They prioritize the following five issues:

1. Adaptation is necessary. Without it, no reading is possible, and in the absence of reading, no text or work is thinkable. Adaptation can, therefore, not be relegated to the margins of the work. If it represents a marginal effect of the work, then it must also occupy the center itself, in the manner of the Derridean supplement. It must be stressed straight away that a simple reading is not equivalent to adaptation, as the latter always involves the idea of change and transformation—in short, an intervention in the text.
2. In essence, what exists is not the work but the adaptation. Put differently: adaptation is not only that which "reveals" the work retrospectively; it constitutes the work itself, which exists only as a chain or network of ceaseless transformations. Instead of the opposition and division between the adapted work and the work of adapting, it is thus more fitting to think of a set of variations in which the concepts of the adapted and the adapting lose part of their value. Any adapted work can also constitute an adaptation. Any adaptation can also be adapted.
3. Although the adaptation process takes place in a chain, it is not necessarily linear. Ever since Borges's famous text on Kafka, we know that writers invent or create their own precursors, at least in the eyes of their readers, and this phenomenon should include adaptation. We can read the original works as adaptations, which is, in effect, something we are doing more and more: to read a novel today is also to imagine the film that could have been its adaptation.[6] In general, one could argue that the current reading practice has become an adaptive reading; we increasingly see the works we are faced with as adaptations (although we do not always have a clear idea of the work they adapt), all the while having in mind the adaptations that could be made in turn (even if the hypotheses we make remain quite vague).[7] The approach holds true in another register, and a theoretically less stimulating fashion, for the

many modern writers influenced by cinema (which they adapt) are eager to be adapted to the screen (to the point that they write with the screenplay that could be drawn from their work in mind). Can we really imagine Stephen King writing his new novel without already thinking of a potential future film version?

4. The phenomena of adaptation are not *technical* processes, even though technique does play a major role. Adaptations are primarily *cultural* facts, that is to say, they are practices saturated with values, some of which are positive (e.g., when the adaptation is intended to pay homage to the person or work one adapts), while others are negative (as when the adaptation is seen as reflecting a lack of originality on the part of whoever is adapted). Adaptation is not just something one can name or identify; it is, first and foremost, something to be *judged* or something inviting the assessment of judgments that determine the stakes.
5. The field of adaptation is much larger and more varied than generally accepted. A number of textual practices can, indeed, be read as belonging to the process of adaptation, like the transition from manuscript to typescript and the final published work, or to take an example typical of traditional comics, the move from pencil drawing to ink drawing and then to the final colored version. That every textual action is a form of adaptation is a fascinating hypothesis, but one which is not without risk. Indeed, if everything is an adaptation, then nothing is.[8] It is therefore necessary to limit with some degree of accuracy our use of the term adaptation so as not to lose the pertinence of the analysis.

What I propose, here, is to use the concept of adaptation to re-examine some classic problems in comics studies. Often, the issue of adaptation—especially the adaptation of literary works into comics—is posed in terms of cultural legitimation, whereby the lower system (comics) taps into the stronger system (literature) for considerations of prestige and the increase of symbolic capital.[9] For various reasons, this motivation is no longer valid. First, on account of a loss of hierarchical markers; literature has ceased to have the same prestige it once did, and thanks to the graphic novel, comics are encroaching on its terrain (as we all know, the most-studied French author in American universities is Marjane Satrapi). Secondly, owing to the widespread phenomenon of adaptation, transmedial transitions have become less conspicuous (it is no longer obvious that analyzing a film adaptation of a novel implies having read or even being familiar with the source).

That said, the trivialization of adaptation and the cultural erosion of the literary repertoire raise other major institutional issues, many of which touch upon the question of the author. In what follows, I will mainly explore the relationship between *style* and the *stance of the writer*,[10] and the way in which this relationship is often the object of value judgments. Indeed, in comics, the style—at least the graphic style—does not always make the man. Some creators develop a personal work while using a relatively neutral style; conversely, the adoption of a highly personal style is not a guarantee that the public will recognize an author in the full sense of the term.[11] As a corollary, the link between originality and value is more complex in comics than, for instance, in literature. In literature, the clear boundary between *restricted* and *expanded* production tends to favor innovation and originality. With comics, which are closer to the industry and broader market, it is not as easy to determine.

In the context of adaptation, these problems are both fundamental and ubiquitous. Three basic situations can be distinguished, which will be examined in the following analysis: (1) original works that are apparently *not adapted*; (2) works that are multifaceted and anything but homogeneous, which are the result of *adaptation*, literary or otherwise; and (3) mixed works that may present themselves as adaptations as well as original creations, whose *continuations* are a widely recognized example in comics.

Originality and Adaptation

Again, we must keep in mind that every work is an adaptation. But what is the use of such a statement to analyze actual works that do not seem derived from any other source? How can the original work be described in terms of an adaptation?

As noted above, every production involves an element of *self-adaptation*. The author transforms an idea, style, form, or structure in order to create a first, still wholly virtual draft, leading to a completed (but never definitively closed-off) work. Sometimes, however, this process becomes public and manifest. In the case of "the alterations by the author," for instance, this fairly conventional form of self-adaptation, in which an author judges himself, has immediate effects on the way the author is judged by the public. A correction judged successful will be credited to the author; a good example would be *The Walls of Samaris* (1982), the inaugural volume in the *Obscure Cities* series by Peeters and Schuiten. When the correction is deemed unfortunate, it will stain the author's reputation—think of the different versions of *The Black Island* (1937), which continue to plunge Tintin fans in the depths of despair. In all of these cases, the object of judgment goes beyond the more or less local transformations in the works and is extended to the larger issue of the writer's stances. For what is judged in these works that initially appear to be "original" is the way in which the author demonstrates discernment and skill at self-adaptation, and more precisely the way in which the adaptation in question can be related to the self-positioning of the artist in the artistic or cultural field. The fact that Hergé made a "bad" self-adaptation is seen as selling out to the pressures of the market; that Peeters and Schuiten made a "good" self-adaptation will be interpreted as a sign of artistic integrity.

This may seem trivial, but it becomes more complex when taking into account that self-adaptation, far from merely registering the strategic considerations of the artist, is increasingly becoming a necessity where the role of the public is anything but *passive* or purely *reactive*. As such, the practice of self-adaptation is not only proof of the author's concern with changing the image he fashions of himself, but also meets the demands of the readers, who, far from merely awaiting this type of self-adaptation, set out to appropriate it.

This can be observed, first, in the audience's reactions to the lack of self-adaptation. An oblique illustration of this same strategy is the reprint, which the public often expects to be accompanied by self-adaptation. For modern audiences, an author who "evolves" can no longer take the liberty of leaving an older work untouched, especially with a work that was not yet up to the standards of the author's current production. The *Obscure Cities* series, which evolves with each re-edition, is a case in point; for them, reprints are always the occasion for improvements. Similarly, and conversely, the artist is permitted with less and less frequency to revise a work deemed satisfactory by the readers. The refusal or inability to self-adapt can sometimes be met with the readers' rather vicious judgments. The latter are no longer content with merely criticizing works as they are found on the market; they now assume the right to demand real changes, a telltale sign of the new context in which the discussion of adaptation is now taking place. The phenomenon is certainly not new and has not changed in nature, yet it has certainly changed its source. In a culture where adaptation becomes the norm, *ne varietur* ceases to be the privilege of producers (and authors and publishers alike—think of the decisive role they played at all stages of Hergé's career). From now on, it is also the reader—and increasingly only s/he alone—who wants to have a say in the *final cut*.

This is even more clearly the case in fan culture, where readers set out to make self-adaptations *in place of the author*, the technical means of new media having toppled copyright barriers; consider the many examples of "fan fiction" (although this phenomenon mainly concerns the third basic category in my typology, i.e., continuations). The trend towards adaptation is thus no longer limited to works in progress or future works; it equally—and often bluntly—touches upon those of the past. That the audience is getting used to reading a work as both adapted and adaptable further reinforces this loss of stable points of reference (icons of popular culture such as Batman and Tarzan are good illustrations of this; readers no longer recognize the chronological relations between novels, comics, movies, series, novelizations, etc., as they also believe that the subject matter belongs to anyone willing to seize it). And as soon as a work is considered to be virtually adaptable, it will function as a standing invitation to the author to self-adapt, so that the demands of the public can be met all the better. Increasingly, the public is directly involved in the production of these adaptations, in a sense participating in the self-adaptation of the author.

The boundaries between self and other, production and reception, reading and writing, become, then, highly tenuous. Regarding the relationship between (original) creation and self-adaptation, we can already conclude that it is no longer possible to "protect" a work from the principle of self-adaptation, and that the contamination of originality by the principle of adaptation can be partly explained by virtue of the mutations in the stance of the writer, wherein the strategies are partially beyond the author's grasp. The context of these changes—clearly formulated by Jean-Christophe Menu in *La Bande dessinée et son double*—is the very questioning of the boundaries between author and reader.

Adaptation: A Tiered Apparatus

Let us now turn to the second kind of adaptation, the deceptively simple case of "pure" adaptations, and take as an example the adaptations of Léo Malet's famous *noir* Nestor Burma series. At first glance, the situation seems straightforward since the (first) adaptations were made by Jacques Tardi, the figurehead of the *(À suivre)* type of narrative comics; what's more, Tardi never denied his debt to Malet. But what actually happens when readers discover this type of adaptation? On the one hand, it is the work of adaptation that is evaluated; it all comes down to seeing how Malet's novel has been converted into a comic by Tardi. On the other, the writer's own stance is equally at stake, and it is just as much a matter of seeing how adapting Malet contributes to better establishing Tardi's own reputation (or, seen negatively, of discarding these adaptations as mere commissions to make a living). In this case, the question is no longer about what remains of Malet in Tardi but about what remains of Tardi in Tardi adapting Malet.

As is widely recognized, this problem is not only Jacques Tardi's, as it is a problem that every writer faces when embarking on an adaptation. S/he is confronted with a crucial dilemma: either to make oneself as invisible as possible or clearly mark one's presence, be it in terms of graphic[12] or narrative style. In fact, the difference between the two is often difficult to pinpoint. However, this way of presenting the adaptation suggests that *the primary issue is always expressed in terms of self-adaptation*. In albums like *Fog over Tolbiac Bridge* (1982) and the four additional volumes that follow, what the public is interested in is not so much how Tardi adapts Malet but instead how Tardi adapts himself by (slightly) changing his diegetic universe. In short, adaptation primarily serves to examine how an author reads himself, as it relies or does not rely on the stance of the writer already or not yet attached to his name.

Each comic is a good illustration of how, in a successful series, the concern with leaving one's personal mark loses its power and urgency as the series gradually advances. The first two, *Fog over Tolbiac Bridge* and *The Bloody Streets of Paris* (1988), were two strokes of genius greeted with unanimous acclaim, thereby relieving the pressure of having to "repeat the trick" in subsequent iterations. From the third volume onwards, one can sense Tardi's mounting lassitude toward the main character and Malet's universe, reflected mainly by the increasing irony that pervades the comics. However, it is important to note that this sense of exhaustion cannot be explained through biographical considerations alone, with Tardi simply losing interest in a character and an author for which he had signed a contract for five installments. Additionally, the symbolic capital the first two versions had generated must be taken into account; it proved difficult to match and yet sufficiently rich to accommodate a number of less intense continuations.

When Emmanuel Moynot took over from Jacques Tardi, who was then drawn to more personal projects, the basic system did not change, even though it became a little more complicated. Indeed, Moynot not only had to seize the opportunity to fully impose his own voice (something not too obvious in the case of a prolific comics artist with a somewhat scattered body of work), but he needed, above all, to prove that he was able to do as good a job as Tardi while also doing something different. Put differently, for Moynot to adapt Malet is mainly to adapt Tardi, with the paradoxical double constraint of establishing the greatest distance from a model that is to be imitated as closely as possible. Again, there is nothing exceptional about this example; even adaptations we initially consider to be "original" are often very complex negotiations between the author who adapts in his own style, and a whole series of "modelisations" that are built around the adapted work. With the adaptation of Kafka's *The Castle* by Belgian author Olivier Deprez (2003), which one would call very free, personal, and original after just a quick read, the reader is nonetheless confronted with a veritable palimpsest: Deprez's woodcuts can also be read as entertaining a highly complex relationship with Kafka's own drawings (and especially the back-and-forth process between writing and drawing that informed Kafka's own approach to his manuscripts) and the tradition of the woodcut novel (from Masereel to today).[13]

A case that is perhaps even more complex but which bespeaks the same underlying principle is that of Martin Vaughn-James's cult book *The Cage* (1975). This unclassifiable book[14] reads simultaneously as a self-adaptation, an original creation, and an adaptation. First, Vaughn-James self-adapts, and in no less than two ways; already famous for his graphic short stories, in 1975 he proved to be an author capable of making the leap from micro-narration to a story of an altogether unusual length. Well established in the French audience's mind for his imaginative variations on Beckett and Pinget in the journal *Minuit*, he had to re-create his image as the in-house illustrator of Editions de Minuit when the book was translated in 1985. Secondly, the singular narrative of this comic, which explores the improvisational possibilities of the formal properties of the book as object, constitutes such an atypical innovation that, to this day, *The Cage* remains one of the major missing links in the history of the graphic novel (a totally unknown label at the time of its first edition in Canada in 1975). Thirdly, the work is also an adaptation in the classic sense of the term, insofar as Vaughn-James transferred many of the views of the first period of the Nouveau Roman to the visual field (an emphasis on the eyes; a refusal of the outdated notion of character; an avoidance of a linear narrative structure; the primacy of spatiality; the exhibition of "generators," that is to say, a formal or thematic nucleus whose transformations replace the actual plot).

Thus, the boundaries between the oeuvre, adaptation, and self-adaptation are blurred, but this observation is no longer by any means surprising. That said, blurring is not synonymous with confusion or leveling, because whatever the operation effected, repetition must always be considered in terms of a gap, while distantiation must always be practiced in terms of a re-telling. A second conclusion that can be drawn, here, has to do with the profound intricacy of the work and its author, or rather the writer's stance. As soon as the strategies of adaptation are examined in the light of how they are read and received by the audience, the appreciation of the object is immediately proven to be inseparable from the evaluation of the relationships that develop between authors—both the adapted or the adapting kind. The third basic situation, that of continuation, charges these relationships with even greater intensity.

Continuations: But Who Is Speaking Anyway?

Even if the phenomenon affects media culture as a whole, including narrative culture in general, few media are as fond of continuations or expansions as comics. Through continuation (which I use to include both continuation and expansion),[15] an author expands an existing work, either in a hidden and mechanical way (as often happens in studio work)[16] or in a creative and quite deliberate fashion (even when the work of continuation is often curbed by legal issues).[17] In many cases, however, the impact of this type of adaptation on the writer's stance is exceptionally complex, and it is through the analysis of a few widespread cases subject to multiple interpretations that I will examine the phenomenon. In very general terms, a continuation does not adapt from the same perspective as a self-adaptation, as when Tardi adapts Malet. While adapting to the style of someone else, the continuation attempts, on the contrary, to be an invention, at least for the writer. But what are the limits and the stakes of such invention by imitation?

The most elementary form of continuation, from the point of view of the writer's stance, is undoubtedly *pastiche* (in the general sense of the term).[18] Through it, an author pursues the work of a different author in a highly singular fashion that cannot be exhausted by calling on the concept of humor. Continuations are made with the intent of parody or homage (or both simultaneously), as well as self-affirmation (since pastiche involves expertise, which the author creating the pastiche wants to take advantage of). What is essential is the combination of these two strategies. Basically, a pastiche only makes sense if it works both ways; a good pastiche simultaneously permits the author to render homage (in a more or less gently ironic mode, of course) and contributes to the affirmation of a personal voice (albeit only as a promise). Any pastiche is therefore both continuation and adaptation. Conversely, every continuation and adaptation may also involve pastiche, at least from the moment the appreciation of the work is coupled with an evaluation of the author's strategies revealed through his continuation. The difficult balance between aligning oneself with the other author and the necessity of not being confused with one's model conjures up a structural relationship between various strategies that deeply affect the reading of any continuation.

As a highly institutionalized mode, pastiche is a practice placed under high surveillance, with targeted responses that are sensibly marked; although pastiche makes one laugh, it is never at the expense of its model (the homage element is supposed to dominate; if not, the pastiche "degenerates" into caricature). Nor is the humor to the sole benefit of the one who makes the pastiche (the modesty with which the authors of pastiches efface themselves behind their models is part of the rules of the game). In practice, however, trickier operations may come to light.

Yves Chaland, for instance, refused to continue Tintin or any other specific genre such as the "Tintin" School of Brussels or the "Spirou" School of Marcinelles (scout novels like *La Patrouille des Éperviers* or science fiction stories in the vein of Edgar Pierre Jacobs) but instead the *ligne claire* (the clear line) itself. What matters is not the generic uncertainty that dominates Chaland's production where pastiche and continuation mix as much as the paradoxical treatment of the writer's stance. In his work as pastiche artist, Chaland discloses certain aspects of the clear line that had remained hidden until then. In a way, his clear line tells the truth about the clear line, both in terms of graphics and content, especially the cultural and ideological aspects, starting with the very complex relation between Belgians—the "Belgian complex" as it were—and their language (*Le Jeune Albert* is a treasure trove in this respect). Chaland is not afraid to emphasize the *belgitude* (the Belgianness) of the clear line, while the whole strategy of the Brussels and Marcinelles Schools had always tended to "de-Belgify" the referents in the works whenever possible (Moulinsart is a French château, the agent in Gaston Lagaffe is a French cop, the characters speak in a highly polished French, and so on). At the same time, he refuses to convert this knowledge and expertise into a personal signature, at least not in terms of style. Chaland's clear line does not so much seek to establish itself as a *ligne claire bis*, contrary to the dreams of those authors called Hergé's heirs, in search of personal and immediately recognizable variations within the frame of the master (an author like Jean-Marie Floch[19] comes to mind). Rather, Chaland's clear line wants to impose itself as "the" clear line *tout court*, although in practice no one is fooled when it comes to the writer's stance; it is through exaggeration, and not through apparent differences, that Chaland stands out.

From this perspective, Chaland's continuation is the antithesis of the continuations of Blake and Mortimer, whereby the faithful imitation of the model, which is probably dictated by their publishing contract, is experienced by the reader as a *renunciation* on the part of the pursuer (especially the artist). In trying (or having) to become "more Jacobs than Jacobs," Ted Benoît and André Juillard apparently pursue the same ambitions as Chaland, at least with regard to the end product, but when it comes to the writer's stance, their strategies are wholly different. First, in continuing Jacobs, they do not want to update Jacobs "himself" or even less to produce an unsuspected Jacobs, a Jacobs beyond what he himself could have done; they simply want to deliver a product that deviates as little as possible from the audience's expectations. Secondly, their imitative project is not at all intended to enable them to impose their own signature. In fact, they are attempting to do just the opposite, that is, try and erase their own voice as best as possible, both directly in the continuations of Blake and Mortimer and also indirectly, since their "own" work is not supposed to be influenced by what they carry out in their continuation of Jacobs. For them, continuation is a break after which they can resume their own business. Chaland, meanwhile, is both a more sly and more humble follower since, by sacrificing his own imagination and his own inventiveness for the sake of the expansion of the oeuvre he continues, his work stands out as an unwavering tribute to the clear line and as the mark of a personality without equal. With Chaland, the writer's stance and personal style are somehow dissociated, but through a ruse, not through ignorance or indifference; it is by doing less (in terms of individual style) that an author like Chaland succeeds, in effect, the most, not the least in terms of writerly stance.

However, there is a further degree in the process of continuation. The basic strategy can be described thus: copying an author, as meticulously and convincingly as possible, but through the style of another author who is credited with the continuation. This is the spirit of the work of British artist Simon Grennan.[20] In a highly remarkable series produced as part of a doctoral thesis, Grennan proposed rewrites—continuations of certain authors, but made not in "their" style, but in that of other artists. He redid a page from *Maus*, trying to imagine how Jim Medway would have drawn it. This type of transposition goes well beyond the replacement of Art Spiegelman's panels with frames drawn in the style of *Teen Witch* (one of Medway's works, which he developed in a spirit of collaboration with the participants of his blog). Indeed, the layout changes, as does the story (Medway does not narrate like Spiegelman, and this difference is no less important than their differing graphic styles). However, it must be emphasized that Grennan's project is, above all, theoretical; his main interest is the question of the dialogism inherent to graphic enunciation.

The result is a far cry from a more famous continuation that was recognized (perhaps a bit prematurely) as groundbreaking: Matt Madden's *99 Ways To Tell a Story: Exercises in Style* (2005). Inspired by Raymond Queneau's *Exercices de style*, as many have been since the book was first published in 1947, Madden offers a graphic reinterpretation. In *Exercices de style*, the variations on the central anecdote are constructed, more or less freely, on the basis of a verbal constraint (each new variation puts forward a new figure of speech). With Madden, they obey a pictorial principle (many variations are made in a different visual style, usually the typical style of a famous comic book writer). However, what is most striking in Madden's work is the often very approximate character of the connection with the author whose work is continued. The "Ligne Claire" page, for example, is only recognizable through its content (it is easy to identify the characters and borrowings from *The Secret of the Unicorn*). Stylistically, the transfer does not seek to convince; the graphic image of this page is not really Hergé's, and the transposition can be described as loose and fast. Obviously, the point of Madden's project is more conceptual than stylistic, and the various aspects of his approach to adaptation tend without exception to emphasize his stance as a writer; variations are not pastiches or, if they had been intended as such, they simply fail. Everywhere we look we see Madden's hand instead of that of the authors who helped him shape the constraint; the somewhat rough transposition of Hergé's style is, in this respect, hardly any different from what can be seen in other variations of this type. In short, these adaptations are clearly adaptation—continuations whose goal is to flaunt Madden's range and, even more, his ability to execute for the very first time a constraint that had not yet been performed (but which in itself is not really original).

To return to Grennan's project, it is much closer to Chaland's, with a few extra turns of the screw. First, Grennan multiplies the number of authors involved in the adaptation. In this respect, he practices a form of overstatement that should benefit his stance as a writer even more, since it exceeds Chaland through the sheer number of styles that he is able to use as he sees fit. His effort is consistent with an ideological aim that goes against the exhibition of the traditional writer's stance, which we invariably imagine as being motivated by a logic of distinction. Grennan rejects pastiche (the adaptations he proposes do not resemble this form of continuation at all), just as he rejects the adapter's approach as a way to show off. What he intends to expose is the element of otherness present in even the most original creation (or, conversely, the most slavishly imitative). By redrawing Spiegelman in the manner of Medway—that is to say, by renouncing the ambition to make "a Grennan"—the author reveals the limits of the notion of originality. He equally foregrounds the necessity to take up, in a creative way, the impossibility not to adapt others when making something personal—in other words, to figure adaptation as a springboard instead of a hindrance. His project opens up a whole new dimension of adaptation that conceives adaptation as dialogism and collective creation.

■ ■ ■

It is impossible to end these reflections on the field of adaptation with a classic conclusion. However, a few general observations and questions can be deduced in the hope that they will result in new readings such as Peter Szendy's in the field of musical adaptations. Three issues in particular warrant further consideration:

1. Adaptation is less a relationship between two objects than a cultural practice that explores new relationships between all aspects of the literary and artistic institution, such as author, originality, and style. It is quite obvious that such an approach is not a substitute for more traditional readings where two semiotic objects are compared (e.g., a novel and a comic), but it must complement the latter so that the functional complexity of the operations involved is not overlooked.
2. Although the concept of the writer's stance is useful in rethinking this dynamic, it alone does not suffice; it is essential to provide a place for the reader and the active intervention of the audience in the permanent reconstruction of the work. Moreover, the reader's participation is not restricted to a consideration of objects. What must also be taken into account is the conceptual study of the author, in particular through Michel Foucault's notion of the "author-function" as a co-construction of the authorial and readerly processes. As a corollary, it is also important to examine the paradox that seems to program the decision to frame reading in terms of an author (if only through the already critical forms of the writer's stance or author-function). It is, indeed, quite curious that the attempt to question the aims or pitfalls of certain authorial positions does not at all produce the effacement of the author to the benefit of his work. From this perspective, the anonymous craftsmen of industrial comics were probably freer than the more high-profile artists of the contemporary graphic novel, who are often the victims of a brand image that muddies or impedes the reading of the work itself.
3. The study of adaptation can never be a goal in itself. The aim of such a study should be to highlight the manifold character of the work as virtually adapted and virtually adapting, as well as to show the multifarious nature of its enunciation. Similarly, adaptation must be read and interpreted in its symptomatic sense, that is to say, as one of the keys that could lead to a better understanding of literary values at any given time. In this sense, it is a resolutely historical concept, in which forms but especially meanings change over time, and it would be ill-advised to take it as an invariant of the literary field. If it were to be confirmed over the coming years, the bolstering of strategies of collaboration and

the multiplication of enunciative instances we have come across in our examples could foreshadow the disappearance, over a short or longer term, of adaptation as a central concept. Adaptation would, then, become an unnecessary hypothesis. Needless to say, we have not reached that point yet.

Notes

1. See, for example, the comments by Christine Geraghty in her article "Foregrounding the Media: *Atonement* (2007) as an Adaptation."

2. See the articles published in the journal *Adaptations*: http://adaptation.oxfordjournals.org.

3. Here I am following the analyses in Dominique Kalifa's book *La Culture de masse en France, 1860–1930*.

4. See Henry Jenkins. In the literary field, which is not Jenkins's main focus but to which comics undoubtedly belong, one may think of the concept of "differential text," i.e., a text that has ceased to exist in a final and definitive form, as Marjorie Perloff proposes in "Screening the Page/Turning the Screen: Poetics and the Differential Text."

5. Transdisciplinarity is a specific approach to interdisciplinarity that combines theoretical perspectives from diverse backgrounds in order to solve practical problems within a given field. It is mainly characterized by: (1) the capacity to combine sometimes entirely different points of view; (2) the elaboration of new tools of reflection or the improvement of existing ones; and (3) an emphasis on the notion of creativity in scientific thinking. Unlike the well-known inter- or multidisciplinary approaches, transdisciplinarity does not necessarily distance itself from established disciplines, though its purpose is not necessarily to create new disciplines (this definition is freely adapted from Michael Gibbons, Helga Nowotny, and Peter Scott).

6. In technical terms, we thus read such books as if they were novelizations or novels made from original screenplays. Moreover, in the field of novelization, the boundaries between novelizations (posterior to the adapted film) and original novels (the source films that are adapted) are becoming increasingly blurry. For more details, see my book *La Novellisation : Du film au roman*.

7. It is possible that the mechanism is not unrelated to the possibility of reading fiction in the manner of the documentary, and vice versa, cf. Gérard Genette in *Fiction et Diction*.

8. One of the most important authors on the subject of adaptation, Linda Hutcheon, is well aware of this danger. Here, I follow her advice to never lose sight of the concrete and contextualized aspects of the object of study.

9. For a sociological analysis of the issue of value in comics, see Thierry Groensteen, *Un objet culturel non identifié*.

10. The concept of the "writer's stance" is taken from Jérôme Meizoz, who has studied it on multiple occasions. See also the paper by Charlotte Pylyser and Steven Surdiacourt ("De gestileerde auteur. Stijl, auteurschap en grafische literatuur. De marges van de literatuur," VAL study day. Leuven, November 16, 2011), which rethinks the concept of the stance in the light of Michel Foucault's author-function (I return to this issue at the end of this chapter).

11. This is not to be confused with the technical concept of the complete author, that is to say, the author who combines the traditionally separate functions of script and drawing, cf. *Case, planche, récit* by Benoît Peeters.

12. Here we touch upon issues of *graphiation*, which Philippe Marion defines as "graphic or visual enunciation" in his book *Traces en cases*. The style of a comic can be described in function of the degree of presence or visibility of this *graphiation*, with, on the one hand, authors who try to erase the intervention of their "hand" as much as possible (e.g., Hergé is an example of this), and on the other, those who instead strive to illustrate as much as possible how their entire body is invested, pushing through into the final result (e.g., Franquin late in his career).

13. Olivier Deprez, who is also an excellent critic and theorist, has often made critical analyses of his own work, notably in the article "Le regard comme projet intersémiotique."

14. For more details, see *La Construction de "La Cage"* by Thierry Groensteen (this text was reprinted as the postscript to the latest reissue of Martin Vaughn-James's book).

15. The difference between "continuation" and "expansion" is a tenuous one, even if it designates two subcategories which, in practice, do not mix that much. With continuation, the adapter extends a work (often a series) where the initial author—or rather, the previous writer in the long chain of those taking turns—had abandoned it. In an expansion, the adapter explores an aspect or dimension of the story that the initial author did not cover. In a nutshell, in the first case, the author narrates what comes next, while in the second, the author narrates what had never been disclosed. Richard Saint-Gelais's *Fictions transfuges* is a real compendium of this type of practice (even if his corpus is primarily literary in the classic sense of the term).

16. The final *Tintin* albums, which were actually drawn by Bob De Moor, are often cited as examples.

17. See, for example, Émile Bravo's work on the *Spirou* series and his reinterpretation of the character in the album *Spirou : Le Journal d'un ingénu*.

18. For a more technical discussion of the notion of pastiche, see *Palimpsests* by Gérard Genette and *A Theory of Parody* by Linda Hutcheon.

19. One can find an overview of "post-Ligne Claire" artists in *Les Héritiers d'Hergé* by Bruno Lecigne.

20. Simon Grennan is a multimedia artist specializing in performances and happenings, that is to say, ephemeral artistic interventions within specific contexts, often carried out in collaboration with groups of users or citizens. Together with the American artist Christopher Sperandio, he is also an author of comics (cf. the website Kartoon Kings http://www.kartoonkings.com/). For more information on the work he completed as part of his PhD project under the supervision of Roger Sabin, see: http://www.wimbledon.arts.ac.uk/ccwgraduateschool/researchdegrees/currentresearchstudentsatccw/simongrennan/.

Works Cited

Baetens, Jan. *La Novellisation : Du film au roman*. Brussels: Les Impressions Nouvelles, 2008.

Borges, Jorge Luis. "Les précurseurs de Kafka." *Enquêtes* puis *Autres inquisitions*. Paris: Gallimard, 1957 [1952]. 147–51.

Bravo, Emile. *Spirou : Le Journal d'un ingénu*. Brussels: Dupuis, 2008.

Chaland, Yves. *The Young Albert*. Trans. Natacha Ruck and Ken Grobe. Los Angeles: Humanoids, 2012 [1985].

Deprez, Olivier. "Le regard comme projet intersémiotique." *Image (&) Narrative* 3 (2000). http://www.imageandnarrative.be/inarchive/illustrations/olivierdeprez.htm. Accessed on July 12, 2013.

Deprez, Olivier, and Franz Kafka. *Le Château*. Bruxelles: Fremok Éditions, 2003.

Foucault, Michel. "What Is an Author?" (1969) *Aesthetics, Method, and Epistemology.* Ed. James D. Faubion. Trans. Robert Hurley et al. New York: The New York Press, 1998. 205–22.

Genette, Gérard. *Fiction et Diction.* Paris: Seuil, 1991.

Genette, Gérard. *Palimpsests: Literature in the Second Degree.* Trans. Channa Newman and Claude Doubinsky. Lincoln: University of Nebraska Press, 1997 [1982].

Geraghty, Christine. "Foregrounding the Media: *Atonement* (2007) as an Adaptation." *Adaptation* 2.2 (2009): 91–109.

Gibbson, Michael, Helga Nowotny, and Peter Scott. "Introduction, 'Mode 2' Revisited: The New Production of Knowledge." *Minerva* 41 (2003): 179–94.

Groensteen, Thierry. *La Construction de* La Cage. Bruxelles: Les Impressions Nouvelles, 2002.

Groensteen, Thierry. *Un Objet culturel non identifié : la bande dessinée.* Angoulême: éd. de l'an 2, 2006.

Hutcheon, Linda. *A Theory of Adaptation.* New York and London: Routledge, 2006.

Hutcheon, Linda. *A Theory of Parody: The Teachings of Twentieth-Century Art Forms.* New York and London: Routledge, 2000 [1985].

Jenkins, Henry. *Convergence Culture: Where Old and New Media Collide.* New York: New York University Press, 2006.

Kalifa, Dominique. *La Culture de masse en France, 1860–1930.* Paris: La Découverte, 2001.

Lecigne, Bruno. *Les Héritiers d'Hergé.* Bruxelles: Magic Strip, 1983.

Madden, Matt. *99 Ways To Tell a Story: Exercises in Style.* New York: Chamberlain Bros, 2005.

Marion, Philippe. *Traces en cases.* Louvain-la-Neuve: Académia, 1993.

Meizoz, Jérôme. "Postures journalistiques et littéraires." *Interférences littéraires* 6 (2011). http://www.interferenceslitteraires.be/nr6. Accessed on July 12, 2013.

Menu, Jean-Christophe. *La Bande dessinée et son double.* Paris: L'Association, 2011.

Peeters, Benoît. *Case, planche, récit.* Paris: Casterman, 1999.

Perloff, Marjorie. "Screening the Page/Turning the Screen: Poetics and the Differential Text." *New Media Poetics. Contexts, Technote'xts, and Theories.* Eds. Adelaide Morris and Thomas Swiss. Cambridge: MIT Press, 2006. 143–64.

Saint-Gelais, Richard. *Fictions transfuges.* Paris: Seuil, 2011.

Szendy, Peter. *Écoute, une histoire de nos oreilles. Précédé de « Ascoltando » par Jean-Luc Nancy.* Paris: Minuit, 2001.

Tardi, Jacques, and Léo Malet. *Fog over Tolbiac Bridge: A Nestor Burma Mystery.* Seattle: Fantagraphics, 2017 [1982].

Tardi, Jacques, and Léo Malet. *The Bloody Streets of Paris (120, rue de la Gare).* Shelter Island Heights, NY: IBooks Graphic Novel, 2004 [1998].

Vaughn-James, Martin. *La Cage.* Bruxelles: Les Impressions Nouvelles, 2009 [1985].

Narrative (De)constructions and the Persistence of the Text: Images of the Cid between Epic Performance and Comics

THOMAS FAYE

In the preface to *A Theory of Adaptation*, Linda Hutcheon argues that "adaptation is not only a formal entity, however; it is also a process" (xv). Adaptation implies the existence of something anterior and is, therefore, a kind of rewriting: "Adaptation is repetition, but repetition without replication" (7). Yet to what extent does the process of adaptation and its result interact with the meaning of what came before?[1] In order to address this question, I believe it is essential to draw a line between hypotext and hypertext (as introduced by Genette) to better define their singular relationship. How does adaptation play itself out? Does it involve putting two things "on speaking terms" so that harmony can reign between the two? Is it just about transforming a work from a specific format to another? At its most elementary, adaptation is always a matter of transmitting a textual object through a different medium to an *a priori* audience that is presumably different. Adaptation always engages to a greater or lesser extent what Roman Jakobson calls an "intersemiotic translation" (114).

From the twelfth century onwards, the life of a knight nicknamed *El Cid* has fascinated Iberian culture and has been the subject of countless adaptations. Although in a fragile state of conservation, the story of his life is scattered among chronicles and even inspired a work of fiction, the *Poema de Mio Cid*. An epic poem of about 3,700 lines divided into three songs (*cantares*), the long poem recounts the warring feats and, more generally, the life of Rodrigo Díaz de Vivar. At the time, the life of the protagonist was made into a historical model, thus paving the way for countless adaptations (translations, movies, animation films, children's books . . .), which follow heterogeneous narrative paths and signifying modes.[2]

Among these rewritings is Antonio Hernández Palacios's four-volume comic adaptation entitled El Cid, issued by several publishers between 1971 and 1984. While the *Poema de Mio Cid* supported the myth of the hero of a unified Spain, the comic presents a fictional rewriting of the events in the life of Rodrigo Díaz prior to the chronological order of the episodes in the *Poema*, offering its readers a "much more authentic" story "than the one we were taught when we were kids," so that we can "truly learn the story hidden from us"[3] (Lara 4). This formal and historical experimentation was driven by the desire to relativize the notion of truth: "You must read everything, sifting through the knowledge transmitted by these beautiful, yet unreliable documentary-wise epics."[4]

First published in 1971 in the magazine *Trinca*—a politically independent publication though affiliated with the *Frente de Juventudes*—it then moved to the Basque publishing house *Ikusager*, based in Vitoria, which published the four volumes in its collection "Imágenes de la historia" in 1982. This collection attempted to provide a new perspective on the agents and events of Spanish history. Hernández Palacios hoped to address a young audience and give the Cid a more everyday image that would break with the legacy of previous rewritings: "El Cid is a story of everyday life and this, in my opinion, is its essential characteristic. It's not a matter of recreating the heroes of the past [. . .] but of ensuring that the past is transformed into the immediate present, alive and recognizable" (Lara 3).[5] In the comic, the Cid is just a background character overshadowed by the presence and charisma of Don Sancho, heir to Ferdinand of Castile, whom he accompanies on his travels. The project thus seems paradoxical: to thwart the established representations of a character who disappears behind the story's other heroes and events. The paradox begins when the origin of the myth is not attributed to the hero himself but to the story's early adaptations. This working hypothesis will allow us to analyze the underlying strategies of Hernández Palacios's adaptation.

The first volume, *Sancho de Castilla* (1971), relates Don Sancho's education; the second, *Las Cortes de León* (1972), is devoted to the sessions of the *cortes*, which established, among other things, the succession to Ferdinand I; the third installment, *La toma de Coimbra* [*sic*] (1973), takes us back to an episode of the reconquest of the west, in which the Cid participated. Finally, the fourth volume, *La cruzada Barbastro* (1984), relates the Reconquista campaigns in Aragon.[6] The plot lines are excuses for introducing a host of secondary characters, and the battle scenes undoubtedly make up the essential part of the story. Yet these same battle scenes were already used in the epic tradition as the backdrop for presenting various characters, and sentimental and political intrigue, in the *Poema de Mio Cid*. Examining the presence, distribution, and interferences of voices and narrative operations in the *Poema* and the comics should give us a better understanding of the place Hernández Palacios's work occupies in the Cidean corpus.

The aim of this chapter is to clarify the links between, on the one hand, the historical character that inspired the poem and made him a hero of chivalry and a mythical figure of the Reconquista, and on the other, the comic that, centuries later, intends to shed new light on the heroes that have become familiar to generations of Spaniards and that history has repeatedly appropriated. Through the dialogue between text and image, Hernández Palacios transposes and questions the source material to ultimately challenge the mythical dimension of the Cid and its transmission.

For a long time, stories about the Cid were transmitted orally, so that markers of orality, which initially functioned as a means for the listeners to visualize the diegetic content, largely influenced the genesis of meaning by leaving their stamp on the transcripts we inherited. The episode of the battle of Alcocer is probably one of the most revealing examples; the famous episode of the first *cantar* recounts one of the very first exploits of the Cid and illustrates the richness of minstrel narrative techniques. One of the Cid's first military successes is chronicled in 250 lines, as he is forced into exile and vanquishes the Moors in the hope of regaining King Alfonso VI's good graces. In the *Poema*, this story of a battle waged more for honor than for the Reconquista is effected through the alternation between narrative and discourse. The voice of the minstrel, the occasional and fleeting incarnation of the legion-author defined by Ramón Menéndez Pidal, takes on the form of reported speech and narrative. The performance was thus an opportunity for the minstrel to make palpable the shift from one narrative modality to another. He could even go further during battle scenes, suggesting a certain interpretation of a story that was meant to be informative and exemplary.

The schematization of alternating voices (fig. 1) highlights the fact that the minstrel, the starting point for all voices, adapts his intonation to the role he assumes and to the story events. I distinguish four situations: the "depersonalized storyteller" (white), when the minstrel provides external focalization; the "individualized storyteller" (black), when he participates directly in the narrative (and thus interrupts the diegesis); "direct mediated speech" (light grey), when a character's words are introduced by a *verbum dicendi*; and finally, "direct non-mediated speech" (dark grey), when words are recounted without narrative interruption.

The storyline is simple: the Cid wins his first victory, after which he is faced with an obstacle, the inhabitants of Alcocer's counterattack. He is thus confronted with a new difficulty before being hailed again for his final victory. The intensity of the "individualized storyteller's" interventions seems to increase after having overcome this obstacle—the minstrel expresses, here, his

Spatial indications ("Cojos Salon ayuso") / Description of the weaponry
"Veyen lo los de Alcocer, ¡Dios, commo se alabavan !"
El Cid's troops withdraw / They talk strategy
Spatial indications / The troops' movements
The lamentations of the besieged of Alcocer
Describes their strategies
Attack order given by El Cid
Describes the assault: "¡Dios, que bueno es el gozo por aquesta mañana" [. . .] "sabet"
El Cid proclaims victory and congratulates his soldiers
Expresses the feelings of the vanquished and evokes El Cid's forced exile ("sabet")
El Cid threatens the king of València
The king of València comes up with a strategy
Describes King Tamin's advances, the composition of Fariz and Galve's armies, as well as El Cid and his men's increasing exhaustion during the siege of Alcocer
Sums up the previous narrative of El Cid and his men's exhaustion
Minaya replies to El Cid and expresses his desire to fight
El Cid then responds to Minaya, thanking him
Marks the transition between two days of siege, a new strategy having been devised during the night
A strategy is defined and attack orders are given by El Cid
Description of the battle scene and of the enthusiasm it arouses in the bard: "¡Que priessa va en los moros ! [. . .] Veriedes armarse moros, [. . .] ¿qui los podrie contar ?"
Combat order given by El Cid
Comments on the reaction to the order just given and introduces subsequent reply
Pero Vermúez describes his own action and attacks
El Cid encourages him
Pero Vermúez becomes even more fiery
Describes the attack, which has just been mentioned by Pero
El Cid calls on the other soldiers to back up Pero

Fig. 1: *Poema de Mio Cid*: speech alternation in the battle of Alcocer episode.

Describes the assault (military technique)
El Cid gives various orders to attack and devises a military strategy
Repeats and develops the orders just given
The bard enthusiastically describes the scene: "Veriedes tantas lanças premer e alçar, / tanta adagara foradar e passar, / tanta loriga falssar e desmanchar, / tantos pendones blancos salir vermejos en sangre, / tantos buenos cavallos sin sos dueños andar"
Describes the Maures' losses
The bard comments on the events from an axiological perspective: "¡Qual lidia bien sobre exorado arzon / mio Çid Ruy Diaz el buen lidiador!"
Lists El Cid's most valorous warriors, then mentions a few warlike deeds that took place during the battle
El Cid orders Minaya to return to combat
The bard reprises the answer to the previous order, then describes the battle again Fariz and Galve ("sabet")
The bard comments on the full impact of what is taking place: "¡Tan buen dia por la christiandad / a fuyen los moros de la e de la part!"
Returns to the description of the battle
Details El Cid's victory
Repeats the full extent of the victory (the number of dead and the symbol)
The bard expresses his admiration for El Cid : "Dios, commo es bien barbado! / Almofar a cuestas, la espada en mano"
El Cid thanks God and his loved ones
Returns to the spoils, evoking El Cid's honor and generosity toward the vanquished
The bard once again expresses his admiration for El Cid: "¡Dios que bien pago a todos sus vassallos / a los peones e a los encavalgados!"
El Cid sends Minaya to give the king some gifts
Minaya accepts the mission with which he is entrusted
El Cid gives Minaya gold and tells him what he must do
The bard evokes Minaya's satisfaction
El Cid dictates the message Minaya is to deliver to the Castillans
Describes Minaya's depature by repeating and expanding on the previously given orders
The bard expresses his admiration for El Cid: "¡Que bien pago a sus vassalos mismos!"
The bard concludes on El Cid's generosity and greatness

euphoria—and until the announcement of the Cid's final victory, sometimes provoking a suspension of the action, a kind of freeze-frame to glorify the protagonist: "This is a good day for Christians! / For everywhere the Moors are fleeing" (Vv. 770–71).[7]

The border between narrated and narrative space is shattered; the intrusion of the narrator in the diegesis merges the two spaces during the performance. As for the image of the *Campeador*, it is constructed through the discourse narrated by the minstrel and his commentary, which never skimps on *admiratio* formulas. The hero is thus defined as much by his acts as a warrior (highlighting his courage and generosity) as by his speeches (whether mediated or not) that express his determination and charisma.

The frequency of the alternating voices testifies to the text's strong oral quality, its dynamic character, and its theatricality, making the storyteller's voice one of the founding elements of epic speech. It allows the narrative levels to take over from, or respond to, each other, thereby strengthening the cohesion of the whole.[8] Heterogeneity and the echoing of narrative voices, elevated to the status of epic narrative techniques, endow the narrative with its continuity. In the battle stories and elsewhere, the alternating voices accompany and actualize the diegesis; at the time of oral transmission, the minstrel's passionate narrative gave way to the diffraction of the narrative voice and, in turn, encouraged the development of representational processes and strategies in the audience.

Text and Voice

Like the *Poema*, the comic uses battle stories to help build the characters and plot. Admittedly, the comic's arrangement differs significantly from the *Poema*, but the organization of narrative voices is not that dissimilar. As Scott McCloud has noted, a polyphony establishes a new narrative balance through the play of sequencing and the visual co-presence of all signifying codes (10). The Cid remains an inescapable historical and literary figure in Spain, and each period tends to recuperate the mythical figure as the embodiment of a national and/or Christian spirit. Hernández Palacios is no exception to the rule and seeks to dust off the image of the knight through an alliance between text and image, in which he sees "a privileged tool to teach others"[9] (Lara 3) and a contribution to the transmission of the myth. Following the comic's opening panel, the omniscient narrative voice welcoming the reader does not hesitate to fragment its speech to the point of suggesting several narrative strata that sometimes overlap or intersect. Two main narrative devices are used: speech balloons and captions. According to Benoît Peeters, captions can be compared to "a full story, linking panels that would otherwise have remained disjointed"; in addition to providing cohesion and coherence, Peeters also points to the caption's ability to "evoke elements that drawings are ill-equipped to portray, such as the thoughts and feelings of the characters, but also sounds, smells, climates" (*Case* 27).

A statistical analysis of the corpus reveals remarkable results regarding the parallel discourse that functions as an adjunct to the main speech, completing or clarifying the frames: 49 percent of the panels contain captions; and in 35 percent of cases, it is the only text in the frame. The more traditional type of speech therefore occupies a mere 65 percent of the panels. The data reinforces the visual dimension of the creation of meaning in comics, but also raises the question of the functions of both narrative speech patterns.

Speech Balloons

The role of the speech balloon could be limited to the transcription of direct speech, which the reader perceives without any intermediary. But the fact that so many captions play the role of a *verbum dicendi* begs for a more detailed analysis of the discursive function of the speech balloon. It has, first and foremost, an *informative status* when its contents mediate an episode of the narrative. The Battle of Graus, the starting point of Volume I, is presented as an event prior to the diegesis, which is added to, and incorporated into, the narrative by two messengers on horseback whose mission is both diegetic (to warn the king) and narratological (to inform the reader of what happened). Throughout the story, there are several other episodes that serve as excuses to erase the narrator's voice in favor of one of the characters: the death of the hermit in Volume II, for example, is a bad omen that foreshadows Don Sancho's death. It is also this unmediated dialogue device that enables an analeptic discourse on Don Sancho's youth, followed by a proleptic discourse on the Cid. In this case, the primacy of meaning and narrative content seems to derive from the unmediated expression of the characters in the episodes that count as true narrative hinges.

Additionally, the speech balloon can play a *structuring role in the narration*, thereby assuming the place and function usually attributed to captions. In such a rare case, the figure is reserved for the development of historical

Fig. 2: *El Cid II : Las Cortes de Léon* (Palacio, 1972): Ferdinand I tells his son that vengeful enemy troops are at the gates of Coimbra, following the city's capture by Almanzor.

events. The extradiegetic narrator thus gives way to one of the characters. The speech of the character of Ferdinand I, for example (fig. 2), is subjectified and is part of a voluntary suspension of the narrative dynamics. The latter is made concrete by arranging the strips in a sequence of almost identical frames, with the royal character as storyteller consistently appearing in superimposition at the bottom of the panel. It is no longer a parallel voice, but an entire narrative that is created.

Captions

As previously stated, captions usually contain some sort of parallel speech, distilling information that supplements or organizes the narrative (Peeters, *La Bande dessinée* 27). In this case, they acquire the status of full speech emanating from a protean voice. This occurs predominantly in a form of speech that is essential to the narrative's coherence, strengthening the unity between the different layers of meaning associated with the text in the speech balloons and the images, respectively. I will group the functions of the captions into four categories:

a. *Editorial framing captions* occur on the boundaries of the diegesis. Present at the opening and closing panels of each volume, they frame the voice of an omniscient narrator who introduces contextual elements, circumscribes the narrative content, and creates continuity between one album and the next. This is the case in the opening panels of each volume where long shots ground the diegesis in a pictorial context (I-1, for example).[10]
b. *Metadiscursive captions* are those that, generally speaking, paraphrase the image (I-23) or text, identify or describe the characters. They open a parenthesis without disrupting the narrative. By providing contextual information, they can emphasize the plurality of views, decrypt an image, reinforce a stylistic twist, or comment on a character's attitudes (IV-26-3). Thus, the voice also participates in the story while remaining in the background; it can sometimes represent a reasoned approach to a type of speech, in which text and image are otherwise difficult to align.
c. *Narrative captions* have a direct impact on the narrative flux in that they expand or condense, interrupt or suspend the narrative, in which they can introduce or conclude an episode, or highlight an action. The caption emphasizes the narrator's presence and allows for the manipulation of key story elements. It is thus possible to stress a particular story element by expanding the time of an action associated with a particular panel layout or by fragmenting the narrative (III-31). Moreover, in many cases, the desired effect of verisimilitude is produced by the suspension of the narrative, into which a contextual element or the voice of an omniscient narrator is incorporated (II-18, III-10). So it is not uncommon for the caption to take on the externality of the voice it features by positioning itself outside the panel; from this intericonic position, it can orchestrate simultaneity (fig. 3) or restore meaning to a series of

Fig. 3: *El Cid I : Sancho de Castilla* (Palacio, 1971): the bard describes how El Cid tried to come to his companions' rescue.

unstructured panels (III-22). The narrative network is thus rendered more complex by the entrenchment of different strata that helps organize the entire discourse. In this respect, the caption may play the role of a *verbum dicendi* and frame the more conventional discourse in the speech balloons (I-40-1, IV-25-2), or present indirect speech, thereby upsetting traditional narrative codes by having such speech spoken by an actant (III-5-3). The caption's common position at the junction of two panels embodies an enunciative position on the border of both discourses, resulting in a mixed speech that is both specific to the diegesis while being external to it, just like the minstrel's voice (II-13-3).

d. The *intermedial caption* effects the convergence between drawing, text, and narration, and, as such, constitutes the mainstay of narration in comics. In responding to dialogue (I-26-1) or establishing continuity between narrative instances (I-48-2), it creates an echo between the different types of speech and generates a confusion between voices and spaces. Consequently, the reader perceives a polyphonic discourse, a generator of meaning and an open space of transmission which is itself integrated into the fiction. By embedding several narrative strata, it operates as a *mise en abyme*, blurring the boundaries between narrated space and the space of mediation, just as original storytellers did in their time.[11]

Polyphony

The distribution of narrative voices works in three main ways:

(1) The caption assumes its traditional metadiscursive function; the extradiegetic, omniscient narrator uses it to open, introduce, or conclude a dialogue.

(2) The intradiegetic omniscient narrator rationalizes the narrative according to his interpretation and produces a stylistic effect interrupting the flow of dialogue (IV-10-2).

(3) The caption mixes with the dialogue and enables the coexisting voices to respond to each other. According to a model resembling the recounting of the battle of Alcocer in the *Poema de Mio Cid*, the alternation between speech balloons and captions, between discourse and story, guarantees the continuity between speech types that can now respond and complement one another. By bursting out of the boundaries of the panel and those of narrative space, and by combining with the image, this "supra-narration" offers the reader a representation of polyphony in a global and multimodal discourse. Captions in the margins of the panel—even those between panels—are the generators that set up a discursive syntax contributing to the recreation within comics of a situation comparable to the narrative performances of old.[12]

Even more clearly than in the *Poema*, visual and textual discourses in the comics adaptation merge in the representation of war. Panels I-42 and I-43 (fig. 4) combine a frame layout and direct speech that follow a parallel pattern, producing an impression of chaos, uncertainty, and danger. On another level, page III-20 demonstrates that narration and its meaning are based solely on the interaction of text and image, with one illuminating the meaning of the other. The succession in Volume IV of the sometimes religious, Orientalist, or dreamlike triptychs, for example, highlights the military and religious dimensions of the battle of Barbastro. The caption is sometimes fragmented (IV-5), facilitating the arrangement of a gallery of portraits and sceneries that suspend the narrative to include the elements required for the development of the diegesis. Visual suspension in I-17 and I-18, established through clichés, produces the analepsis of Usúa's childhood, while a similar suspensive technique in IV-38-3 creates an information gap that amplifies the suspense of the next scene. In short, it is always the affinity between, and accumulation of, image and text that create meaning in III-20 (fig. 5): the

Fig. 4: *El Cid I : Sancho de Castilla* (Palacio, 1971): Don Sancho's men try to free their leader, who has been imprisoned after launching an attack on the castle of Usua.

rising power of an aggressive army is made palpable through the juxtaposition of a scene depicted in long shots and more fragmented representations of the same scene in narrow panels offering different perspectives, where continuity is maintained exclusively through the representation of heavy rain, and ending with the return to direct speech in a fragmented panel. The intericonic space no longer indicates temporal ellipses, which instead become overwhelming; it is the agent of cohesion in an almost cubist portrayal of the scene, which the redundancy of conjunctions and accumulative adverbs ("y," "también" . . .) reinforces.

Between Subject and Object of Representation: The Character of the Cid

Like the speech balloons, the images seem to be the manifestation of a narrative entity's voice that reveals and integrates itself within the polyphonic network, generating both direction and interpretation. In this regard, the view on the character of the Cid offered by the image warrants discussion. As mentioned above, the Cid occupies a rather marginal place despite his eponymous status. The knight is conspicuously absent from the four albums in which he often only appears in the background. When the text evokes him, it is through the lips of another character who, calling him by his first name, Rodrigo, makes it possible for us to identify the "main" character in spite of

Fig. 5: *El Cid III : La toma de Coimbra* (Palacio, 1973): Fernando I's increasingly powerful army.

Fig. 6: *El Cid IV : La cruzada de Barbastro* (Palacio, 1984): When Sancho, El Cid, and their men arrive to fight against Moctadir, they receive a message from their enemy demanding they return his niece, whom they had captured, and leave.

the distance. In his other appearances, it is the image alone that depicts the character of the Cid, either as subject or object of the gaze.

With the Cid as a subject of the gaze, the reader is encouraged to adopt his point of view and become emotionally involved in the story. As an object of the gaze, the distribution of panels, the framing of the action, and the multiple perspectives reveal clues as to the state of mind of the hero, whose temperament is sketched through representations that reveal him to be combative and determined. In so doing, his image evolves throughout the series, showing him as he becomes not only more mature, thus ensuring the consistency of the comics, but also more unrecognizable, as if his only role were to be the other characters' sidekick in the events he takes part in. It is necessary, however, to point out that, though almost entirely absent from volume one[13] where he always appears in the shadow of Don Sancho, he is gradually endowed with an identity, origin, and social status. Through images and speech, the successive volumes portray a man whose appearance and temperament become increasingly worn: long hair and a beard—highly symbolic in the Middle Ages[14]—and the reactions of a combative, determined man facing his future (II-26). Anyone familiar with the legend of El Cid will identify in both the setup of the images and the voice's statements allusions to the famous episodes that contributed to the creation of the myth, and which can be found in the *Poema de Mio Cid*, as well as in chronicles and romances[15] (fig. 6).

So what exactly is being adapted here? Certainly not the legend of the historical hero, relegated as he is to Don Sancho's shadow.[16] The story advances only when text and image merge, but ultimately it is the speech in the captions that organizes it. The sources of focalization are centered more on the leading characters (Don Sancho, Basurde, Usúa, Aixa) than the Cid. The Cid is but mentioned in passing, and when he does intervene, he is introduced by the image or in direct speech and never by the ever-evasive narrative voice. Should we see this as the fulfillment of Hernández Palacios's desire to radically break with the existing corpus? It would ultimately be incorrect to do so. The portrayal of the battle of Alcocer highlights salient aspects the comic seems to hinge on as well: the accuracy of topographical references and the temporal organization correspond to the *Poema* and the comic, both of which tap into the legend to derive the consistency required to make it intelligible to different audiences. The twelfth-century text already recommended a measure of fidelity to certain representational aspects of the Cid, which was reinforced by attention to verisimilitude. For if the epic genre imposes the exaggeration of the hero's military exploits in battle, it must always be offset by elements that make the whole more believable. In addition, was the epic not intended as a means to disseminate information? By saturating the text with comments made by the omniscient narrator's learned voice, Hernández Palacios reinforces the presence of the godlike narrator, emphasizing the oral quality and thus making the modern storyteller's personality more convincing.

This voice manipulates the representation of time and space (expansion, compression, sequencing) and produces a complex chronology, alternating story time and narrating time, flashbacks and prolepses, which add even more density to the diegesis: the characters have a past, present, future; each action is bounded by a beginning and an end, with phases occurring at different rhythms, as determined by the linking of word and image. As Patrizia Violi (2013) points out in her work, the visual dimension is essential to the meaning of the text. Though virtual, the act of depiction by the minstrel, meant to ensure the vitality and truthfulness of his performance, is now accomplished by the image. This "transfer of power" is accompanied by an explosion of narrative networks; the signifying units are distributed across the panel, the strip, and the page. While all the voices in the *Poema* originate from the same point to construct a continuous narrative that could only be broken down into subordinate narrative layers thanks to the talent of the storyteller, the comic brings the voices together. The channels of meaning multiply, are superimposed, cross, and merge autonomously by resorting to a more subdued mediation. The image formulates what the text cannot show, and vice versa. Owing to its rich narrative potential, the comic impresses both as fiction and as a representation of reality. However, the story was already alive and kicking well before its adaptation into images. More than meaning alone, it is this generative process that matters, and the adaptation only has meaning because "[i]t is interesting to note [. . .] how the humble images silently accompany these words, these texts, helping them say the same things with the same irony, either affirming or refuting their meaning" (Lara 3).[17]

The tension between text and image, hypotext, and hypertext (in this case the adaptation) is constant. It is a tension amenable to what Benoît Peeters calls "suturing" (*Case* 101); the story is reconstructed, illuminated by new techniques capable of giving a new direction—new meaning—to the diegesis without erasing the trace of the first, anterior, and foundational text. Thus, Hernández Palacios did not completely free himself from the semiotic influence of the *Poema de Mio Cid*, which still haunts his update of the myth of the Cid, suggesting that the myth springs from the text rather than the hero.

Conclusion

Joseph Courtès taught us that the representational mode must speak to a particular group to generate a process of interpretation. In this case, the interpretive process remains ambiguous; through the time lag and dissolution of the original semiosphere, the relationship with the referential world entails modifications in the signs owing to the shift in the relation between audience, medium, and object. From the *Poema* to *El Cid*, the affinity between diegesis and referential world has changed very little, while the narrative tools in both are quite similar, as they meet the expectations of an audience well-versed in epic narrative. However, thanks to the specific narrative set-up of comics, Hernández Palacios complicates the transmission channel, so as to increase the liveliness of the work for an audience that is more used to its language. In this case, it is not orality itself that arouses the adapters' interest, but its representation. Did Hernández Palacios succeed in dusting off and demystifying the Cid? I believe he has, in part, achieved his goal. As the first rewriting of the myth after the death of Franco,[18] *El Cid* recalls and highlights the myth and the values it defends. The emphasis on the representation of battles is a pretext for showing the Cid as "[lord and victim] of war, [a Spaniard] learning how to survive on the battlefield, with a bloodlust"[19] (Lara 4). Given that there are certainly no direct links between the *Poema* and *El Cid*, there are, however, some thematic and formal similarities that invite us to consider them in the light of hypertextuality. Neither the author of the comic, nor his audience, can ignore the existing corpus and simply turn way from the preexisting path the source material bestowed. Any new reworking seems invariably marked by the significant trace of orality, regardless of the mode of representation. This not only testifies to the persistence of the text in its semiotic function, but also to the resilience of the myth. The persistence of the first text in any adaptation would therefore support the theory that the myth—or the "mythic energy," in Michel Serceau's phrase (92)—does derive its force not so much from its hero but from its successive rewritings and representations.

Notes

1. Hutcheon explicitly associates the practice of adaptation with intertextuality: "adaptation is a form of intertextuality: we experience adaptations (*as adaptations*) as palimpsests through our memory of other works that resonate through repetition with variation" (7).

2. In 2007, on the 800th anniversary of Per Abbat's manuscript, which is still at the Biblioteca Nacional de España and remains the only tangible trace of the poem's existence, many editions were released, targeting all types of audiences, from the most erudite philologists to young Spanish and Latin-American readers.

3. Original text: "mucho más auténtico que el que nos enseñaron de pequeños [para] volver a aprender, de verdad, la historia que se nos escamoteó."

4. Original text: "Hay que leerlo todo, desbrozando el conocimiento a veces transmitido por los cantares de gesta, hermosos, pero poco fiables como documento."

http://alasombradelasabina.blogspot.com/2010/07/antonio-hernandez-palacios-el-arte-del .html. Accessed on April 24, 2012.

5. Original text: "El Cid es una historia cotidiana y ésta es, a mi juicio, su característica más importante. No se trata de recrear héroes del pasado [. . .] sino hacer que ese pasado se convierta en presente inmediato, vivo y reconocible."

6. The previous editions were published by Trinca (*Sancho de Castilla*) and Doncel (*Las Cortes de León* and *La toma de Coímbra*).

7. Original text: "¡Tan buen dia por la christiandad / ca fuyen los moros de la [e de la] part !"

8. This is the case, for instance, when the Cid himself (on line 667) expresses his soldiers' exhaustion, summing up the story of King Tamin's strategic advances that has just been related.

9. Original text: "una herramienta privilegiada para enseñar a los demás."

10. The Roman numeral refers to the volume, the number to the plate. A third number is indicated when referring to a specific image.

11. On Spanish bards, see Edmund de Chasca's *El arte juglaresco en el "Cantar de Mio Cid,"* Alan Deyermond's *El « Cantar de Mio Cid » y la épica española*, and Paul Zumthor's *Introduction à la poésie orale*, among others.

12. On performance, see, for instance, Jean Rychner's *La Chanson de geste*.

13. In the first installment, the Cid is only mentioned in fairly evasive phrases ("ese mozo Rodrigo," "un tal Rodrigo") that insist on his utter lack of fame at this stage of the diegesis.

14. For further discussion of epic discourse, see Ramón Menéndez Pidal's *Cantar de Mío Cid. Texto, gramática y vocabulario*.

15. These comments echo Wolfgang Iser's theories on reader response: the reader can recreate a narration s/he is already familiar with, based on a certain number of references suggested by the transposition into the comic medium.

16. This view of adaptation recalls Michael Serceau's comments on film adaptations: "adaptation subjects itself [. . .] to the mythical energy of another text or another adaptation" to the point of "constituting its own system" (91).

17. Original text: "Resulta curioso comprobar [. . .] cómo las humildes imágenes acompañan, calladamente, a esas palabras, a esos textos, ayudándolos a decir las mismas cosas, y también con la ironía de prolongar su significado o negarlo."

18. "What the artist is offering, here, is a rite of passage from childhood-adolescence to man which, in Spain, has always been associated with blood and death. Too much human blood has been spilled onto this bull skin for thousands of years. Let's hope that none shall ever be spilled again. As in the days of Rodrigo, in Antonio's [Hernández Palacios] youth, the young were also sent into the streets wielding weapons. The coincidences and parallels between what we could call a secret biographical identity between the young Rodrigo and the young Antonio seem quite obvious to me, though that would be the topic of another discussion, of course" (Lara 4). Original text: "Lo que nuestro dibujante nos propone es una ceremonia de iniciación, ese paso de niño-joven al hombre que en España ha estado asociado a la muerte y a la sangre. Sobre esta piel de toro se ha derramado demasiada sangre humana desde hace miles de años y ojalá no se vuelva a verter más. Como en tiempos de Rodrigo, en la juventud de Antonio [Hernández Palacios], también los jóvenes fueron lanzados a la calle con un arma en las manos. Las concomitancias y las idas y venidas de lo que podríamos llamar una oculta identidad biográfica entre el Rodrigo y el Antonio jóvenes me parecen claras, pero eso sería, por supuesto, otra historia."

19. Original text: "[señor y víctima] de la guerra, [hispano] que aprend[e] a sobrevivir en el combate, con el sabor de la sangre."

Works Cited

Courtes, Joseph. *Du lisible au visible. Initiation à la sémiotique du texte et de l'image*. Bruxelles: De Boek Université, 1995.

De Chasca, Edmund. *El arte juglaresco en el "Cantar de Mío Cid."* Madrid: Gredos, 1972 [1955].

Deyermond, Alan. *El « Cantar de Mío Cid » y la épica medieval española*. Barcelona: Sirmio, 1987.

Deyzieux, Agnès, and Marcel Philippe. *Le Cas des cases. Informations, études et bibliographie sur la bande dessinée*. Paris: Bulle en tête, 1993.

Eisner, Will. *Comics and Sequential Art*. Expanded edition. Tamarac, FL: Poorhouse Press, 2000 [1985].

Groensteen, Thierry. *La Bande dessinée : une littérature graphique*. Toulouse: Milan, 2005.

Groensteen, Thierry. *Un Objet culturel non identifié*. Angoulême: l'An2, 2006.

Helbo, André. *Sémiologie de la représentation : Théâtre, télévision, bande dessinée*. Bruxelles: Complexe, 1975.

Hernández Palacios, Antonio. *El Cid I. Sancho de Castilla*. Vitoria: Ikusager, 1982 [1971].

Hernández Palacios, Antonio. *El Cid II. Las Cortes de León*. Vitoria: Ikusager, 1982 [1972].

Hernández Palacios, Antonio. *El Cid III. La toma de Coímbra*. Vitoria: Ikusager, 1982 [1973].

Hernández Palacios, Antonio. *El Cid IV. La cruzada de Barbastro*. Vitoria: Ikusager, 1984.

Hutcheon, Linda. *A Theory of Adaptation*. New York and London: Routledge, 2006.

Iser, Wolfgang. *The Act of Reading: A Theory of Aesthetic Response*. Baltimore, MD: Johns Hopkins University Press, 1978.

Jakobson, Roman. "On Linguistic Aspects of Translation." *The Translation Studies Reader*. Ed. Lawrence Venuti. London and New York: Routledge, 2000 [1959]. 113–18.

McCloud, Scott. *Understanding Comics: The Invisible Art*. Amherst, MA: Kitchen Sink Press, 1993.

Menéndez Pidal, Ramón. *Cantar de Mío Cid. Texto, gramática y vocabulario. Obras completas III–V*. Madrid: Espasa-Calpe, 1964 [1908–1911], 3 vols.

Ory, Pascal. *L'Histoire culturelle*. Paris: PUF, 2011 [2004].

Peeters, Benoît. *La Bande-dessinée. Un exposé pour comprendre, un essai pour réfléchir*. Paris: Flammarion, 1993.

Peeters, Benoît. *Case, planche, récit. Lire la bande dessinée*. Paris: Casterman, 1998 [1991].

Pernin, Georges. *Un Monde étrange : la bande dessinée*. Paris: Clédor, 1974.

Rychner, Jean. *La Chanson de geste : Essai sur l'art épique des jongleurs*. Genève: Droz, 1955.

Serceau, Michel. *L'Adaptation cinématographique des textes littéraires*. Liège: Céfal, 1999.

Violi, Patrizia. "Enonciation textualisée, énonciation vocalisée : arts du dire et sémiotique de l'oralité." *Nouveaux Actes Sémiotiques*. Conference proceeding, 2006, "Arts du faire: production et expertise." http://revues.unilim.fr/nas/document.php?id=3119. Accessed on May 2, 2013.

Xavier, José-Manuel. *La poétique du mouvement suivie du Carnet de l'animateur*. Angoulême: Centre National de la Bande Dessinée et de l'Image, 2003.

Zumthor, Paul. *Introduction à la poésie orale*. Paris: Seuil, 1983.

Absent Humanity: Personification and Spatialization in "There Will Come Soft Rains"

NICOLAS LABARRE

Ray Bradbury's short story "There Will Come Soft Rains" was first published in *Collier's* magazine in 1950, with a substantially revised version appearing in his 1953 short story collection *The Martian Chronicles* (Eller 154–58). Writer Al Feldstein and artist Wallace Wood published an eponymous adaptation in the bimonthly *Weird Fantasy* no. 17 (January–February 1953) in the then-dominant comics format, the short story anthology. Although science fiction comics were not the bestselling EC publications at the time (Gabilliet 39), the seven-page story colored by Marie Severin has since been frequently re-edited and reprinted, owing as much to its association with Bradbury as to its artwork, with Wallace Wood at the height of his artistic abilities.[1]

Both versions tell the same story. Set in August 2026, it features a fully automated house that continues to function long after the disappearance of its inhabitants. A Cold War narrative and post-apocalyptic reading of E. M. Forster's 1909 novella "The Machine Stops," "There Will Come Soft Rains" recounts the survival of machines that continue to function even though they have become useless: the kitchen continues to prepare meals, cigars still burn out in the ashtray, and so forth. A chain of external events will eventually disrupt the entire mechanism and destroy the place.

This chapter seeks to demonstrate that Feldstein and Wood's adaptation follows the logic of a paradoxical supplement, since, at first glance, their version seems to merely add illustrations to Bradbury's original text, which is present almost in full. However, this supplement, in turn, creates a new work that cannot be regarded as the result of a mere addition (Stam 11). The supplement creates, in effect, multiple gaps in the story, inviting contemplation and nonlinear reading trajectories. If spatialization is an inherent feature of comics (McCloud 100), in "There Will Come Soft Rains," it is exploited to suggest stasis, history that has come to a halt. As I will show in the final section of this chapter, the drawings also bring the story closer to the present, diminishing the allusive power of the original, while simultaneously bringing it to bear on the contradictory discourses on automation and the role of domestic space during the Cold War. By separating and spatializing the functions of narrator and enunciator, the adaptation ultimately changes the status of the house. Finally, I will demonstrate how the house's transformation into a possible protagonist possessing its own distinct voice prompts a reflection on the relationship between man and machine. The adaptation thus radically alters the story's reading contract by adding an ostensibly empty space, enabling multiple temporal trajectories and creating a tension between an almost tangible present, contained in the represented objects, and the end of the world, made all the more terrifying by the fact that it has already happened. The multiple modalities of comics turn Bradbury's text into one voice among many others, even as the adaptation and its paratext foreground signs of fidelity to the original. This chapter explores how the transition from a linear to a multimodal narrative engenders a diversity of interpretations and reading strategies.

The Spatiality of the Page and the Representation of Time

The idea of a world ruled by automated machines after the death of their creators is not particularly original. John W. Campbell, writer and editor of *Astounding Stories*, who exerted an unmistakable influence on Bradbury's early career, had already explored the theme at least twice: in "Twilight" (1934) and "Night" (1935). In "Night," a traveler from the thirties is projected into the distant future where he discovers an abandoned and useless automated city before learning that a few robots have survived and are willing to help him. Also of note is a short story published only a year after Bradbury's, Ward Moore's "The Flying Dutchman," which features a fully automated robot plane flying over the Earth; the reader eventually discovers that the planet has been destroyed in a nuclear disaster.

Thus, the central idea in both versions of "There Will Come Soft Rains" is neither new nor unique to its time. Its austere tone, however, is what makes Bradbury's story stand out: there is no narrative framework to explain the fate of the house; no human character; no time travel to justify the presence of a narrator. While Campbell's hero wanders across a vast city for millions of years, Bradbury's story centers on a single day in an enclosed space, reconstructing an Aristotelian poetics for a theater of destruction, where the setting is the sole protagonist.

The adaptation does not alter any of this. It is ostensibly characterized by an extreme fidelity to the original text. The task of adapting the story fell to Al Feldstein—a prolific author who wrote most of the stories published

there will come soft rains...
THE SUN CAME OUT FROM BEHIND THE RAIN. THE HOUSE STOOD ALONE IN A CITY OF RUBBLE AND ASHES. THIS WAS THE ONE HOUSE LEFT STANDING! AT NIGHT, THE RUINED CITY GAVE OFF A RADIOACTIVE GLOW WHICH COULD BE SEEN FOR MILES. THE ENTIRE WEST FACE OF THE HOUSE WAS BLACK, SAVE FOR FIVE PLACES. HERE, THE WHITE SILHOUETTE OF A MAN MOWED A LAWN. THERE, AS IN A PHOTOGRAPH, A WOMAN BENT TO PICK FLOWERS. STILL FARTHER OVER, THEIR IMAGES OUTLINED IN ONE TITANIC INSTANT, A SMALL BOY, HANDS FLUNG INTO THE AIR... HIGHER UP, THE IMAGE OF A THROWN BALL... AND OPPOSITE HIM, A GIRL, HANDS RAISED TO CATCH THE BALL WHICH NEVER CAME DOWN...
ADAPTED FROM A STORY BY RAY BRADBURY
THE FIVE SPOTS OF PAINT... THE MAN, THE WOMAN, THE CHILDREN, THE BALL REMAINED! THE REST WAS A CHARCOAL LAYER...
WOOD
THE MORNING HOUSE LAY EMPTY. IN THE LIVING ROOM, THE VOICE-CLOCK SANG, REPEATING AND REPEATING ITS SOUNDS INTO THE EMPTINESS...
TICK-TOCK! SEVEN O'CLOCK! TIME TO GET UP! TIME TO GET UP! SEVEN O'CLOCK...
IN THE KITCHEN, THE BREAKFAST STOVE GAVE A HISSING SIGH AND EJECTED FROM ITS WARM INTERIOR EIGHT PIECES OF PERFECTLY BROWNED TOAST, EIGHT EGGS SUNNYSIDE UP, SIXTEEN SLICES OF BACON, TWO COFFEES, AND TWO COOL GLASSES OF MILK...
SEVEN-NINE! BREAKFAST TIME! SEVEN-NINE...
1
©1950, 1990 by Ray Bradbury

Fig. 7: "There Will Come Soft Rains . . ." (Feldstein and Wood, 1953): "Ruins and ashes," the opening page.

in *Weird Fantasy*—and he retained the original virtually word for word. EC reserved a considerable amount of space for captions, usually placed at the top of panels to accommodate narrative cues. This preexisting layout made it possible to include more than two-thirds of the 2,000 words of the short story without the narrative looking particularly verbose compared to the rest of the publisher's output. The compatibility between the form of the adaptation and the length of the story facilitates the impression of fidelity.

Fidelity is a central feature, here, given the divide between the reputation and legitimacy of Bradbury, the respected author, and that of the comics medium. While adaptation arguably benefits both the source and the new work,[2] Bradbury's name figures prominently in the adaptation, while Feldstein's isn't even mentioned. Similarly, a caption on the cover boasts "EC's adaptation of a story by Ray Bradbury, America's top science-fiction writer," but fails to mention the comic book's regular authors and illustrators. Even if this is mostly advertising rhetoric, a textual hierarchy is clearly established, with fidelity to the source an implicit promise. The adaptation of "There Will Come Soft Rains" thus follows the logic of the supplement; with a text reproduced almost verbatim, the comic only seems to add a graphic rendering of the descriptions that remain allusive in the original. However, Robert Stam—invoking Derrida—has shown that the propensity of literary adaptations to "fill in the lacunae" of the original stories is a way to draw attention to "their structuring absences" (10). In turn, the supplement modifies our reading of the text, which is also slightly altered in places, by breaking down the story into panels and by spatializing narrative time. This becomes apparent if we compare the first page of the graphic version with the opening paragraphs of the short story.

Whereas Bradbury opens his short story with the empty house waking up, delaying the disturbing revelation of the setting—it is the only house left standing in a city "of ruins and ashes"—Feldstein eliminates the revelation. The graphic narrative begins with a splash panel showing a ravaged world and the burned façade of the house (fig. 7). With this exception, the sequence of the story is kept intact, and most of the changes are elisions, minor reformulations, or deletions of introductory clauses, which are integrated in the narrative in the form of balloons.

The focal point of the first panel is a black wall bearing the negative imprint of the silhouettes of the house's former occupants, echoing the traces of vaporized objects and people in Hiroshima and Nagasaki after the atomic bombings. The perfect contours depict contemporary America and include a symbol of an extravagant yet domestic future: a lawnmower bristling with coils and wires. The machine, made noticeable by its insertion in a family scene, immediately introduces a dissonance in the opposition between the human form and the perfect geometry of the house. In the lower righthand corner of the panel, where our visual exploration is likely to end, a bluish skull leaves no doubt as to the fate of humanity.

The two following panels present what remains of normality inside the house. In the first, a living room with knickknacks is outlined in vertical and horizontal lines, which are only interrupted by the soft contours and the deep shadows of the furniture. A white ladder takes up the center of the panel, reinforcing the sense of balance. Both windows are opaque and colored light blue, while an ordinary curtain parallels the panel border on the right. Only through the text can we know that this is the same house as in the first panel, since neither the geometry of the room nor the shape of the windows seem related to the previous image. On the right, a speech balloon announcing the time of day points to a metallic oblong aperture, the distant cousin of a loudspeaker. The enigmatic machine introduces the mechanical universe of the next panel. There, the entire space is taken up by the machine-kitchen, with no trace of humanity. The corrugated surfaces, multiple buttons, and chrome pipes form a futuristic vision where space has been softened, solid but comfortable, neither rough nor threatening. The invisible floor and the cramped atmosphere underscore the suspicion that mankind has no place here.

As early as the first page, the adaptation strategy appears clear and can be described as both a virtuoso treatment of emptiness and a spatialization of time. Wallace Wood is renowned for his drawings of voluptuous women, as well as fantastic and complex machines.[3] Here, the former is reduced to a sign on a wall, while the latter takes center stage. To Bradbury's recounting of the absence of humans, Wood and Feldstein add the rhetoric of the gap. The illustrations add nothing but emptiness: elegantly functional spaces devoid of purpose. The balance of the story is profoundly altered by the addition of these depopulated spaces, which, through their detail and graphic quality, invite a substantial reading time. Their presence gives rise to a contemplative dimension that lengthens every moment and disrupts the narrative's regular temporal rhythm. Jonathan Eller writes that the story evokes "the deconstruction of our chronological sense of time, which has now become meaningless" (Eller and Touponce 154). One of the strengths of the adaptation is that it intensifies this theme by multiplying the possible readings of a panel, mobilizing the tension between what Pierre Fresnault-Deruelle has called the panel's "linearity" and "tabularity" (121–38).

The homology between the grid in comics and architecture has been noted on more than one occasion (Groensteen, *System* 69; Bartual 2011). "There

Will Come Soft Rains" taps into this property by turning the lines between the panels into a mark of separation between two locations. The curtain and speaker in the second panel repeat the grid and integrate it within diegetic space. Consequently, the page cannot be read in a linear fashion exclusively; it can also be read in a tabular way, with juxtaposed rather than successive spaces. The adaptation thereby introduces an additional narrative temporality. To the chronology of the day described by Bradbury, an effect of immobility or nonlinearity is added; it is enabled by a tabular reading, which is arguably an intrinsic property of comics.[4]

The story also relies on variations in representation (design, color, etc.) to delimit three distinct spaces. The first is the exterior, a horrific vision of a contemporary world where the future is just a fleeting trace, the explosion having "drawn" the outlines of the lawnmower on the wall. The motif of the blue skull, present throughout the story, serves as an explicit encoding of this setting. The second space is the empty house where everything still recalls humanity's recent disappearance. It is an intermediate space, juxtaposing contemporary aesthetics with futuristic artifacts hurriedly hiding from sight. Finally, the third space is that of the machine itself, with its shiny surfaces and soft angles, which soon becomes the story's protagonist.

The vision of an uninhabitable environment and automated, claustrophobic interiors present in Forster's novella "The Machine Stops" is an obvious inspiration for Bradbury's work. Forster's story also presents three distinct spaces, invisible machines at work behind the walls, and an inventory of modern commodities, suggesting that the ideals of domestic comfort had remained fairly constant from 1909 to 1950.

> There were buttons and switches everywhere—buttons to call for food, for music, for clothing. There was the hot-bath button, by pressure of which a basin of (imitation) marble rose out of the floor, filled to the brim with a warm deodorized liquid. There was the cold-bath button. There was the button that produced literature and there were of course the buttons by which she communicated with her friends. The room, though it contained nothing, was in touch with all that she cared for in the world. (Forster 90)

Bradbury's story can be read as a rewriting of Forster's, a connection furthered by the fact that both texts also use an immutable, mechanically repeated sequence. Forster achieves this effect through parataxis, while Bradbury systematically mentions the passing hours throughout his story. As a matter of fact, Forster's tale had already been adapted by Wallace Wood a year prior to "There Will Come Soft Rains." In addition to its role as hypotext

Fig. 8: "Blobs" (Kurtzman and Wood, 1952): the year 1952.

for Bradbury's text, it also provides a point of comparison for gauging the specificity of the artist's graphic treatment.

"Blobs!"—a satirical adaptation of "The Machine Stops" written by Harvey Kurtzman and illustrated by Wood—appeared in the first issue of *Mad*. As in Forster's narrative, it shows how humanity has become utterly dependent on a technological arsenal fulfilling every need, until a malfunction causes a breakdown of the entire system (fig. 8). "Blobs" adds a chronological depiction of human dependence on technology to the original narrative, starting with prehistoric times and including a depiction of 1952, when a "working man's office was a mass of switches and buttons." The year 1952—as portrayed in "Blobs!"—is endowed with just a few futuristic traits in the soothing interiors where comfortable armchairs are set against rectilinear walls. However, the vision of the future developed later in the story exhibits the same meandering perspectives, the same uninhabitable spaces that characterize the third panel of "There Will Come Soft Rains." "Blobs!" thus underscores that, in his adaptations, Wood deliberately constructs two juxtaposed but distinct spaces, one of which displaces a portion of Bradbury's futuristic tale towards the present.

Anchoring the story in the recognizable present further emphasizes the emptiness within the graphic narrative. By refusing to create an outright science fiction world, Wood creates a tragic atmosphere in which history has already been played out, and the distinction between present and future is no longer relevant. He thereby elaborates upon a latent thread in Bradbury's text, which can be fully worked out in the graphic narrative's production and reception. In a publication devoted to short graphic tales, often with twist endings, each panel is valuable and even necessary to the story's development; devoid of technological wonders and shock effects, the frontal representation of an almost banal interior constitutes an unparalleled break with the rest of the stories in the issue of *Weird Fantasy* and the science fiction comics published by EC in general. While Bradbury already foregrounds the banal in his science fiction setting and mentions the emptiness of the house three times, this emptiness is disclosed in all its terror in Wood's adaptation. The emptiness of this familiar interior, devoid of any fantastic, retroactive explanation, creates horror through absence, a feeling that overused apocalyptic images could no longer arouse; that issue alone comprised no less than two stories relating the end of the world. As early as the first page, the focus of the narrative is not on destruction—which is not used to produce suspense since its aftermath is already evident in the first panel—but on absence.

Man and Machine

The history of American comics has called attention to the specificities of these short narratives published in magazine anthologies. Using the term *nouvelle graphique* ("graphic short story"), borrowed from Jean-Pierre Dionnet, Daniel Riche and Boris Eizykman suggest that they present a rare attempt at doing away with the figure of the hero (78–79). Nevertheless, EC stories are invariably structured around a more or less identifiable protagonist, sometimes reduced to his/her narrative function. It must be borne in mind that the play of similarities and differences with other stories published by EC is an almost indispensable component in the reading contract of the adaptation of "There Will Come Soft Rains," shaping the horizon of expectation of many readers. Even contemporary reprints usually juxtapose Wood's reworking with other EC science fiction stories.[5] Therefore, even minimal differences with existing codes of representation in EC's other titles and issues are significant. Whether we read the story within this paradigm, or more generally within the frame of narrative comics, in which the existence of a central character is a structural component (Groensteen, *System* 190–91), our attention is mechanically drawn to the one voice capable of playing—if only temporarily—the role of the protagonist: the automaton in charge of the house.

In the story's second panel, the chosen narrative system turns the machine into a speaking agent through a speech balloon pointing to the loudspeaker on the wall. The use of a balloon is significant considering that comics have a wealth of means to represent speech, especially that of non-human agents. Onomatopoeia written directly in the panel are rather rare in *Weird Fantasy*, but captions abound and can relate with the content of the panels in a variety of ways, ranging from redundancy to meta-narrative commentary. The type of speech balloon used here—a white, rounded bubble—is usually reserved for words originating from living, human characters. In other EC comics, when a voice is transmitted through an electronic communication channel, as in another adaptation of Bradbury's work, "Zero Hour" (Al Feldstein and Michael Kammen, *Weird Fantasy* issue 18, March–April 1953), the bubble is jagged and yellow.

The construction of a human-like protagonist through this medium-specific device implies a shift away from the original story. Bradbury immediately evokes a "second voice" after the house stops announcing breakfast and indicates the time of the day aloud. Feldstein and Wood's adaptation ignores this distinction, eliding introductory clause and inserting the spoken text in a speech balloon with the same form as in the two previous panels. As each voice no longer has its distinct function, the successive enunciations come to constitute a discourse. The machine that controls the house is thus put in the position of a single enunciator, whose physical form is that of the various loudspeakers. The rest of the story will confirm the first signs that point to the possible substitution of the human by the machine. The classic device of the "talking house" involves pointing a speech balloon at a building shown from the outside. It is a conventional way to create a dramatic setting where speech is attributed to a protagonist inside the building (Campbell 2011). "There Will Come Soft Rains" reveals the ambiguity of the convention, with the house as the source of the spoken words (2).

The double play on codes, which relies on both the specificities of EC comics and the function of speech balloons in general, turns the machine-house into a highly ambiguous potential substitute for—and even metonymy of—humanity. Furthermore, the story submits the machinery to two tests that will reveal its limitations and, through this opposition, make it appear more human. These trials, already featured in the short story, are once again transfigured by the play on the ambiguities of the comics grid.

The story quickly introduces some mouse-robots, "invaders" scurrying out from the entrails of the machine, blindly penetrating the living space of the vanished humans (2) (fig. 9). However, the animality evoked by the "small

Fig. 9: "There Will Come Soft Rains . . ." (Feldstein and Wood, 1953): robots in the guise of animals.

cleaning animals" is a misdirection, an illusion akin to the savage beasts moving on the walls of the nursery further on in the story.[6] Wood draws them as quasi-organic shapes, rounded with chrome curves, but their color (they are blue with white highlights) gives away their machinic nature, as did the skull in the opening panel. When faced with a real animal, the home-robot reacts with hostility. It does recognize the "voice" of the dog and grants it right of entry but nothing more, chasing it instead with the "angry" mechanical mice (3, panel 3) and locking its food away until the animal dies. The machine's hostility is reflected in the layout, which gradually crushes the animal in the first strip of the page. It is in the space between two panels that the carcass disappears (3, panels 8–9), suddenly replaced by a multitude of cleaning robots, which we have now come to realize are simply *imitating* life. The rhythmic function of the grid dominates this sequence, which begins and ends on a single page, composed of three strips of three identically shaped panels. The passage also invites a tabular reading (Fresnault-Deruelle 121–38): the kitchen the dog wants to come into occupies the central panel, with the

THE DOG RAN AROUND, HYSTERICALLY YELPING TO EACH DOOR, AT LAST REALIZING, AS THE HOUSE REALIZED, THAT ONLY SILENCE WAS HERE! IT SNIFFED THE AIR AND SCRATCHED AT THE KITCHEN DOOR...

BEHIND THE DOOR, THE STOVE WAS MAKING LUNCH...PANCAKES WHICH FILLED THE HOUSE WITH A RICH BAKING ODOR AND THE SCENT OF MAPLE SYRUP...

THE DOG FROTHED AT THE MOUTH, LYING AT THE DOOR, SNIFFING. ITS EYES TURNED TO FIRE...

Fig. 10: "There Will Come Soft Rains . . ." (Feldstein and Wood, 1953): the grid as prison.

animal unable to cross the gutter space that separates it from the room (fig. 10). The grid is a prison, and the narrative's spatial organization underscores the sterility of preserved mechanical life. The house is not the animal, even if it sometimes mimics its shape. While part of the narrative structure constructs the machine-house as a tragic protagonist—its fate sealed ("At ten o'clock, the house began to die," as the caption on page 4 announces)—the grid and the layout maintain the difference between the artifact and the living. The multiple expressive modes of comics, sometimes referred to as *multimodal* (Groensteen, *Comic* 122), thus allow for several simultaneous discourses, and Bradbury's text is just one of them, now inscribed into a complex discursive scheme that affords multiple interpretations of the story. If adaptations are, in effect, dialogues between two cultural objects (Christa and Ray 19), then retaining almost the entirety of Bradbury's text facilitates the back and forth between the adaptation and its source within the comics version itself. The inherent dialogue, or tension, between text and image in comics thus mirrors the tension between the adaptation and the "original."

The house is later confronted with nature itself, as a tree branch shatters the window, tearing down the boundaries between the different narrative spaces. At the heart of the machine, in the automated kitchen, a fire starts, eventually engulfing the entire house. The voices no longer mechanically repeat their messages, but instead "wail," becoming explicitly "tragic" only to "die" (7). As in most science fiction, emotion becomes "the last sign of a desperate humanity" (Telotte 21). The destruction that strikes the home echoes the unseen disaster that precedes the narrative. By letting only the automated home survive, the destruction produced a blurring of preexisting boundaries, which had remained hidden by the permanence of spatial divisions. The fire collapses all hierarchies. The space vacated by humanity becomes the battleground for the struggle between the house and the flames (6), with the electronics that had been so discreet becoming ubiquitous; it is also at this moment that we see that the house clearly has eyes (7, panel 1), in addition to its many mouths.

Like the dog, the tree and the fire establish—in the negative and through metonymy—the essence of the house: it is neither animal, nor elemental. The missing test, which cannot be staged in the story, is the confrontation with the human, which, like in a large-scale Turing test, would have separated man from machine. Instead, ambiguity lingers, supported by the use of multiple narrative devices.

Commenting on the transition from novel to film, narratologist Seymour Chatman observes that adaptation transforms the process of description as film evinces visual "plenitude" (38–41). A comic that is "realistic" in its representation, if not its content, like the EC adaptation of "There Will Come Soft Rains," occupies an intermediate position. Spatial completeness is promised, but quickly dissolves because of the peculiarities of drawn images. Drawn images call for simplification and abstraction of everything that is not strictly necessary for the story action (Groensteen, *System* 190–91). For example, in several of Wood's other science fiction stories, the decor is sometimes erased completely. In "There Will Come Soft Rains," that decor has to be maintained at all times, since there is nothing else in the panels, endowing the representation of places and objects with greater weight. Every single detail is meaningful, even more so since the reader is unable to forget the conscious decision behind the marks on the page. The mimetic contract, which can no longer rely on conventional elisions, transforms the house into an artificial place where the reader follows the development of an "artifact" on both the level of the diegesis and the page itself (Groensteen, *Comics* 93). The opacity of the comics medium, which never allows us to forget the artist's hand, is thus in tune with the narrative's theme. As Bill Mason has pointed out, the affection Wood shows for objects and their design implies a powerful emotional charge: "'Soft Rains' is profoundly moving because Wood obviously loved the doomed inanimate objects that are all that remains of the men and women who made them" (97). The link between the human and the machine-home is, then, affirmed on the level of the narrative structure.

Textual changes work in unison with the graphic and structural treatment. Although there are few omissions from the original text, they remain consistent. In addition to a passage devoted to the animated animals on the walls of the nursery—an allusion to the short story "The Veldt"—these omissions include a poem and a recurrent religious subtext, which spelled out the relation between humans and their machine-house. The omission of the poem is, perhaps, the most surprising of the two, since Sara Teasdale's text—published in 1920 and evoking the uninterrupted continuation of nature after the disappearance of humankind—provides the short story with its title. The main effect of this omission is to add an element of mystery to the story's title, now linked to an absent text without any footing in the diegesis. Pragmatically, the limited space and the difficulties of the graphic treatment may explain this elision. However, my hypothesis is that the removal plays a role in the adaptation's legitimatization strategy. The comic is presented as the adaptation of a short story, but by revealing that this text was, in turn, inspired by a hypotext, Wood and Feldstein's version would be relegated even further from an admittedly mythologized "original" underpinning any claims to fidelity an adaptation may have (Hutcheon xiii). The other omission is more significant, as the missing passages detailed the relationship between the house and its owners, making the place the altar of an obsolete religion in which the incinerator is enthroned like the devil. The original passages read:

> The house was an altar with ten thousand attendants, big, small, servicing, attending, in choirs. But the gods had gone away, and the ritual of the religion continued senselessly, uselessly. [. . .] The offending dust, hair, or paper, seized in miniature steel jaws, was raced back to the burrows. There, down tubes which fed into the cellar, it was dropped into the sighing vent of an incinerator which sat like evil Baal in a dark corner. (Bradbury, "There Will Come Soft Rains" 168–69)

By emphasizing the role of ritual and presenting the house as a meaningless vestige, Bradbury turns it into a mere décor that fulfills a different narrative function than in the graphic retelling. The narrator draws attention to the futility of the daily gestures of the automatic installations, and in adopting this voice, Bradbury also condemns interpretations linking these gestures to the occupants of the house before their disappearance. Feldstein's cuts take the story beyond the haunted house trope, making the boundary between human and machine an uncertain one. Basing their analysis of Bradbury's version on the reference to the altar, Eller and Touponce suggest that the aspiration of the machine to become human is doomed from the start (154–55). The graphic version downplays such a strict separation and leaves the possibility of crossing the divide open.

With the line between man and machine now so tenuous, the passage also echoes the debates on the role of automation in the domestic space that were taking place at the time of the story's publication (Oldenziel and

Zachmann 2009). The anxiety "Blobs" expressed in an openly satirical vein is more implicit in "There Will Come Soft Rains." The perfect perspectives of Wood's ultimately uninhabitable spaces suggest that the disappearance of humanity as we know it preceded the nuclear catastrophe.

The Machinic and Domestic Ideal

During the so-called "kitchen debate" between Nixon and Khrushchev at the American Exhibition in Moscow in 1959, the rivalry between the two superpowers centered on their advances in home appliance technology. Although none of the "kitchens of the future" of the fifties reached the perfection of those drawn by Wood, a robot vacuum cleaner like the one featured in the story did exist and became the symbol of Whirlpool's "Miracle Kitchen" presented in 1956. As Ruth Oldenziel and Karin Zachmann have shown, the exchange between the vice president of the United States and the first secretary of the Communist Party was not an isolated oddity, but the expression of the political and diplomatic role of representations of domestic space since the end of World War II. In the fifties, the kitchen and domestic space in general "served as models of technological change, as metaphors for modernism, and as microcosms of new consumer regimes of the twentieth century" (Oldenziel and Zachmann 10). Above all, the modern kitchen serves as a counterweight to an outspokenly negative view of technology, with the atom bomb as its emblem.

It is thus no accident that Mrs. Robert West, the housekeeper who presented the "kitchen of the future" in a commercial for General Electric in June 1945, is cast as the wife of a pilot (fig. 11). The army and the kitchen both figure in a comic-like, nine-panel sequence in which the kitchen is described as "uncanny"—in this case, meaning "extraordinary," but which is also the usual translation of the Freudian *Unheimliche*, the "disquieting strangeness," the anxiety at the heart of the everyday. The fascination with the kitchen of the future and technology in the domestic sphere precedes World War II (Bucher 1939), but it takes on a different meaning in a world where science can lead to mutual destruction. In the Cold War context, mastering one's home serves as a proof of patriotism; ads urged consumers not to let their bathroom become a nest for Communists—"Is your bathroom breeding Communists?"—associating all forms of microbial contamination with the red menace (Ross 45). Wood conveys the fascination the future exerted on advertisers, as well as on people like Tex Avery, whose short features on the technology of the future—"House of Tomorrow" (1949), "Car of Tomorrow" (1951), and "T.V.

'Positively the most uncanny thing I ever
aw!" exclaims this attractive Air Corps
ife after previewing General Electric's
ll-Electric Kitchen-of-the-future. "Im-
gine! The new G-E Dishwasher is com-

pletely automatic! It washes, rinses, and dries a dayful of dishes in
a few minutes—and *you* don't lift a finger! The G-E Disposall dis-
poses of garbage *electrically!* After the war, you'll be able to buy
the Dishwasher and the Disposall separately. But I want the whole
time-saving works—the complete G-E Electric Sink!

"My goodness! wasn't that a *chicken bone?*" asks Mrs.
West in amazement, as a load of food waste disappears
down the magic G-E Disposall. Yes, the Disposall
takes it all—even bones. Shreds it up and whirls it
down almost while you count to twenty.

Fig. 11: Advertisement published in *Life* (1945): "Mrs. Robert West of New York applauds new G-E electric sink."

of Tomorrow" (1953)—appear more rapt than satirical. Wood juxtaposes these idealized and laudatory representations with the critical voices who felt that these automated homes would be impossible to live in despite, or because of, their technological marvels (Oldenziel 327–28). The image of a futuristic home was thus simultaneously ubiquitous and ambiguous when the two versions of "There Will Come Soft Rains" appeared; the prospect of the "push-button housewife" was greeted with a mixture of hope and fear. The automation of domestic space, with technology explicitly in the service of humanity, is thus not simply a bright counterpoint to the fear of a destructive science represented by atomic weapons; it is in itself potentially dangerous.

The story's graphics contribute to this critical reading of technology. The two spaces Wood creates—the space of humanity and that of the machine—have in common their absolute perfection, making them ideal model homes, like those Khrushchev and Nixon visited during their famous debate. With their fully integrated equipment, such model homes seem far removed from all social relations. The integration of automatic appliances in the walls suggests that they are integral elements of the house. They have not been purchased, but seem to have been built right into the walls. The status of the machine and domestic equipment as consumer products is thus absent in the story. Like all the kitchens of the future presented by General Motors and Whirlpool in the 1950s, it is not a model meant to be mass-produced and then sold, but a prototype, a unique demonstration model, just as unique as the paintings by Picasso and Matisse on the walls (6, panel 2). Wood captures the idea of the "artist's rendition" of the future that was so ubiquitous in popular magazines at the time, only to render it problematic. As the architects and designers creating modernist interiors had experienced, designing an ideal home without input from its inhabitants was sure to meet with protest, prompting a dialogue between occupants and designers (Oldenziel and Zachmann 20–21). In the house designed by Wood, the modernist ideal is exalted to be ultimately questioned. While there are some knickknacks and personal items in the house, they are all tidy and well-organized, and whatever threatens this order soon disappears, as the dog finds out. The machine's passive violence toward the animal underscores, yet again, that this house is uninhabitable and that humanity has already been expelled. As I have noted above, it is at the moment of destruction that emotion crops up and the modernist dream is confronted with the unexpected. By arranging the evisceration of this domestic space with such relish, Wood introduces another reading of the story that emphasizes the interconnection of the two equally destructive visions of technology. The story humanizes the machine, all the while hinting at humanity's prior reification. The skull in the opening panel is of the same blue as that of the wall and ruins in the closing panel.

Conclusion

It seems to me that, even more than other Bradbury adaptations in EC comic books, "There Will Come Soft Rains" keeps the source text legible in almost its entirety, integrated as it is in the comic. The compatibility between the short story's length and that of the graphic narrative offers a rare example of a transposition that demands no addition or subtraction from the original text; though confined to captions at the top of the panel, almost all the original text has been retained. Through this virtually complete repetition, the story's graphics are freed from the obligation to be faithful, despite the weight of Bradbury's name and the claims in the promotional paratext. The graphics and layout do not need to repeat anything; instead, they offer complex and ambiguous additions. To Bradbury's imaginative tale, Wood and Feldstein add alternative readings and different temporalities, while never outright contradicting the original text. Rather, the adaptation questions the original and its binaries: the tension between routine and immobility, present and future, language and absence, and man and machine are explored through the drawings and the apparatus of the comics medium.

Evidently, this interpretation grounds the graphic narrative in the time it was made, the fifties, while Bradbury's text aims to be timeless. Bradbury's story verges on the fairy tale, its main strategies recalling those of dystopian fiction. Indeed, in utopia, a perfectly ordered world is sealed off from the outside world through a hermetic enclosure "as a kind of enclave within which Utopian fantasy can operate" (Jameson 15), the loss of which immediately leads to a collapse of the system. To borrow Linda Hutcheon's concept

(150–51), the graphic version "indigenizes" Bradbury's text, leaving clear traces of the present in this utopian enclave. Seeing reality catch up with his stories, Bradbury decided in 1997 to shift the timeline into the future, changing the dates of all the stories out of our reach once more. Meanwhile, the future of Feldstein and Wood's version is firmly anchored in 1951. The adaptation is a temporary, remarkably accomplished reflection of a text whose brevity is an invitation to appropriation.

Notes

1. The comic can be found in *The Ray Bradbury Chronicles* no. 3 (Byron Press, November 1992), a reformatted version of the comic in the paperback collection *Tomorrow Midnight* (Ballantine, 1966), as well as in numerous reissues of *Weird Fantasy* from the late 1970s onward. The story is also reprinted in full in monumental books celebrating the career of Wood aimed at collectors, i.e., *Woodwork: Wallace Wood, 1927–1981* (IDW, 2013) and *Wallace Wood: The Artist's Edition* (IDW, 2012). In French, the beautiful black-and-white edition in large format *Bradbury : planète rouge* (Albin Michel, 1984) also features the story.

2. Part of my affection for the author derives from reading his stories in comics versions as a child.

3. Later in his career, Wood would also publish erotic and semi-erotic stories like *Sally Forth* (1968–74).

4. Commenting on the difference between temporality in films and comics, Groensteen observes: "[W]e already have sight of the following panels, and we can see that the future is *already there*. If the future that pulls our reading towards it is already present, then the present inevitably tends to slip back towards a past to which, in fact, it already belongs" (*Comics* 2013, 87). The strict chronology and scansion of the short story are supplemented with the necessarily synchronic reading of the space of the page.

5. See note 1.

6. "Blobs!" includes humanoid robots, which are absent here.

Works Cited

Aggelis, Steven L. *Conversations with Ray Bradbury*. Jackson: University Press of Mississippi, 2004.

Bartual, Roberto. "Architecture and Comics: Jimenez Lai's Citizens of No Place." *Comics Grid Blog*, August 15, 2011. http://www.comicsgrid.com/2011/08/citizens-of-no-place. Accessed on March 13, 2013.

Bradbury, Ray. "There Will Come Soft Rains." *The Martian Chronicles*. Toronto: Bantam Books, 1985 [1950]. 166–72.

Bucher, George A. "Electric Home of the Future." *Popular Mechanics Magazine* 72.2 (August 1939): 161–66.

Campbell, Eddie. "A Big Spread-2." *The Fate of the Artist*, July 16, 2011. http://eddiecampbell.blogspot.com/2011/07/fter-yesterdays-post-about-upcoming.html. Accessed on March 13, 2013.

"Car of Tomorrow." Dir. Tex Avery. Written by Roy Williams and Rich Hogan. MGM, 1951. *Looney Tunes: Golden Collection, Vol. 4*. DVD. Warner Home Video, 2006.

Chatman, Seymour. *Coming to Terms: The Rhetoric of Narrative in Fiction and Film*. Ithaca and London: Cornell University Press, 1990.

Christa, Albrecht-Crane, and Dennis Ray Cutchins. "Introduction: New Beginnings for Adaptation Studies." *Adaptation Studies: New Approaches*. Eds. Christa Albrecht-Crane and Dennis Ray Cutchins. Cranbury, NJ: Fairleigh Dickinson University Press, 2010. 11–24.

Eller, Jonathan. "The Body Eclectic: Sources of Ray Bradbury's *Martian Chronicles*." *Ray Bradbury*. Ed. Harold Bloom. New York: Chelsea, 2010. 141–64.

Eller, Jonathan, and Touponce William. *Ray Bradbury: The Life of Fiction*. Kent and London: Kent State University Press, 2004.Feldstein, Al, Wallace Wood, and Marie Severin. "There Will Come Soft Rains." *Weird Fantasy* 18 (January–February 1953), n.p. [Facsimile by Gemstone Publishing, 1997].

Forster, E. M. "The Machine Stops." *The Machine Stops and Other Stories*. London: André Deutsch, 1997 [1909]. 87–118.

Fresnault-Deruelle, Pierre. "From Linear to Tabular (1976)." *The French Comics Theory Reader*. Eds. Bart Beaty and Ann Miller. Leuven: Leuven University Press, 2014. 121–38.

Gabilliet, Jean-Paul. *Of Comics and Men: A Cultural History of American Comic Books*. Trans. Bart Beaty and Nick Nguyen. Jackson: University Press of Mississippi, 2009.

Groensteen, Thierry. *Comics and Narration*. Trans. Ann Miller. Jackson: University Press of Mississippi, 2013.

Groensteen, Thierry. *The System of Comics*. Trans. Bart Beaty and Nick Nguyen. Jackson: University Press of Mississippi, 2007.

"The House of Tomorrow." Dir. Tex Avery. Written by Jack Cosgriff and Rich Hogan. MGM, 1949. *Looney Tunes: Golden Collection, Vol. 3*. DVD. Warner Home Video, 2006.

Hutcheon, Linda. *A Theory of Adaptation*. London and New York: Routledge, 2006.

Jameson, Fredric. *Archaeologies of the Future: The Desire Called Utopia and Other Science Fictions*. New York: Verso, 2005.

Mason, Bill. "A Thousand Rays in Your Belly." *Against the Grain: Mad Artist Wallace Wood*. Ed. Bhob Stewart. Raleigh, NC: TwoMorrows Publishing, 2003. 73–100.

McCloud, Scott. *Understanding Comics: The Invisible Art*. New York: Kitchen Sink Press, 1993.

"Mrs. Robert West of New York Applauds New G-E Electric Sink." *LIFE*, June 18, 1945: 7.

Oldenziel, Ruth. "Exporting the American Cold War Kitchen." *Cold War Kitchen: Americanization, Technology and European users*. Eds. Ruth Oldenziel and Karin Zachmann. Cambridge, MA: MIT Press, 2009. 315–39.

Oldenziel, Ruth, and Karin Zachmann. "Kitchens as Technology and Politics: An Introduction." *Cold War Kitchen: Americanization, Technology and European Users*. Eds. Ruth Oldenziel and Karin Zachmann. Cambridge, MA: MIT Press, 2009. 1–29.

Riche, Daniel, and Boris Eizykman. *La Bande dessinée de science-fiction américaine*. Paris: Albin Michel, 1976.

Ross, Andrew. *No Respect: Intellectuals & Popular Culture*. New York: Routledge, 1989.

Stam, Robert. "Introduction: The Theory and Practice of Adaptation." *Literature and Film*. Eds. Robert Stam and Alessandra Raengo. Malden, MA: Blackwell Publishing, 2005. 1–52.

Telotte, J. P. *Science Fiction Films*. London: Cambridge University Press, 2001.

"T.V. of Tomorrow." Dir. Tex Avery. Written by Heck Allen. MGM, 1953. *Looney Tunes: Golden Collection, Vol. 4*. DVD. Warner Home Video, 2006.

Nestor Burma, from Léo Malet to Jacques Tardi, via Jacques-Daniel Norman: *120, rue de la Gare* and Its Adaptations

CHRISTOPHE GELLY

It is never easy to propose a "comparative" reading that takes into account both the possibilities offered by different media and the decisions made by the "authors'" by focusing exclusively on the works themselves. Criticism is often fraught with methodological obstacles: what is the meaning of the practice of adaptation from the perspective of the "fidelity" to the source? How much attention should be paid to the works' production and reception contexts? Through which particular framework should one address the issue of intermediality? If one were to believe Tardi's own comments on this part of his oeuvre, one would not have to look too far: "The word adaptation should suffice to understand what it is about . . . It's just an A-DAP-TA-TION!" (Sadoul 85).[1] In short, authors should be allowed to exercise their creative freedom. However, one cannot help wondering about the mechanisms that govern the passage from one work to another, from one medium to another, not because of any vain desire to analyze the second work, but to better understand the concerns behind the adapter's deliberate choices, as well as the artistic and historical constraints.

The case of *120, rue de la Gare* is symptomatic in this regard. Published in 1943 during the German occupation of France, it is the first novel that features Léo Malet's recurring hero Nestor Burma, who was inspired by the American detective thrillers so popular among French readers after being forbidden during the war. For Malet, it was an opportunity to present a new kind of detective, rooted primarily in contemporaneous French reality, but without overtly politicizing its discourse in those troubled times when censorship prevailed. This is why the few references to the historical context are not explicit and thematic but lie hidden in the text, as in this episode where Burma implicitly accuses Commissioner Bernier of complacency towards the Vichy regime:

"Let's not be flippant, Monsieur Burma. You do understand I'm trying to catch the man who killed your employee, don't you?"

"Colleague."[2]

"What? As you like." (28)

Tardi, who adapted the novel in 1988, will clearly emphasize this aspect—the 1980s are, indeed, another period, with different customs and freedom of expression. In 1946, Malet's novel was made into a film by Jacques-Daniel Norman; filmed during the Occupation, the adaptation guarded itself against overt politicization. Taking into account this historical constraint repeatedly noted in criticism,[3] the aim of this study is twofold. First, it will show how the transition from novel to film to comics effects a movement of redefinition of the genre of the postwar "noir" novel. In Tardi's case specifically, this entails a historical distancing from the source text that is generally favored by this type of re-appropriation. Secondly, I will show how the emergence of a kind of "noir" comics, predating the publication of Tardi's work, relates to a specific aesthetics on the one hand, and to the specific format of the graphic novel on the other.

Noir: From Malet to Tardi via Norman

Although not the main focus of this study, the writing of Léo Malet can be read as a "cheeky" variant of the hard-boiled style practiced by American writers of the 1930s, which the author had already spoofed under the pseudonym "Frank Harding" before the creation of Burma. Like Dashiell Hammett's heroes (especially "the thin man") who constitute a deviating and mocking rereading of the *armchair detective* archetype, Nestor Burma—the man who, in his own words, "knocks mystery out"—likes to caricature himself as a private eye who is all too ready to resort to heavy-handed methods, while denigrating the excessive refinement of his predecessors' deductive logic:

"Shut up," I said. "Someone tried to throw me in the river. That's all that matters as far as I'm concerned. But I am prepared to free this little angel's wrists just long enough to show you why I'm called Dynamite Burma."

My fist shot out and caught him squarely on the chin, dropping him to the floor just next to his hat. I threw a scarf to Covet.

"Tie him up," I said. This room isn't big enough for him to let him wave his arms about. And pop a cork in him. He might want to sing when he wakes up, and I don't much care for his repertoire. (Malet 76)

This somewhat mocking generic reference is reflected in Norman's film by the presence of Burma's servant/employee, Kimura (an addition to the novel). The latter, a second-rate Fu Manchu, drops his mask once he finds himself in familiar territory, as in the scene where Burma realizes—while in the company of Hélène Chatelain, the woman he followed from Lyon and whom he intends to hire as his secretary—that Kimura merely puts on oriental garb to impress the clients:

> HÉLÈNE: I refuse to accompany your carnival servant.
> BURMA: Yes, go put on a jacket. Anyway, quibbling with Mademoiselle is useless. She's my new secretary.
> KIMURA: I like the sound of that! I'm fed up with playing pretend. Well, c'mon, doll, let's get you your bags . . .
> BURMA: You better get used to it: he's from the Batignoles. [57:50–58:02]

The tendency to ironically stage genre affiliation is not only one of the main ingredients of the humor in Malet's writing; it is also the driving force of any generic tradition. What Tardi's adaptation highlights is, among other things, the prominence of references to the genre and other media in which the genre is incarnated—to the point of endowing these references with a function, i.e., what Roland Barthes referred to through the notion of "plot."[4] The play on generic references is visible in Tardi through numerous cinematic allusions, which have been analyzed by François de la Brétèque. They sometimes lead the adapter to create visual quotes of "real" movies, such as *Remorques* (Jean Grémillon, 1941) and *Münchhausen* (Josef von Báky, 1943), whose posters (portions actually) appear on page 187, with the poster of the second film largely covering that of the first, as a visual sign for (geo) graphic occupation. Sometimes these allusions invoke fictitious films or actors, such as the actress Madeleine Morlain (Michèle Hogan in Malet) or the film *Brouillard au Pont de l'Alma*, "invented" by Tardi (fig. 12). Similarly, the "realistic" illustrations that abound in the comic—such as the propaganda posters or the adverts for the exhibition *Le Juif et la France*—are also mixed with overtly fictional posters, like the one appearing in the course of a panel, announcing the death sentence of a certain . . . Jacques Tardi.

In addition, the artist peppers his story with personal references in the form of private jokes: Burma's secretary looks like his wife Dominique Grange, and the lawyer Montbrison is reading an edition of Poe's tales illustrated by Jean-Michel Nicollet, Tardi's classmate at the School of Fine Arts in Lyon.[5] In each of these examples, one gets the sense that the adaptation has become a site for the expression of a cinephile and genre culture. Yet it

Fig. 12: *The Bloody Streets of Paris* (Tardi and Malet, 1988): Burma walks past the movie posters of *Münchausen* (von Báky, 1943) and *Remorques* (Grémillon, 1941), referencing both the cinema and the political context.

is more than just a matter of "enhanced" generic reflexivity, as Tardi literally incorporates *extra-generic* elements in his work, such as the face of his friend Lebedel, whom he uses to create the character of Mark Covet, the journalist who comes to Burma's aid during his investigation (Douvry 44). Other examples include the frame in which Pétillon's detective Jack Palmer is described as "not too bright" compared to Burma (Tardi and Malet 64), or the one in which Burma delves into the autobiography of Palmer he found at Jo Parry's place (Tardi and Malet 135); the generic references reinforce the ironic treatment of a detective who was already offering a pastiche of the genre, to such an extent that we almost lose sight of the pastiche's primary source.

But these posters and filmic references are unique to Tardi's comic insofar as they appear as illustrations (images within the image) that are made in the same graphic style that is characteristic of intradiegetic characters such as Burma, inspector Faroux, and Hélène Chatelain. For example, Tardi does not seek to imitate the real poster of *Münchhausen* when it appears in the frame. Instead, he integrates it in the overall graphic style of the adaptation. This might seem obvious, given that an attempt to mimic the "photographic" image regime inspired by the poster for the actual film would entail a break in representation. Yet this kind of break has been practiced by other comics artists, notably those who incorporate photos in their panels.[6] But in the context of the detective story, the graphic continuity of the film references mainly makes the same image—that of Hélène Parry/Madeleine Morlain—simultaneously reappear on the purely diegetic level and the meta-narrative level constituted by the film posters. This is particularly striking in the poster

Fig. 13: *The Bloody Streets of Paris* (Tardi and Malet, 1988): the fictional film, *Brouillard au Pont de l'Alma*, participating in the comic's narrative and meta-narrative.

of the "fake film" *Brouillard au Pont de l'Alma*, in which actress Madeleine Morlain accurately reproduces Hélène Parry's pose and outfit at Perrache station during the murder of Bob Colomer (Tardi and Malet 27, 39) (fig. 13). This continuity—the reprisal of the same image rather than the repetition of a general graphic style in the comics—even appears on a third level, i.e., the dreams Burma has on two occasions (pages 20 and 61, as well as page 155 where Burma is confronted with the "real" Hélène Parry and mentally compares his image to the one at Perrache station), which emblematize his obsession with the mysterious woman. The striking repetition of the "frames" of reality and dream, along with the poster as image within the image, reveals that the image has lost its simple illustrative function within the story. In Malet, Burma only refers to a movie star to convey a visual representation in a non-iconic medium (Malet 24); what is at stake in Tardi's adaptation is the *incarnation* of the enigma through the image. It is in this sense that the photograph of Madeleine Morlain becomes a function in the Barthesian sense, as it motivates narrative progression: without it, there is no narrative.[7]

The role played by the poster as a self-reflexive element in Tardi's adaptation of Malet involves several criteria. Not only is there reflexivity because the image "reflects" (in the sense that it reproduces) the original image in several copies (the dreams, the daughter of criminal Jo Parry—with the reflection making the image the nodal point, the function where the enigma is concentrated—but the graphic continuity of the poster with the diegesis of the story (the meta-image of the first narrative) also acts as a reminder of the artifice of the drawn images. Indeed, it is because Tardi represents—in an artificial way—the characters of Hélène Parry (the disappeared gangster's daughter) and Madeleine Morlain (the movie star) not as likenesses, but as literally the same characters on the page that we recognize the artifice for what it is: a reflexive play on our belief in realistic representation (where Malet's text could rightly insist on a simple resemblance whereby the degree of reality would remain vague).

In short, Tardi's adaptation of Malet via Norman can be read as a generic reference on three different levels. First, as an indefinite reference that places the hero (and the reader) in a nostalgic relationship with reality—hence Burma's obsession with an image he seeks to identify, which would count as the epitome of the real. Second, as a reflexive adaptation that exhibits its own artifice and its character as a work created by an artist who instills his own personal, sometimes familial references. Finally, as a truly generic reference aiming to expand and develop the frame of the noir novel—the play on genre conventions, the detective's ironic attitude towards himself, the role of "femmes fatales" (like Hélène Parry who manipulates Bob Colomer), and so on—into a distanced rereading already present in Malet but exacerbated by Tardi. Note that the dialogues added by Tardi often tend to recall the dimension of the genre's facetious rereading. While he is in the process of performing a classic *lecture d'objet* by examining the will Jo Parry left to his daughter Hélène, he asks inspector Faroux what can be deduced from the document:

> Did you notice anything strange about this envelope and the letter inside?
>
> Sure! The assassin has one eye, flat feet and suffers from a six-year-old ulcer every day between 6 p.m. and 7:22!
>
> Very funny! No, look again . . . (Tardi and Mallet 161)

This type of joke, addressed to the connoisseur of "classic" detective novels, is a clear sign of distance from the initial generic model, as well as a token of the work's return—in both novelistic and graphic terms—to its characteristic logical presuppositions.

The scene of the final confrontation with the suspects and revelation of the murderer's name can serve as a point of comparison to show how the adaptation inflects the genre overall. In Malet, this scene is presented in a rather classical way, while in Norman it does not constitute the film's ending but is displaced to the infamous house on 120, rue de la Gare, with the movie closing with a shootout rather than providing any real explanation.[8] Tardi treats this scene canonically and quite literally delays it (which means that it is visibly not inspired by the 1946 movie), since he announces and then pushes the narrative forward by representing Burma being dropped off at his place by Faroux *after* the finale. At the end of the comic, we follow Burma wandering through Paris as, he reveals, quite strangely (since he seems to be talking to himself in the street, and it is only *a posteriori* that we realize he is accompanied by his secretary, Hélène Chatelain), the different stages of his reasoning before passersby who are undoubtedly just as bemused as . . . we, the readers, are, faced with a character who so deliberately breaks the conventions of dialogue in a realistic story (fig. 14).

This displacement is a sign of Tardi's re-appropriation of the genre with the aim of surprising the reader. Another sign that similarly breaks away from genre conventions is the panel in which Burma announces very theatrically (and yet again quite conventionally, since such scenes abound in crime fiction) that the murderer is present amongst the small crowd he gathered at his home, upon which the characters express their astonishment through speech balloons containing only question marks (Tardi 178). However, these question marks have different shapes for each of the three characters (Douvry 35): Hélène Chatelain who still holds her employer's bullying earlier in the story against him; the police officer who is incognito but is eagerly expecting the "big reveal"; and the guilty Montbrison whose surprise is, of course, infused with apprehension.

For the attentive reader, this way of marking the differences between the characters' apprehension of the situation is a semantic surplus the adaptation adds to the narrative. At the same time, however, it is also a mode of expression typical of the comics medium, engaged as it is with a rereading of the conventions of the detective story. It is this mode of representation specific to Tardi's comic that I will now address and that will lead me to a consideration of both the comics medium and the graphic novel.

Fig. 14: *The Bloody Streets of Paris* (Tardi and Malet, 1988): Burma's final account of the crimes.

The Bloody Streets of Paris: Almost All of Tardi?

The question of the *style* of Tardi's adaptation of Malet—which shows little trace of the influence of Norman's film, the latter being quite dated and subservient to the studio politics of the time, and wholly geared towards putting the contemporary star, René Dary, in the limelight—touches on the essence of Tardi's comics artistry. The latter is expressed through an adaptation that allows the artist to highlight his own aesthetic choices more directly, precisely because we are dealing with an adaptation that has "rid itself" of the writing of the plot: "The plot of the detective story is just a pretext. All that is easy. [. . .] I no longer worry about the story, whether it's worth being told or not" (Sadoul 85).[9] Graphically speaking, these adaptations thus offer the "complete Tardi." The focus on style allowed him to work on two independent levels: on the one hand, the transposition of a "noir style" inspired by the detective genre to drawn images, and on the other, the treatment of those aspects specific to the comics medium.

The question of a particular mode of representation typical of the detective genre first crops up in the treatment of one of the genre's prerequisites: the representation of clues. These are either "drowned out" by the flow of Malet's text or simply ignored in Norman's case. Thus, in Norman's film adaptation, the key to the famous house so many people are looking for, located at 120, rue de la Gare, just happens to be concealed inside a Punchinello offered by the criminal as a present to his daughter, a "transparent" sign that the residence in question is located in the city of . . . Pantin (the French word for "puppet"). As one can see, there is nothing special about this representation of

Fig. 15: *The Bloody Streets of Paris* (Tardi and Malet, 1988): the close-up of the clue, the criminal's American cigarette.

the key to the mystery, which is simply a remarkable clue (since the viewer's attention is repeatedly drawn to this object in the dialogues) and which is filmed quite routinely. Its significance is revealed at the end of the narrative in a manner that should come as no surprise to the audience.

Instead, what characterizes Tardi's treatment of clues is a change in the angle, often highlighted by a close-up.[10] The way the perpetrator's (Montbrison's) hand is depicted crushing a cigarette butt in an ashtray is one telling example (89) (fig. 15). It is not only a sign of his incessant smoking, but also constitutes the crucial clue that will lead Burma to the truth, since the culprit forgets to pick up his cigarette butts from the crime scenes—the American brand he smokes, Philip Morris, was extremely rare during the Occupation. Apart from changes in viewing angles, Tardi sometimes draws the reader's attention to clues that turn out to be false leads, like the presence of a suitcase or the large number of gloves in the culprit's accomplice's (Carhaix-Jalome's) apartment (86, 100). It is true that, as far as the suitcase is concerned, the clue in question is mentioned in the text and does not appear in the image itself. On more than a few occasions, the adaptation captures visual clues mostly intended to fool the reader. The use of the close-up that we just observed in the case of Montbrison evokes a traditional cinematographic practice[11] and may reflect the influence of cinema on comics, a worn-out theme if ever there was one. However, despite the recurrence of this type of debate, the rarity of these angles of view in Tardi's adaptation of Malet (angles also associated with another culprit, Commissioner Bernier) is, in fact, the equivalent of Burma's highly subjective reading of the storyline; it is, no doubt, the detective himself who notes these clues that remain invisible to the other characters. These instances would, therefore, constitute rare moments when we are allowed to penetrate the detective's consciousness, with the added effect of emphasizing this particular stylistic device more common in cinema than in Tardi. It is also a means of endowing the adaptation with a playfulness that will lead the reader to go back to the work and hunt down all the clues placed by the artist but whose true import had eluded us. The "fetishism" of the adaptation is, thus, already at work here, a point we will return to below.

Notwithstanding visual perspective, which is just as relevant to film, the question of the frame arises in more specific terms in comics, as Thierry Groensteen has pointed out. On another level, this is where we will encounter the same issue of adapting a literary style to a graphic register, since the particular way *The Bloody Streets of Paris* treats the frame involves a generic reference. In his adaptation, Tardi has deliberately multiplied the panels and varied their form, sometime even placing a central frame at the heart of a series of panels.

Similarly, the speech balloons are used in many different ways, exploiting the full range of possibilities noted by Groensteen (49): several panels can be connected to the same balloon, and two or more speech balloons are shared by several characters, etc. For example, Tardi often tends to include two images separated by a strip of text in the same panel, as when Commissioner Bernier holds a coffee pot up to Burma before pointing the revolver of the character who tried to kill him on the Quai de Saône at Burma; this link also expresses the ambivalence between protection and aggression in the character of Bernier, an ambivalence that will make sense at the end of the comics when he is proven guilty (fig. 16). Tardi's propensity for multiplying variations of the shape of the frame and (almost logically and consequently) significantly altering the shape and integration of the speech balloons in the frame (as in the crucial example of the comic's cover, which features Burma smoking a pipe out of which a question mark emerges, in yet another variation on the principle of the balloon) is not only a way to infuse the adaptation with his own style; it also serves to introduce variations in perspective, allowing the interaction between the different characters and their dialogues to appear on a graphic level. A similar logic governs the very obvious presence of numerous "texts within the text" in the comic: Jo Parry's letter to his daughter, the postcard Bob Colomer's parents sent to their son read by Burma, Colomer's notes on the books he consulted in the Lyon library, the excerpt from a medical treatise cited by Burma before Faroux, and so on.

Fig. 16: *The Bloody Streets of Paris* (Tardi and Malet, 1988): Bernier's extremely ambivalent behavior with Burma.

This last point takes us from the dialogism that is perhaps typical of the serial adventure novel (which, after all, inspired Malet so profoundly that it gave him the idea of reimagining the work of Eugène Sue in a new light, under the title *Les Nouveaux Mystères de Paris*) to a different phenomenon, undoubtedly more significant in terms of the "personal" quality of Tardi's adaptation, involving a form of competition between the texts within the same comic. These texts within the text, in effect, seem to invade the frame and demand the attention of the reader, thereby highlighting another phenomenon noted by Groensteen (121–26)—that is, the difficulty for a comics author to determine the *order* and *priority* with which his work will be read. Which speech balloon or which feature of the drawing will the reader focus on first? These texts also show that the detective's reasoning process and the solution to the riddle ultimately refer to voices other than his own. Thus, they highlight the narrative instability symptomatic of the detective genre. Who essentially solves the mystery—is it Burma or the texts he cites? Who is it that speaks in the scenes that underscore the "triumph" of reason? Is it really Burma talking all alone in the street, as one is led to believe at the beginning of the final scene, or is it another Burma who addresses his secretary, as she had initially been relegated to the off-panel space?

Elsewhere (Gelly 2010), I have analyzed how the instability of enunciators is a generic characteristic of film noir, in that it touches on the questioning of identity that is so central to the detective genre. But it is notable that the presence of the texts within the text transcribes this process very efficiently to the field of comics, in the sense that Burma's discourse—and, more generally, the work's enunciation—seem to escape a single enunciative authority, as in the panel where inspector Faroux takes a jibe at Burma by saying: "You're boring." Here, we witness an implicit questioning of the authority of the detective narrator, whose "perorations" exhaust the patience of his colleague from the official police precisely because so many (too many?) other texts are embedded in this scene, complicating, and establishing a distance with, any direct relation to diegetic relationship.

The question of the position of the text and Burma's ultimate authority over it reappears in the final scene (added by Tardi) when Hélène Chatelain, his secretary, refers to the question of origins by asking Burma to elucidate the meaning of the name of his agency, *Fiat Lux*, something which the detective is at a loss to explain. Thus, there is always an original text that escapes enunciative authority, and this opening up of the work can be read as a clever questioning of the detective genre itself, one that challenges its "self-sufficient" logic, a questioning that, of course, has its origin in Malet's text, which critiques the purely deductive detective novel.

■ ■ ■

In closing, let's return to the concept of the graphic novel, which, though it was not born with *The Bloody Streets of Paris*, maintains a special relationship with Tardi's comic mainly because of its length and narrative "density," which were still unusual in the 1980s. Without really attempting to hold forth on the concept, and by limiting our scope to the sheer magnitude of the story (which runs almost two hundred pages), one can point out that it is a condition that allows and encourages the reader to return to the text, to its past and especially to the images that were interpreted inadequately on a first reading. Despite the development of new viewing modes, it is a revisiting of the work that remains more typical of written or drawn narrative than of film narrative, where revisiting past episodes of the story is more difficult, materially speaking. Yet the length of the story also enables Tardi to develop meaningful resonances from one end of the plot to the other, thus making Covet and Burma "twins" whose physical appearance is similar both in Paris and Lyon (where Covet lends his clothes to Burma). Both the narrative density and the development of correspondences and contrasts eventually invite the reader to surrender to the fetishism of the image, through which s/he will perceive the extradiegetic reality reflected in Tardi's drawings, which are so well-documented (as the interviews with Numa Sadoul demonstrate). Tardi's attraction to the picturesque and realism of his documentary sources (even if the drawings themselves do not evince a documentary quality) confirms the interpretation of Francis De La Brétèque, who has noted an evolution toward "hyperrealism" in Tardi's work (278). However, it seems that this tendency in adapting Malet refers, above all else, to the fact that Tardi is adapting a *genre*, the detective genre, which also tends to fetishize the real as a place and source of clues that accrue meaning.

Notes

1. Original text: "Le mot adaptation devrait suffire pour comprendre de quoi il s'agit . . . Il s'agit d'une A-DAP-TA-TION!"

2. The French text reads: "Collaborateur."

3. See Claire Gorrara in particular.

4. Incidentally, Thierry Groensteen has already suggested that the reflexivity specific to comics is not only a characteristic trait of the genre but also of the medium itself, although he does not go into the causes of this phenomenon (82). By adapting Malet, Tardi was undoubtedly already "doomed" to instill this reflexive dimension.

5. These comments, as well as those on intertextual and "personal" elements in the adaptation, originate in the work of Jean-François Douvry.

6. Art Spiegelman's *Maus* comes to mind, as the author includes photos of his father whose life during the war he recounts.

7. Tardi has Burma mockingly address Gérard Lafalaise, who interrogates him about the reason for his attachment to Madeleine Morlain's double: "I met her one night in a bus, and I've had the hots for her since" (82). Lafalaise's car driving into the night is shown when Burma says this instead of his face: it is logical, in the sense that the identity covering up this image is bound to be unknown; Burma's reply cannot at this stage contribute to any real progress in the story, but aims at prolonging the suspense surrounding this identity.

8. Norman's film also plays with the viewer when, during the end sequence, the characters Burma and Hélène Chatelain kiss and glance at the camera. It is a kind of address to the viewer, one that no doubt refers to the familiarity between the characters and the typical readership of serial novels.

9. Original text: "L'intrigue policière n'est qu'un prétexte. Tout ça est reposant. [...] Je n'ai plus l'angoisse de l'histoire, savoir si elle vaut le coup d'être racontée."

10. Indeed, Tardi admitted how reluctant he was to use high-angle and low-angle shots, as he makes clear in the book of interviews with Numa Sadoul (140–42).

11. On this point, see the argument put forward by Julien Guieu in his PhD dissertation.

Works Cited

120, rue de la Gare. Written and directed by Jacques-Daniel Norman, based on the novel by Léo Malet. With René Dary (Nestor Burma), Gaby André (Suzanne Parmentier), and Sophie Desmarets (Hélène Chatelain). La Société des Films Sirius, 1946. DVD. René Chateau Vidéo, 2004.

Barthes, Roland. "An Introduction to the Structural Analysis of Narrative." Trans. Lionel Duisit. *New Literary History* 6.2 (1975): 237–72.

De La Brétèque, François Amy. "Les références cinématographiques dans l'univers de Tardi." *Les Cases à l'écran*. Ed. Alain Boillat. Genève: Georg, 2010. 265–82.

Douvry, Jean-François. *Rendez-vous . . . 120, rue de la gare—Autopsie d'une adaptation*. Paris: Casterman, 1988.

Gelly, Christophe. "Reflexivity in three films noirs: *Laura* (Otto Preminger, 1944), *Double Indemnity* (Billy Wilder, 1944), *Sunset Boulevard* (Billy Wilder, 1950)." *Generic Attractions: New Essays on Film Genre Criticism*. Eds. María del Mar Azcona and Celestino Deleyto. Paris: Michel Houdiard, 2010. 357–71.

Gorrara, Claire. "Malheurs et ténèbres: Narratives of Social Disorder in Léo Malet's *120, rue de la Gare*." *French Cultural Studies* 12 (2001): 271–83.

Groensteen, Thierry. *The System of Comics*. Trans. Bart Beaty and Nick Nguyen. Jackson: University Press of Mississippi, 2007 [1999].

Guieu, Julien. *Esthétique de l'indice dans le cinéma américain des années 2000*. Diss. Université de la Sorbonne Nouvelle Paris 3, 2012.

Malet, Léo. *120, rue de la Gare*. Trans. P. Hudson. Paris: Pan Books, 1991 [1943].

Sadoul, Numa. *Tardi: Entretiens avec Numa Sadoul*. Paris: Niffle-Cohen, 2000.

Schulman, Peter. "Le 'Stylo-Caméra': Léo Malet vu par Jacques Tardi." *De l'écrit à l'écran: Littératures populaires : Mutations génériques, mutations médiatiques*. Ed. Jacques Migozzi. Limoges: PU de Limoges, 2000. 523–34.

Tardi, Jacques, and Léo Malet. *The Bloody Streets of Paris* (*120, rue de la Gare*). Shelter Island Heights, NY: IBooks Graphic Novel, 2004 [1998].

Doctor Jekyll & Mister Hyde by Mattotti-Kramsky: Shattering Figuration

LAURA CECILIA CARABALLO

This chapter proposes an analysis of the adaptation of the literary classic *The Strange Case of Dr. Jekyll and Mr. Hyde* by Robert Louis Stevenson, drawn by artist Lorenzo Mattotti and written by Jerry Kramsky, published in France by Casterman (2002). Their work on this graphic novel highlights the problem of the distance between figuration in the image and the possibility of a partly non-narrative comic. In this sense, Gilles Deleuze's discussion of the work of painter Francis Bacon provides useful elements for iconic analysis, especially the notion of the *figural* as a counterpart to figuration. Discussions of a non-linear reading of comics, the concept of *amalgam* as complementary to that of *sequence*, and the existence of a purely abstract comic, all tend towards an erasure of the narrative. The distance from figuration is materialized in Mattotti and Kramsky's comic through the occasional progressive deformation of forms and figures in different panels. The gap between the story related in the album and the source narrative is effected through a radical variation; the literary and linear narrative becomes something else once transposed into the comic medium. Adaptation involves a consideration of the source text and foregrounds a distinct reading, as well as a number of decisions made at the production stage. These issues relate to the tension between the virtual and the actual, where reading is conceived as an actualization, the solution to a specific problem.

Following the discussion of theoretical concepts, two divergent and complementary issues will be addressed based on the analysis of the comic. First, a comparison of the literary and comics narratives will be undertaken with particular attention to the segmentation of sequences and the link between word and image. This starting point will make it possible to consider the image beyond figuration. These two non-figurative and narrative instances, or properties, are not mutually exclusive within the same work, and it would be a mistake, as far as literary adaptations are concerned, to prioritize the narrative's literary or scriptural dimension.

Transposition and Moving Away from Figuration: A Conceptual Explication

The term "adaptation" sometimes carries negative connotations, leading one to oppose the original work to one that is considered secondary or even merely accessory. Such considerations lead to the assumption that the original somehow inexorably exercises its ascendancy over its descendants. Similarly, the comparative approach, associated with the idea of "fidelity," leads all too often to the conclusion that the secondary or posterior work is by the same token inferior to the "original." Nevertheless, the act of adapting also admits an active reading grounded in a specific historical and cultural moment. By examining both ends of the operation, it becomes clear that Mattotti and Kramsky's comic offers a complex view of its source(s) as a re-creation that creates anew. Both authors take the literary referent merely as a starting point and pick up at least three other non-literary hypotexts: Alberto Breccia's comics adaptations of "El otro yo del Dr. Jekyll" and *L'Homme et la bête*, and Jean Renoir's TV movie *The Doctor's Horrible Experiment* (RTF, 1959).

The notion of "transposition"—associated with that of intervention, movement, transfer, and the foregrounding of a distinct reading—is a valuable analytical tool. As the passage from one apparatus to another is correlated to the specificity of the creative process of comics, a comparative approach makes it possible to define the expressive and technical resources of each art form. The phenomenon of transposition, linked as it is to the characteristics of each medium, effects various metamorphoses that respond to different readings. Oscar Steimberg reminds us that transposition, as an act of reading, is historically and stylistically circumscribed:

> We live in a world of stories, riddles, information, poems and sermons torn from their spaces, invoked for no apparent reason from one language or medium to another. [. . .] In the course of this transition, these stories, puzzles, bits of information and sermons tend to be reduced, elongated, distorted or assume nuances which, in some cases, seem destined to highlight the specificity of a medium, to reproduce a fad or to recall our embeddedness in a tradition. [. . .] The mundane aspect of such transitions of stories from one medium to another recalls the partially inevitable and fatally conditioned character of any reading undertaken in the times in which we live.[1] (95, 98)

Transpositional readings generate new reading habits that favor fragmentation in relation to the book as a whole. Hybrid languages like comics underscore the necessarily incomplete nature of reading, which is mainly defined by the technical apparatus.[2]

The graphic composition of comics actually makes the reading of the text more complex, since it must submit to a particular visual sequence through images selected beforehand. The process of displacement/replacement leads to a shift from the literary text, an apparatus devoted to scriptural narration, to comics, which shows and tells simultaneously. Linda Hutcheon thus defines three modes of audience engagement characteristic of different media: *telling*, *showing*, and *interacting* (22). The first, *telling*, focuses on the narrative and plunges the reader into the fictional world, while the second, *showing*, immerses the viewer in the domain of perception and the visual. Comics are situated between these two modes, and studying transpositions entails appreciating the difference between aspects that approximate its literary referent and others that require an autonomous analysis. The concept of *monstration* (from *montrer*, the verb "show" in French) has been applied to comics by Philippe Marion and Thierry Groensteen (1998), as initially formulated by André Gaudreault,[3] who emphasized the "monstrative" function of images: *showing rather than telling* (Gaudreault, *Du littéraire* 87). He attributes the equivalent role assumed by the "fundamental narrator" (*narrateur fondamental*) in literature to the "monstrator" (*monstrateur*) in film and the performing arts; more than an intermediate consciousness presenting space and action, the *monstrateur* presents itself (Gaudreault, *Du littéraire* 91). Applied to comics, the theory of monstration concerns the medium's enunciative specificity; geared towards the iconic representation of an object, it allows for an overall, synthetic, and immediate appropriation (Groensteen, "Entre monstration" 42). Monstration can be understood as a virtual description achieved thanks to the reader's participation. The image is subjected to two readings: one that is descriptive, in which the frame is isolated to produce a repertoire of what it presents, and one that is narrative, in which the only elements that are selected are those that participate in the chain of events, which functions within the narrative's dynamics, that is, constant elements and contingent ones (Groensteen, "Entre monstration" 46). However, in each case, the reading process entails an operation of actualization. Comics are endowed with great potential, a virtual force that can undergo a process of resolution thanks to the reader's intervention: "Contrary to the possible, which is static and already constituted, the virtual is, like the problematic complex, the nexus of tendencies or forces accompanying a situation, an event, an object, in short any entity that calls for a process of resolution: that is, actualization" (Lévy 14).

Transposition can be thought of in terms of actualization, that is to say, the solution to a particular problem: "a solution that was not already present in the utterance (*énoncé*). An actualization is a creation, the invention of a form starting from a dynamic configuration of forces and finalities" (Lévy 15). This initial actualization of the work, which involves transposition, will then be re-actualized by the reader.

In comics, the process of actualization is partly guided by certain pre-established and partly contingent rules. The possibility of a non-narrative reading arises during what Groensteen calls a descriptive reading, a process in which narration and figuration do not necessarily intervene. Unlike the sequential reading of the comic page, in which the narrative function is predominant and during which the reader cannot escape the predetermined linear order of the discourse, the isolation of an image allows the reader's eye to perform a visual journey, lingering to a greater or lesser extent on one or more details in a random and erratic fashion (Groensteen, "Entre monstration" 46). Despite the intrinsic narrativity of the comics apparatus, readers are free to pause and enjoy the visual qualities of the image:

> Reading, of whatever kind, releases the narrative. But you can also simply view the drawing—as it offers a simulacrum of nature—and thereby enjoy the pleasures of figuration. Reading can be performed within a single image or, conversely, start from braiding (*tressage*), that is to say, the gathering of distant images and image fragments. It can be the outcome of a non-linear route, even of an overall familiarity with the iconic material. (Morgan 34)

Beyond comics' general license when it comes to nonlinear reading, Groensteen resumes the discussion on the possibility of abstract comics, a phenomenon linked to experimentation that exceeds predefined borders. It tests the widespread, common definition of comics as a sequential, multiple, visual, narrative, and so on, apparatus. Abstract images, pure forms, consist of plastic elements and their mutual relations; to account for when the lack of causality between panels becomes concrete, Groensteen proposes the notion of the *amalgam* instead of the *sequence*, since it implies a cohabitation between images without continuity or causal relationships: "The 'zero degree' of the distribution of panels [...] is defined as mere juxtaposition of disparate images" ("La Narration" 55). This notion is relevant when dealing with capricious frames/icons that appear to lack logical order or causality. In this manner, Mattotti and Kramsky's *Dr. Jekyll* at times moves away from figuration to offer a series of panels that engage in pure iconicity, to the extent that the connection to the mimetic disappears. It favors abstract escapades between sequences and panels: "Statistically, abstract comics represent only a minute proportion of production as a whole, but they bear considerable symbolic weight because they suggest that comics can banish narration and figuration without ceasing to be comics" (Groensteen, *Comics and Narration* 13). In Mattotti and Kramsky's work, the move away from figuration through a progressive deformation of forms can be considered beyond the simply pure or abstract image. Deleuze's reflections on Francis Bacon's paintings will lead me to address specific aspects of the comic, in which forms are visualized with remarkable graphic force. For Deleuze, the Figure is not necessarily figurative; it may take other routes, such as abstraction (pure form) or the purely figural, where it acts as a direct force emanating from the image's surface and provoking pure sensation in the viewer. The isolated Figure, devoid of narrative links with other elements of the image (the only possible relationship is the fact of its coexistence, what Deleuze calls after Bacon the "*matter of fact*"), escapes its figurative condition.

Narration and Visualization: The Aborted Enigma

Narrative images are part of a larger group of images characterized by a particular relation to time. In comics, the chronological course of events can be observed in the linear sequencing of representations running from left to right and from top to bottom. The distribution of panels plays a fundamental role in the construction of the narrative, together with iconic content (construction of space, the presence of the characters, framing, and so on). Groensteen explains the process (narrative reading) by which the reader differentiates constant elements from new elements within each frame to follow the story ("Entre monstration" 46). The reading process adapts to the unfolding of the narration, allowing the reader to reconstruct the story. The idea that there is a rhythm to comics also plays a part in the actualization of the narrative, implying a dynamic related to the experience of time in the perception of the image. Rhythm constitutes one of the images' structural parameters, where the notion of repetition is crucial, as well as that of periodicity (compromising the reiteration of elements or groups of elements) and structure (the mode of organization of those elements).

In terms of narrative, Mattotti and Kramsky's *Dr. Jekyll* effects a reversal of the source text by modifying the development of the plot. In the new version, the story's construction is based on its continuity; the key to the mystery is only made manifest at the end of the story. As for the images in the comic, they invert this structure, and the mystery disappears, since the reader knows from the start the origin of the enigma. Jekyll's voice in the captions establishes two main temporalities in the narration: the first concerns the moment when he writes the letter, the second when he recounts the various events taking place in the image. The two—the time of the image and the time of the text—merge in the final panel where Jekyll-Hyde dies. After the introductory sequence, which represents the character of Hyde in an indeterminate time, the narrative is constructed as a kind of flashback. Like a voice-over, Jekyll's words in the captions accompany Hyde's actions on the iconic plane. The first sequence presents Hyde strolling through the city. The first panel immediately reveals his dark presence in the form of an urban shadow cast across buildings, trams, and the street. It is an elliptical figure, between the chromatic and achromatic, with the shape tracing a sinuous visual route. The captions present Dr. Jekyll's words, his regret, and his relationship to his cruel and despicable side. It is here that the reversal in the narration occurs, as from the outset we can see the doctor's devilish side embodied in Hyde. The following panels focus on the monstration of the monster's wickedness, depicting an event where he attacks a girl for no apparent reason. This is the event that triggers the renewed concern and curiosity of Mr. Utterson, the lawyer whose role is to uncover the intrigue. Like a detective, the latter will gradually unveil the mystery of the shadowy creature in order to save his friend Jekyll. In the comic, however, the character's duality is highlighted early on; the braiding of panels 8 and 9 determines a fundamental sequence and marks the symbolic and physical fusion of the two characters when Jekyll's body is visible in Hyde's eyes. Throughout the successive panels, the shot closes in to frame Hyde's eye. The face expresses hatred and disgust, the body becomes a dark mass between the chromatic and achromatic—a gray shape arrayed in a disturbing chromatism. The third panel of the page displays his cornea in close-up, reflecting the figure of Jekyll, who is writing, his body bent over. The confrontation between culture and bestiality is explicit in the story and is symbolically reproduced and intensified in the comic. Hyde's duality and cruelty are intensely thematized by the images: the distinction between good and evil, consciousness and unconsciousness. What is emphasized are Jekyll's desires as they are channeled through Hyde. How can desire be released from the control of consciousness and acted upon? The materialization of a drive beyond all restrictions (i.e., internalized social rules) is incarnated by the beast devoid of control or self-consciousness. The monster appears in the artist's drawings: the brusque line, unexpected marks, and intense colors. Animality is conjured up in two ways: lack of self-consciousness and the brute physicality merging into one.

Deleuze's analysis of the monstrous figures painted by Bacon is highly relevant, here, especially given that the processes of construction (or deconstruction) of forms in Mattotti's work are clearly influenced by the Irish artist. It is the treatment of pictorial matter that explains, according to Deleuze, the operations of rubbing and brushing, as well as the deformation of facial features. The animal traits that mark the commonality between man and animal can thus emerge:

> The deformations which the body undergoes are also the animal traits of the head. This has nothing to do with a correspondence between animal forms and facial forms. In fact, the face lost its form by being subjected to the techniques of rubbing and brushing that disorganize it and make a head emerge in its place. And the marks or traits of animality are not animal forms, but rather the spirits that haunt the wiped off parts [. . .] Bacon's techniques of local scrubbing and asignifying traits take on a particular meaning here. Sometimes the human head is replaced by an animal; but it is not the animal as a form, but rather the animal as a trait. [. . .] In place of formal correspondences, what Bacon's painting constitutes is a zone of indiscernibility or undecidability between man and animal. Man becomes animal, but not without the animal becoming spirit at the same time, the spirit of man. [. . .] It is never a combination of forms, but rather the common fact: the common fact of man and animal. (Deleuze 21)

According to Deleuze, the meeting point between man and animal is located in the flesh, transposed by the brushed and deformed Figure. This commonality is found in Mattotti's Figures, in which animal and bestial traits arise from the movement of matter against the surface. While the comic tends to present Hyde directly—his brutal side being present throughout the album, forcing the reader to witness his actions—the beast is only referred to indirectly in the report, and it is through the words of the characters that his actions are revealed. The mystery thus gives in to the conspicuousness of the image, where a double inversion takes place; from the start, the reader sees Hyde and all his actions. We are thus made aware of the ambiguity of Jekyll's feelings right away, since the text expresses the regret of having to endure this irreversible bond with the animal.

The Dissolution of Forms: Figuration/Figural

The plastic elements do not just serve the narrative, but also evoke image-ideas related to pure sensations and non-figuration. Mattotti develops the thematic thread of the album—the protagonist's becoming formless—through the plastic treatment of bodies and the color scheme. Lines with colorful contours, chromatic saturation, simultaneous contrasts, chiaroscuro, and shading participate in the comic's plastic and graphic richness. The main character is twisted and dematerialized through patches and blots. This loss of form is sublimated by the softness of Mattotti's bodies, which are flexible and plastic. They shift along a vector projecting them in a unidirectional movement. Three different panels in particular illustrate this. On plate 48 (fig. 17), Hyde's body is leaning over a horizontal surface, extending towards another human figure. The whole figure moves in one direction, and the head becomes a kind of arrow. To reinforce this tension, the face remains indistinct, a mere distribution of shadow and shaded light. Similarly, in the next plate, the body becomes a homogeneous, solid black mass. The force directs it towards a specific point, and the face expresses tension. Plate 52 depicts a running silhouette, once again recalling the shape of an arrow; all the tension is channeled into a curve directed at a single, identical objective. The treatment of Hyde's body evokes spasmodic and violent movements that make the character unpredictable and uncontrollable; each spasm is accompanied by a change, a modification of form. Such deformations temporarily steer the comic away from figuration. It thus becomes necessary to isolate the plates and panels that are prone to engage in a play on forces that take us beyond the figurative and representation. A non-narrative reading is possible, but it is less common for comics which are usually read as narrated stories, since narrative coherence is one of the medium's conventions. Yet in certain comics (this is a fairly contemporary phenomenon), the non-narrative dimension is acutely present—most obviously in abstract comics.

Any comic can lend itself *a priori* to a "non-narrative" reading, with the tension between the virtual and the actual indicating that a reader can ignore the text completely and stick to single images and their specific visual qualities. The meaning of images is activated by the reader. Deleuze's approach to semiotics separate signification from discourse, inviting a consideration of images beyond all signification: "Deleuze calls 'Ideas' complexes of sensation that are not reducible to discursive signification, but that stimulate thought. These images do not say anything; they give rise to thought" (Sauvagnargues 10).

Fig. 17: *Doctor Jekyll & Mister Hyde* (Mattotti and Kramsky, 2002): Hyde writes a letter to Lanyon in Jekyll's name requesting a specific substance.

The dissolution of form ensuing from these image-ideas is revealed especially towards the end of the comic (fig. 18), as the character progressively turns into a blot. The deformation goes *crescendo* in an amalgam of five panels where the twisted and amorphous body is still recognizable. In the first image, the body leans on a winding axis; one can still identify certain parts of the face and tormented arms. A powerful white light, coming from the left and almost at ground level, sets the mass on a horizontal plane, casting

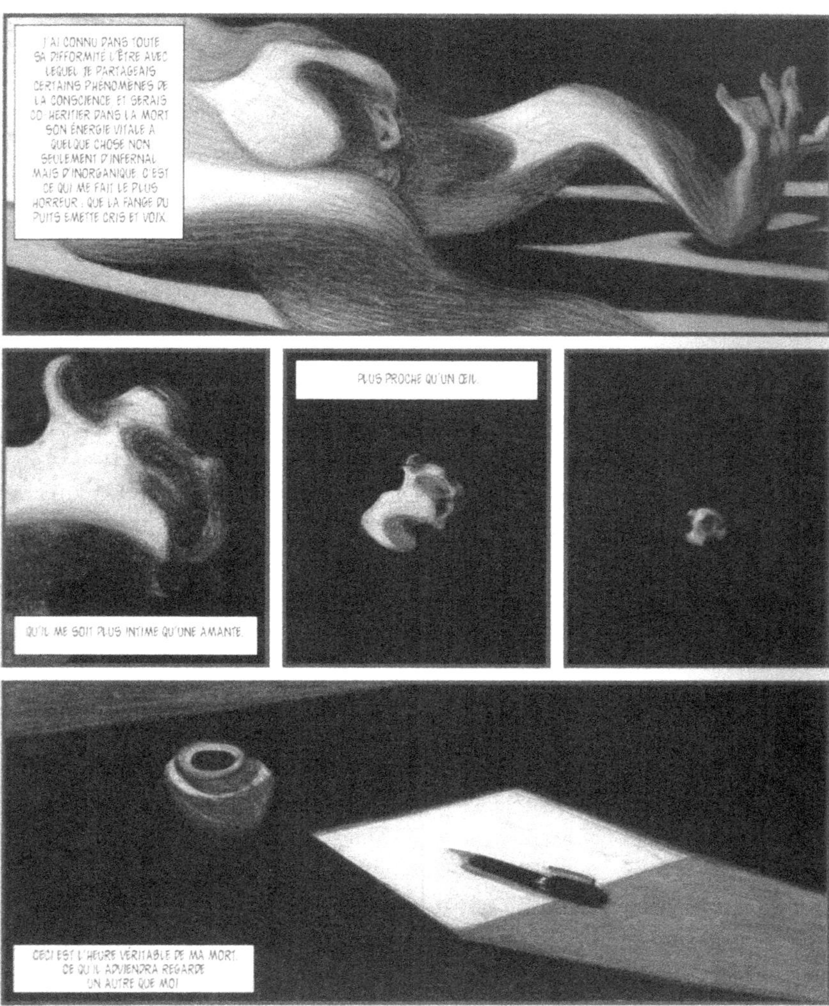

Fig. 18: *Doctor Jekyll & Mister Hyde* (Mattotti and Kramsky, 2002): Jekyll/Hyde's body dissolves, turning into a blot.

its shadow over the flat tints. In the following three frames, the figure loses its form, density, and color scheme, only to find itself consumed, as though swallowed up by the black void. This informal transformation recalls the issues analyzed by Deleuze in relation to Bacon's work, when the author lists the artist's pictorial elements: the Figure (human form, character), solid areas, chromatic zones and space, the traits that place the Figure, etc. In these circumstances, the form of the purely Figural (through extraction or isolation) exceeds the illustrative character of representation that always ties the form to an object acting as referent, as well as to other forms. Isolation is non-figuration's response, the liberation of the Figure. While there are several Figures, the abolishing of narration is effected following a distinct relationship between the Figures, namely, through what Deleuze calls *matter of fact*, which does not engage in relationships between ideas and objects. To illustrate this concept, we can invoke the example of coupling (between two distinct Figures): "There is one Figure common to two bodies, or one 'fact' common to two Figures, without the slightest story being narrated" (Deleuze 66). In the case of multiple images—triptychs in particular—the link between separate parts is there, yet it is neither logical nor narrative: "The triptych does not imply a progression, and it does not tell a story. Thus it too, in turn, has to incarnate a common fact for diverse Figures. It has to produce a 'matter of fact'" (Deleuze 69). The "fact" of copresence, of the incarnation in the image of the deformed body, is, for instance, evident in the single panel on page 41 (fig. 19), which occupies the entire width of the strip. Situated on the horizontal plane, it represents a Figure composed of two floating bodies in a space composed of areas of solid color as well as achromatic tints. The two bodies are intertwined, following a curve and counter-curve (*contre-courbe*), their intensity rendering them uncontrollable and powerful forms. Mattotti creates a relation of forces that binds the forms to one another beyond narrativity and renders them visible. As Deleuze maintains, the Figure is the "sensible form related to a sensation; it acts immediately upon the nervous system, which is of the flesh" (Deleuze 27). Sensation is thus attached to the body; it is a carrier of color and form: "As Valery put it, sensation is that which is transmitted directly, and avoids the detour and boredom of conveying a story. And positively, Bacon constantly says that sensation is what passes from one 'order' to another, from one 'level' to another, from one 'area' to another. This is why sensation is the master of deformations, the agent of bodily deformations" (Deleuze 36).

As Deleuze argues, while this sensation is transmitted in a direct manner and must be understood as something instantaneous, it is also concerned with changes and distortions. In the comic, the sequence of transformation when Jekyll becomes Hyde unfolds in plates 14 and 15, in a multiplicity of juxtaposed images, shaping the progression of one body to the other; the character suffers the pain of the physical metamorphosis. If we isolate the plate, we cannot see the causal relationships but only a succession of capricious Figures. The first panel shows the fragmented body, the scattered parts floating in abstract space, while the last panel presents a Figure in tension and torsion (fig. 20). The panels on the following page stage a series of amorphous

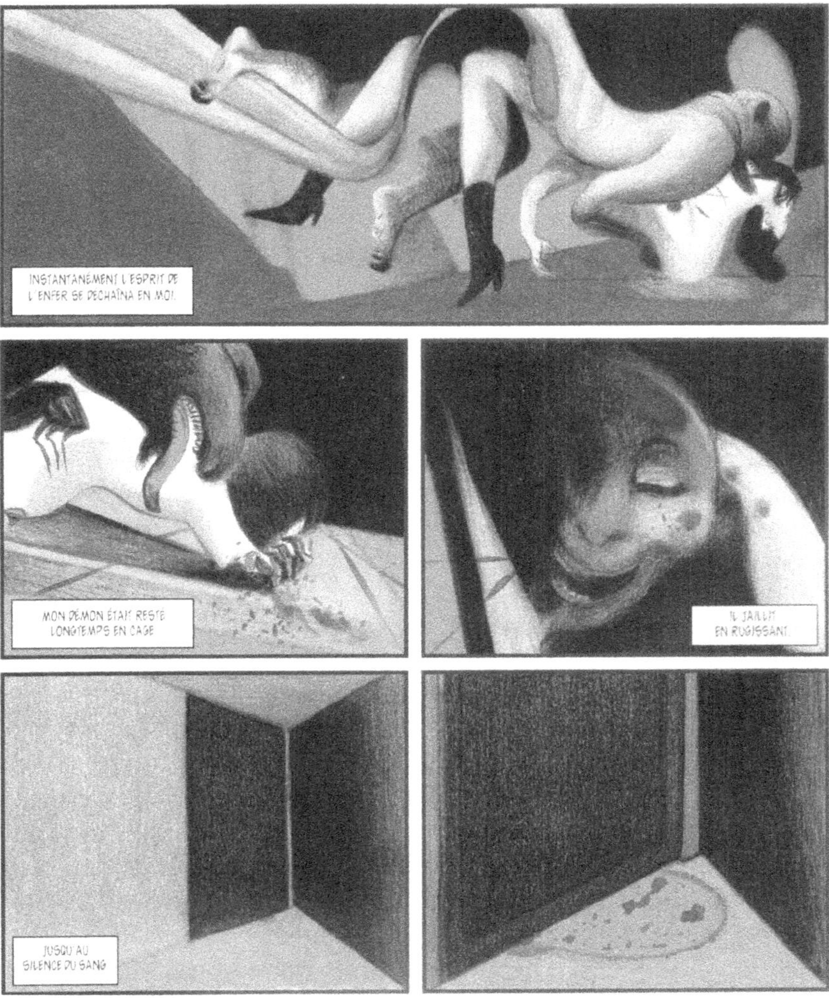

Fig. 19: *Doctor Jekyll & Mister Hyde* (Mattotti and Kramsky, 2002): Jekyll pictures the dark force taking over his body and self.

shapes, with body, face, and hands twisting and undergoing deformation. The circumstances leading to these different states, where the forms and spasms are isolated into distinct images, unveil a body that wants to escape from itself, very much like the Figural in Bacon's work:

> The entire series of spasms in Bacon is of this type: scenes of love, of vomiting and excreting, in which the body attempts to escape from itself

> through one of its organs in order to rejoin the field or material structure. Bacon has often said that, in the domain of Figures, the shadow has as much presence as the body; but the shadow acquires this presence only because it escapes the body. [. . .] And the scream, Bacon's scream, is the operation through which the entire body escapes through the mouth. (Deleuze 16)

The escape of the body described by Deleuze is visible in the barely identifiable pointed shadow in the first frame of the second plate. The intense cries evoked further give the impression of a body escaping through the mouth. The third panel depicts an animal form, with an undulating head sticking out and a mouth emitting a bright red scream. Sensation is materialized in living flesh:

> The Figure is not simply the isolated body, but also the deformed body that escapes from itself. What makes deformation a destiny is that the body has a necessary relationship with the material structure: not only does the material structure curl around it, but the body must return to the material structure and dissipate into it, thereby passing through or into these prostheses-instruments, which constitute passages and states that are real, physical, and effective, and which are sensations and not imaginings. (Deleuze 18–19)

Figures tangle and then blur with the background until they become one. Regarding the transformation, we can see how the animal shape approximates Hyde's construction as human beast. Deleuze insists that, in Bacon's work, the body is flesh or meat. As noted above, this materiality is the common zone linking man and beast: "The head-meat is a becoming-animal of man. In this becoming, the entire body tends to escape from itself, and the Figure tends to return to the material structure" (Deleuze 27). In this figure-ground, relationship, form, line work, and color intervene. The chromatic atmospheres created in each sequence are rich and varied, as are the line and the treatment of the surface. In certain sequences, the line is clearly identifiable, displaying its nature as a drawn image (in the manner of Otto Dix or George Grosz), while in others the shading and chromatic surfaces bring the image closer to the pictorial (the many references to expressionist painting and fauvism). In addition, strained perspectives and the construction of space evoke the scenery of the German expressionist film *The Cabinet of Dr. Caligari* (Robert Wiene, 1920). The sequence on page 13 shows Dr. Jekyll working in his laboratory. The simultaneous presence of highly saturated colors creates a dynamic atmosphere and increases the intensity and tension of the situation. The background elements are rendered in warm hues, while the character is represented in cold tints. By contrast, plate 28 does not exhibit great color contrasts, as it conforms

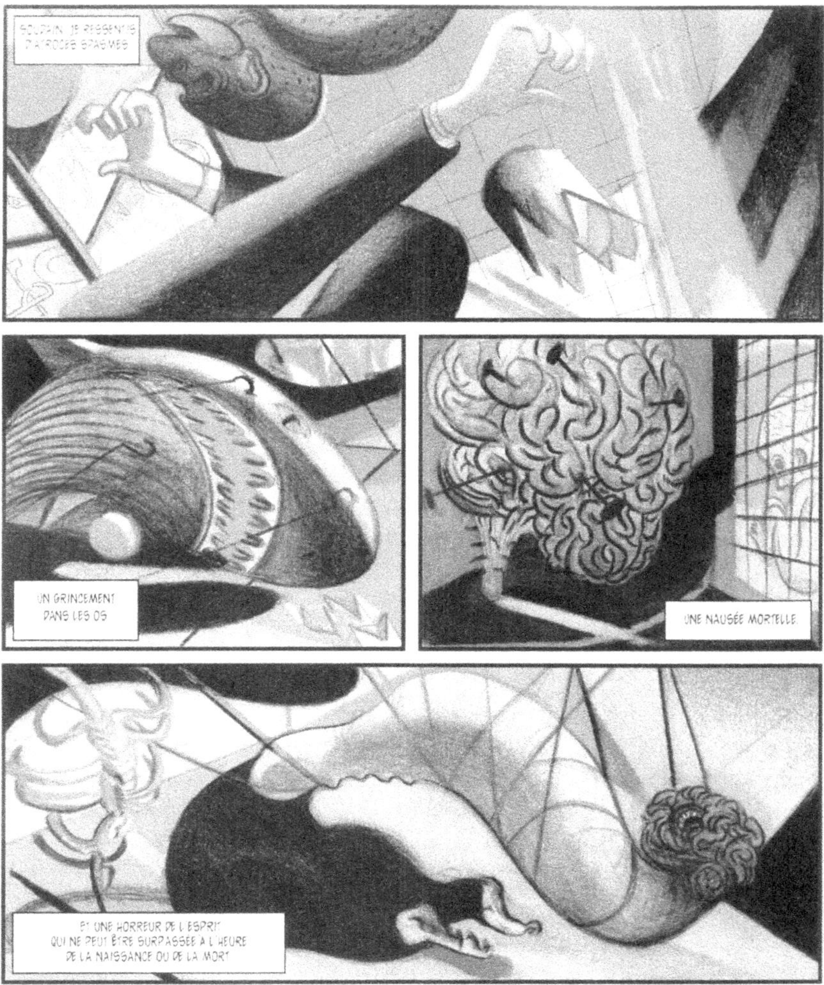

Fig. 20: *Doctor Jekyll & Mister Hyde* (Mattotti and Kramsky, 2002): the Baconian imagery evoking Jekyll's painful transformation.

to a form of monochromaticity. Shadows and grayish light, coupled with the presence of a yellow-green light, create a strange and dark atmosphere. Proceeding to page 31, we can notice the presence of white in the chromatic surface; solid grays and whites occupy large areas within the images and combine with bright colors. Together with the emptiness of space, the chromatic harmony conjures up a certain metaphysical atmosphere reminiscent of the landscapes of Giorgio De Chirico.

Conclusion

This approach to Mattotti and Kramsky's *Doctor Jekyll*, a work that is as fascinating as it is complex, has been made possible by a combination of elements of comics theory and certain analytical principles from visual studies. Studying the narrative and non-figurative aspects of the comic revealed how narrative can become a force so that its opposite can be understood and enable us to delve into the abstract and non-representational potentialities of the work. Shattering figuration thus implies a certain emancipation from the requirement of representation in comics images. The "-ing" form of the verb contains the potential for action, while at the same time the *monstrator* authorizes all deviations from *mimesis* through drawing. This potential takes concrete form thanks to the diverse readings that actualize new meanings and sensations every time. The authors' strategy testifies to a double stance: first, creating an assumed adaptation that also refers to previous readings of the source text; second, exceeding representation and figuration by combining images without apparent continuity or resorting to striking images that set themselves apart from the rest of the page or even graphic novel. The diversity of references in this comic participates in a dynamics of transposition, which it presents as a process. From this perspective, one can no longer think in terms of separate objects, but rather of a series of substances that shift and take form, of a synergy between the texts and their possible positions. Incarnation implies a becoming-material of the original story through line, color, and form-Figures.

Notes

1. The original reads as follows: "Vivimos en un mundo de relatos, acertijos, informaciones, poemas y sermones arrancados de su lugar, llamados sin razón aparente de un lenguaje o de un medio a otros. [. . .] En ese tránsito, relatos, acertijos informaciones o sermones suelen además reducirse, o inflarse, o achatarse, o teñirse de matices que, en ciertos casos, parecen destinados a exhibir los poderes de un medio, y en otros reproducir una moda, o recordar la insistencia de una tradición. [. . .] La relación cotidiana con el pasaje de los relatos entre medios despliega ante nosotros el carácter inevitablemente parcial y fatalmente condicionado por algún estilo de época de toda lectura."

2. In *L'Image*, Jacques Aumont provides a broad definition of apparatus (*dispositif*), reflecting its internal configuration, as well as its modes of circulation and relation to the public: "These social determinants include in particular the means and techniques of image production, their modes of circulation and possible reproduction, the places where they are accessible, and the formats used to disseminate them. It is to this set of material and organizational features that the term *dispositif* refers. [. . .] The *dispositif* is what regulates the viewer's relation to images

within a specific symbolic context." This concept is relevant because it takes into consideration both the material qualities of comics (technical, means of dissemination) and also the modes of circulation and thus also the relationship with the reader.

3. Gaudreault applies the concept of *monstration* to the performing arts and film.

Works Cited

Aumont, Jacques. *L'Image*. Paris: Nathan, 1990.

Deleuze, Gilles. *Francis Bacon: The Logic of Sensation*. London: Continuum, 2003 [1981].

De Rueda, María de los Ángeles, ed. *Múltiples / múltiples. Pasajes entre las artes, la tecnología y la cultura visual*. La Plata: UNLP, 2006. https://issuu.com/lelederueda/docs/m__ltiple-_m__ltiples. Accessed on August 7, 2017.

Gaudreault, André. *Du littéraire au filmique : système du récit*. Québec: Nota bene, 1999 [1988].

Gaudreault, André, and Philippe Marion. "Transécriture et médiatique narrative : l'enjeu de l'intermédialité . . ." *La Transécriture. Pour une théorie de l'adaptation: littérature, cinéma, bande dessinée, théâtre, clip*. Eds. André Gaudreault and Thierry Groensteen. Québec: Nota bene, 1998. 31–40.

Groensteen, Thierry. *Comics and Narration*. Trans. Ann Miller. Jackson: University Press of Mississippi, 2013 [2011].

Groensteen, Thierry. "Entre monstration et narration, une instance évanescente: la description." *L'image BD = Het stripbeeld*. Ed. Pascal Lefèvre. Leuven: Centre belge de la bande dessinée, 1991. 41–55.

Groensteen, Thierry. "Fiction sans frontières." *La Transécriture*. Eds. André Gaudreault and Thierry Groensteen. 9–20.

Groensteen, Thierry. "La narration comme supplément. Archéologie des fondations infranarratives de la bande dessinée." *Bande dessinée, récit et modernité*. Ed. Thierry Groensteen. Paris: Futuropolis, 1988. 45–69.

Groensteen, Thierry. *The System of Comics*. Trans. Bart Beaty and Nick Nguyen. Jackson: University Press of Mississippi, 2007 [1996].

Gubern, Roman. *La mirada opulenta. Exploración de la iconosfera contemporánea*. Barcelona: Gustavo Gili, 1987.

Hutcheon, Linda. *A Theory of Adaptation*. New York and London: Routledge, 2006.

Lévy, Pierre. *Qu'est-ce que le virtuel ?* Paris: La Découverte, 1995.

Mattotti, Lorenzo, and Jerry Kramsky. *Docteur Jekyll et Mister Hyde*. Paris: Casterman, 2002.

Morgan, Harry. *Principes de littératures dessinées*. Angoulême: Editions de l'An 2, 2003.

Sauvagnargues, Anne. *Deleuze and Art*. London: Bloomsbury Academic, 2013.

Steimberg, Oscar. *Semiótica de los medios masivos, El pasaje a los medios de los géneros populares*. Buenos Aires: Atuel, 2005 [1993].

Stevenson, R. L. *The Strange Case of Dr Jekyll and Mr Hyde*. London: Penguin, 2008 [1886].

In Defense of Freedom of Adaptation: The Case of *El hombre descuadernado*, an Adaptation of "The Horla"

BENOÎT MITAINE

> Like Eisenstein in his day, I am still convinced that the best way to approach reality is by transcending realism.[1]
>
> —FELIPE HERNÁNDEZ CAVA

Guy de Maupassant is one of the the most adapted French authors, with his work having been turned into plays, films, television series, and comics.[2] Although it is difficult to explain the power of attraction of his work in the twentieth and early twenty-first centuries,[3] there are at least a few hypotheses that could account for the author's "adaptability," or *adaptogénie*, as André Gaudreault calls it (271).

One of the main factors is undoubtedly Maupassant's renown as one of France's foremost canonical authors. As the author of several classic masterpieces (*Bel Ami*, "Dumpling," "The Horla," etc.), he is remembered through his works, to paraphrase the title of Judith Schlanger's book, *La Mémoire des œuvres*. Fame itself is already a source of capitalization[4] ("only the rich get credit," or so the saying goes), the number of adaptations of a given work often being proportional to an author's reputation. Adaptation (especially film versions, accompanied as they often are by ballyhoo in the media) serves the interests of the adapted work by updating it to current tastes, while the adapted work, because of its notoriety, serves the interests of the adaptation by endowing it with legitimacy. A second factor can be added to Maupassant's renown, namely, the brevity of most of his stories, be they erotic, realistic, or fantastic. This brevity seems to have found favor with comics artists (and this is probably not true of filmmakers) to the extent that throughout the sixties and seventies, before the album became the dominant format in Europe, comics artists published their works in magazines,[5] which forced them to create short works suitable for serial publication. The third and final factor contributing to Maupassant's *adaptogénie* is genre: the author excelled in tales of the Fantastic. In his introduction to the special issue of *Otrante* devoted to the relationship between comics and the Fantastic, guest editor Jean-Paul Gabilliet (2003) suggests that "historically, the Fantastic has been a *structuring* force in comics" to the extent that, through their semiotic hybridity, comics "seem [. . .] to generate intense phantasmal powers." Furthermore, unlike literature, comics can "*represent* without necessarily *signifying*" (7). In sum, it is this capacity inherent in abstraction—Gabilliet calls it the "disequilibrium of expression"—that is supposedly at the basis of the natural affinity between comics and "strictly 'non-referential' stories," which is precisely the defining feature of the Fantastic (Gabilliet 7).

None of these hypotheses is valid in the case of *El hombre descuadernado* (2009) by scriptwriter Felipe Hernández Cava (Madrid, 1953–) and Argentine artist Héctor Sanguiliano aka Sanyú (Neuquén, 1951–). Indeed, the authors took great care to remove all intertextual references to the title (in Spanish, Maupassant's short story is known by the same title as in French, "El Horla") in order to insist on the autonomy of the comic vis-à-vis its source. They deliberately chose not to exploit the fame of the adapted work and the commercial potential that such adaptations (sometimes) generate.[6] Regarding brevity and genre, the authors deliberately transformed the source text in order to produce the opposite effect; they lengthened the original by adding biographical facts about Maupassant, thereby defusing the story's fantastic dimension. The third hypothesis is partially valid (as with works of fantasy in general), but has no explanatory force as far as this adaptation is concerned.

In short, instead of trying to account for a "Maupassantmania" by investigating profitability and the convenience of a ready-made story, it might be more relevant to first ask ourselves what makes a work a "classic." Classic texts are grounded in issues that offer both universality and timelessness, qualities that make them flexible and adaptable to "contemporary issues," which is the basis for "the plurality of readings throughout time" necessary for their survival (Schlanger 107).

I will address the latter question in the first part of this chapter, which is devoted to the reasoning that drove (a strong word, perhaps, but the adaptation was practically made under constraint) Felipe H. Cava to adapt "the Horla," a monster that each generation reshapes and adapts according to the social fears of their time. The second section of this chapter will focus, first, on the script and then on the drawing in order to explore some of the major changes introduced in Cava's script compared to the hypotext (including the expansion of the genre through the addition of biographical material from Maupassant's life). This will facilitate the analysis of three major graphic and narrative strategies—what Philippe Marion refers to as "graphiation" (294)—used by Sanyú to convey madness: (1) the shifts between baroque and expressionist styles; (2) the visual *mise en scène* of the themes of the double and fragmentation; (3) effects of deformation (surprising variations in size) and multiple *trompes l'œil* that predominantly exploit sequentiality (the illusion of sequential progression and its opposite, the illusion of sequential stasis); the play on narrative conventions ultimately culminates in Cava and Sanyú's daring disconnection of the storylines within the same panel, generating narrative disjunctions that disturb the reader's senses, as well as the meaning and the act of reading.

Adaptation as Pharmakon

In his preface to *El hombre descuadernado*,[7] Felipe Hernández Cava relates how the adaptation was the driving force behind a difficult mourning process. Cava offers an account full of restraint of how his mother's Alzheimer's gradually changed and ultimately took her. Ana Juan and Keko, two artists who are among Cava's closest friends, were afraid of the impact his mother's declining health would have on the writer. They eventually found, by way of a remedy, an unusual way to keep him occupied—they entrusted him with the creation of a new collection for Edicions de Ponent, one of the three major independent comics publishers in Spain. Cava got to work with his loyal friends, and in 2007 founded *El cuarto oscuro*, the collection that would include *El hombre descuadernado*. This anecdote would be insignificant were it not for the fact that the collection specializes in adaptations of classic horror stories.[8] Besides Cava and Sanyú's loose adaptation of "The Horla," it also comprises an adaptation of a passage from Bram Stoker's *Dracula* by Ana Juan, an adaptation of E. T. A. Hoffmann's "Sand-Man" by Felipe del Barrio and May Prol, and Keko's adaptation of Henry James's *The Turn of the Screw*. The name of the collection, "El cuarto oscuro,"[9] comes from the eponymous punishment that owes part of its efficacy to the combined effect of confinement and fear of the dark. A kind of domestic "jail cell," "el cuarto oscuro" is a windowless room (closet, storage room) where disobedient children are locked up. Although the term (and punishment) are no longer widely known, it owed its effectiveness to the evocative and ominous combination of the words "room" + "dark." In addition to this first meaning, there is a more profound one tied to Cava's experience at the time. It doesn't take a psychoanalyst to make the connection between the title and the name given to those "mental closets" where our traumas are repressed; *el cuarto oscuro* is a mental crypt (a junk room) where we get rid of what we are unable to integrate psychologically (Hachet 2000).

In this case, the choice of the "Horla" is no accident, as Cava immediately points out. In the second paragraph of his preface, the author compares

Alzheimer's to something alien that has grown roots in his mother's brain, feeding off her thoughts until her collapse ("It was as if something unfamiliar had taken possession of [her brain] and fed off her consciousness, leaving her memory blank").[10] This comparison recalls the Horla, an alien being that snatches humans and causes them to go insane. On the third page of the preface, Cava candidly acknowledges that he used the adaptation of "Horla," the most terrifying story he ever read, as "a good excuse to [. . .] talk about what was happening to [him]."[11]

Where Cava's confessions become truly remarkable is when he adds that his adaptation explores both the association between the Horla and Alzheimer's as well as his own identification with Maupassant: "I was the protagonist of this story and at the same time the writer who imagined him when he already felt the threat of reason slipping away."[12] He then adds: "I had to give free rein to the fears that plagued me and let them spill out into the medium I have always had the most faith in: comics."[13] Judging from these statements, *El hombre descuadernado* would be the transcription of an inner experience, an emotional shock, which almost pushed the author beyond the brink of madness. In this case, at least, adaptation seems to have been a cultural practice with cathartic and therapeutic value.

How to Go about Adapting?

During the creation of an adaptation, two major questions naturally arise: "Which work should one adapt?" and "How should one adapt the work?"

All in all, the preface of *El hombre descuadernado* answers the first question: it is a matter of heart and soul. The second question has more to do with textual mechanics: selection, condensation, transformation. However, all too often we forget that comics adaptations involve two moments: they begin with the adaptation of a text into a new text by a scriptwriter, followed by a second adaptation by the artist who gives visual form to that script. The relation between the textual adaptation and the graphic adaptation is asymmetrical in the sense that the writer and artist are separate individuals, especially when the artist is granted more freedom. If, as semiotician Oscar Steimberg argues, the writer often has the upper hand (Berone and Reggiani 2010), *El hombre descuadernado*, by contrast, testifies to the absence of a hierarchy between an Author with a capital A and an artist who would just be the latter's puppet. *El hombre descuadernado* is the work of two authors, two artists who each in their turn have adapted "The Horla" with their own tools, knowledge, and sensibility.

1. Cava Adapts Maupassant

Cava, who is often considered "the most important writer in Spanish comics" (according to Peeters and Baetens on the website of their publishing house Impressions Nouvelles), is a self-confessed "elitist" writer driven by reflection and not by dreams of commercial success. Averse to classic, conventional creations, Cava is one of those authors who revels in ambiguity and declines to offer his readers straightforward stories. He does so deliberately, and it is often difficult to figure out what lies behind it: "I wanted to make a declaration of principle on how to tackle a personal drama while not portraying the disease from a supposedly realistic angle, which is all the vogue today. Like Eisenstein in his day, I am still convinced that the best way to approach reality is by transcending realism."[14]

For this master of the unsaid, a text like "The Horla," whose plot revolves around the motifs of the double, dispossession, and vampirization, easily wins over any realistic script about Alzheimer's. In addition, *El hombre descuadernado* does not tell the tale of a disease so much as the suffering of someone torn to pieces, be it Cava or Maupassant. This makes the comics a maze of sorts where multiple narratives are intertwined: that of the "Horla" with the theme of Alzheimer's woven in, and that of Maupassant's life mixed with Cava's. In short, we are dealing with an adaptation animated by a form of generic migration; it gives the "Horla" more autobiographical weight (Maupassant as chronicler of his own life) than the original tale, which was ultimately meant to read more like a form of autofiction. However, the autofictional component has not completely disappeared. Indeed, Cava has removed the mask of the narrator of the "Horla" to make it appear behind the figure of the author (Maupassant) and hide himself all the better behind the mask of the narrator of *El hombre descuadernado*. In so doing, Cava appropriates the enunciative tactic of Maupassant by hiding/splitting behind a narrator whose emotions he shares.

In addition to these genre transformations, Cava has also changed the form of the "Horla" by relieving his own text of the calendar constraint imposed by the diary form. The forty-two dates extending from May 8 to September 10 in the original have given way to twenty-one three-page chapters, which, if one compares the adaptation to the source text, refer, through textual or graphical citation, to twenty-one of the forty-two dates of "The Horla."[15] Although the temporal anchors are gone, the chronological progression remains faithful to the sequence of events in the "Horla."

Moreover, the intertextual debt uniting these two texts is never concealed. For example, the second page of *El hombre descuadernado* refers to the first day in the "Horla" diary, May 8: "Just like the character of your story, I, too, could see the black barges full of coal pass by on the Seine on their way to Rouen [. . .] and the comings and goings of the three-master which seemed to glide by my garden, drawn by a small tugboat buzzing like a fly in the middle of the fumes."[16] The words "story," "three-master," "tugs buzzing," and so on are all unequivocal references to Maupassant's story.

The phrase quoted above is an excerpt from a conversation between Flaubert and Maupassant. Fussy readers might be surprised to hear Flaubert mention "The Horla," as it was only published in 1887, seven years after the death of the author of *Madame Bovary*. This is not an anachronism, but rather a conversation hallucinated by Maupassant who is at death's door, ravaged by syphilis. Maupassant's conversations with the dead, notably Flaubert, Gérard de Nerval, Nietzsche, and his brother Hervé, evoke the daily life of a man who has gone insane and, owing to his condition, inhabits both worlds, as he readily admits: "I talk a lot and often with the dead"[17] (Cava and Sanyú 50, C1).

Though difficult to understand on a first reading, the first chapter plunges the reader into Maupassant's world of hallucinations. Certainly, the first page of the book contains a significant clue as to the author's life, at least for those in the know; he is depicted prostrate, in a straitjacket with his arms tied behind his back, held up by two men as they cross the main entrance to Dr. Blanche's mental hospital.[18] Maupassant was, indeed, committed on January 8, 1892, following a suicide attempt on the night of the first and second of January (Satiat 567–75). He would not leave the institution until the day of his death (July 6, 1893). Without specifying this at any time in the comic, Cava begins his story on January 8, 1892, just days after Maupassant's suicide attempt. This explains the curious anticipatory caption formulated in the first person that introduces the first panel: "Today I announced that I am dead. Although this will only happen in a few months."[19]

The second panel immediately refers to another important character in the story, the invisible twin who will later be designated as the Horla: "But he, however, did not die. He's lying on the grass in front of his house."[20] "He," so the narrator tells us, "is not dead"; what is more, he has even won the war, as this sentence, taken from the entry dated May 8, is not originally in the third person but in the first: "I have spent all the morning lying in the grass in front of my house" (Maupassant, "The Horla," 100).

The first four pages of the comic set the stage and multiply the references to the events of May 8. Reprising the rapid pace of the short story, the fever episode quickly follows (chapters 2, 3, and 4). This allows Cava to introduce the themes of disease (syphilis), madness, and the double.

Fig. 21: *El hombre descuadernado* (Cava and Sanyú, 2009): the Horla torments Maupassant in bed at night.

With the reader now fully aware of Maupassant's torment, the story switches to horror with the irruption of the Horla starting on the third page of chapter 4 (following the chronology of the short story, this would refer to the events of May 25). Strangely enough, on numerous occasions, the graphics are at odds with the text, thus producing a *narrative disjunction* (fig. 21). Cava soberly renders the text as: "He sleeps two or three hours until the arrival of the next crisis. He wants to scream but he cannot. He wants to move but cannot. He wakes up covered in sweat"[21] (Cava and Sanyú 13, C2). Whereas Cava withholds the name of the monster, Sanyú depicts a most striking scene that took place on the night of May 25: the Horla climbs onto the diarist's bed, kneels on his chest, and tries to strangle him. Though both Cava and Sanyú narrate the events of the same day (May 25), they do not focus on the same passage, with each artist seeming to keep only what suits him best. This separation is quite destabilizing for the reader, since it generates a double narrative process in which the drawings become independent from the text and vice versa. The traditional pattern in which the artist is the faithful double of the writer no longer holds. It is as if the writer had lost control of his double, who has become a Horla.

The presence of the Horla grows from chapter to chapter. Chapter 5, entitled "Maupassant and Maupassant," clearly indicates that the double has

Fig. 22: *El hombre descuadernado* (Cava and Sanyú, 2009): a series of close-ups of the Horla's eyes, mouth, and hands.

usurped his master. His grip on the writer is now complete, and it is the Horla who ends up dictating the story (Cava and Sanyú 15, C6). The writer has become the "writing," a kind of human typewriter. As he points out to his host, "[t]he writer does not always choose his themes, sometimes the themes choose him"[22] (Cava and Sanyú 15, C4). This comment, more than any other in the comic, applies as much to Maupassant as to Cava, who lets his guard down for these three panels. After reading the preface and considering the many inner demons he is fighting, we are justified in thinking that the Horla is, in effect, the one who has picked Cava and not the other way around.

The double-page spread, where the Horla is shown leaning over the shoulder of Maupassant at his desk holding a quill, brilliantly illustrates both the physical and mental influence of the double on the original. Besides the Horla's towering presence that domineers the writer, it is difficult not to link the Indian ink Maupassant uses to write his short story with the Horla's physical appearance, which is portrayed in thick black stripes resembling ink strokes. It is as if the Horla surfaced from the page itself, still dripping with the ink the author used to write this romantic being into existence. We are confronted with the familiar scenario of the mad scientist or divinely inspired writer, overwhelmed by the creature he has created.

In addition to the Horla's posture and physical appearance, Sanyú's clever and original framing are especially noteworthy, both in this excerpt and throughout the comic. Emphasizing body parts through extreme close-ups effectively emphasizes the evil and monstrous aspect of this otherworldly being; this malevolent eye can only inspire fear (fig. 22), like the close-up of the hand which simultaneously refers to the hand of the strangler and to the monstrous fantasy of the severed limb that seems to have a will of its own. This streaked, clenched, and flayed hand[23] is no longer human; it is at best animal, at worst supernatural or extraterrestrial.

By entitling this chapter "Maupassant and Maupassant," Cava goes beyond mere adaptation and proposes a psychoanalytic reading of the "Horla." Like others before him, he suggests that this hallucinatory tale owes as much to the author's madness as to his imagination. Throughout the remaining fifteen chapters, Cava continues to blend the story of the "Horla" with Maupassant's life, taking the reader through each phase of the author's madness up until the final page, which shows a realistic representation of the tomb at the Montparnasse cemetery where the author was laid to rest.

Though more can be said of Cava's script, it is now necessary to turn to the artwork, which, from beginning to end, is affected by the madness and suffering of the central character. The Argentine artist's graphic adaptation is twofold, as he simultaneously interprets the Horla and Cava's script; it is enigmatic and often makes the reader think the drawings could only have been the work of a madman. If indeed it seems crazy, it is only in the sense that Sanyú has devoted an insane amount of time to the work—five years of his life, in fact (admittedly, he was simultaneously working on other projects).

2. Sanyú Adapts Cava and Maupassant

Sanyú uses three major graphic-narrative devices to give form to insanity.

The first is immediately striking: his unconventional drawing style, which merges the Baroque and Expressionism. Sanyú readily recognized the power of water, air, and fire in Maupassant's short story, and has given free rein to what Gaston Bachelard (1941) calls "the imagination of matter." The sinuous lines, endless whorls, and arabesques—an aesthetics of the fold that endows the drawings with a baroque patina (particularly visible in chapter 1)—owe much to the decisive presence of the three elements of the universe (fig. 23). These baroque caprices are not only numerous, but also quite fragile; at any moment, they can be swept away by the Horla's irruption or Maupassant's bouts of madness. Sanyú's black brush lends itself quite readily to Expressionism. The fusion or occasional alternation between two styles that are both demanding and difficult to read sometimes ends up turning the drawings into obstacles in the progression of the narrative. The use of Indian ink and a No. 3 marten brush, both for the lettering and the drawing, adds to the plastic density of a work where the eye gets bogged down in the volumes and whorls. Worlds away from the clear line, Sanyú is a practitioner of the dark line, making his drawing sometimes so opaque that it oscillates between figuration and abstraction.

Fig. 23: *El hombre descuadernado* (Cava and Sanyú, 2009): the baroque arabesques evoke the three elements (air, fire, water).

The second graphic technique Sanyú uses to embody madness also stems directly from Maupassant's short story. It concerns the exploitation of the theme of the double, which is so central to "The Horla." From page 2 on, the specular and distorting properties of water are used to visualize the inverted and undulating reflections of Maupassant and Flaubert strolling along the Seine. Their bodies distorted by their reflections, they appear imprisoned by their clothes, wrapped around their figures like straitjackets, reinforcing the link with the previously mentioned page in which Maupassant is depicted in a straitjacket. This reversal of top and bottom, coupled with the anamorphic and baroque world of folds, anchors the story, from the outset, to a realm where the laws of perception are turned inside out.

From chapter 4 onwards, the classic doubling generated by reflective surfaces (like water in chapter 1) is followed by a form of duplication that is no longer physical but psychological. On page 11, Maupassant's face appears in close-up, split over two panels: the left, marked by multiple scratches, suggests the presence of evil, while the other half appears normal (fig. 24). It is only after symbolizing the subjective schism through this iconic fracture, and after candidly naming the disease in a dialogue,[24] that Sanyú finally introduces the Horla. The latter bursts forth quite dramatically onto the page in the final panel of the third and final page of chapter 4: he appears squatting on

Fig. 24: *El hombre descuadernado* (Cava and Sanyú, 2009): Maupassant's face split in two, the scratches on the right side suggesting the presence of evil.

Maupassant's body, with one hand around the author's neck in an attempt to strangle him. His nakedness, hirsutism, and prominent musculature make him Maupassant's primitive double, a kind of archaic figure escaped from the depths of the unconscious. A true *Doppelgänger*, a morbid, evil, and rival emanation of Maupassant, the Horla will not stop harassing his master, driving him to suicide before taking his place.

The third and final major graphic device is by far the most sophisticated and requires more attention. As I have already indicated, *El hombre descuadernado* testifies to a rigorous composition in which each of the twenty-one three-page-long chapters follows the same cadence; as a rule, the first two pages contain six panels, while the third page only has two. This might lead one to conclude that the story is embedded in a multiframe[25] that is monotonous on both narrative and rhythmic levels, leaving no room for variation or the unexpected. Yet this is not the case for at least two reasons.

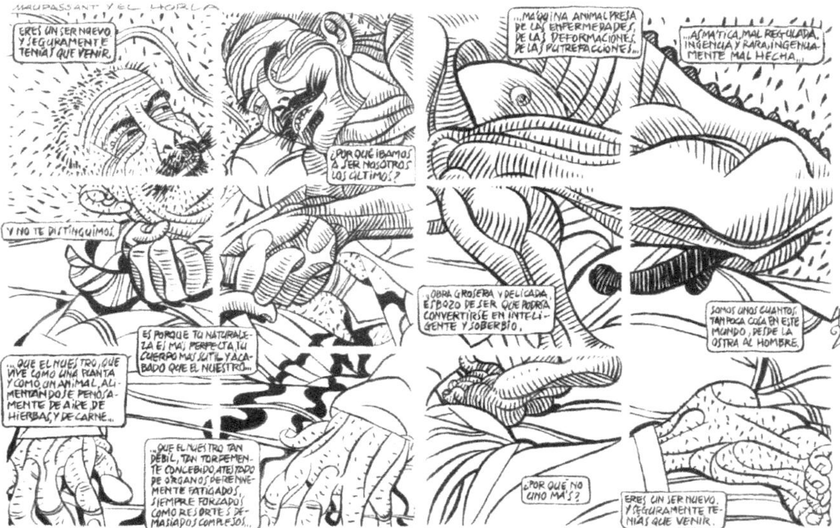

Fig. 25: *El hombre descuadernado* (Cava and Sanyú, 2009): "Maupassant and the Horla" or the writer's nightmare about the evil being.

First of all, and even after acknowledging that the chapters quite faithfully adhere to the chronological progression of "The Horla," what is highly significant is that their self-contained format resembles a book of poems[26] more than a graphic novel. The patterning of 2x6 panels + 2 that many artists would have used to play things safe and resort to the academic "waffle iron" grid, is reinterpreted by Sanyú as if it were serial music where atonality and syncope prevent a regular beat from setting in. The main trick to successfully thwart this obsessive pattern is to divide a single image or scene into two, three, six or sometimes twelve panels (fig. 23–26). It is thus not unusual to see a face or a body divided into several panels or, more precisely, dismembered. Given the work's theme, the fragmented representation of the body is highly effective to convey the psychological alterations Maupassant suffers, which are at the heart of "The Horla."[27]

The play with sequential codes has other unexpected effects. The two-page spreads on pages 41–42 and 59–60 are, in this respect, the most remarkable.

The first (fig. 25), entitled "Maupassant and the Horla" (chapter 14, 41–42), illustrates the nightmare of July 5, as described in the diary entry in the short story: "Imagine a man asleep, who is being killed, and who wakes up with a knife in his lung, with a death rattle, covered in blood" (Maupassant, "The Horla," 106). Surprisingly, while Sanyú's drawing unambiguously refers to the same nightmare, Cava's text contains exact quotes from the diary entry of

August 19, making no reference whatsoever to what the comic depicts. Word and image are linked exclusively through the chapter title: "Maupassant and the Horla." Everything suggests that the artist has just followed his whim and merely implemented the six panels per page rule as he saw fit. However, nothing is further from the truth. Sanyú has, in fact, followed Cava's script to the letter.[28]

A rare sight in comics, the authors, here, exploit the natural semiotic split between the text and the drawing to generate a narrative disjunction. By dividing the diegetic sources, the reader is confronted with the sheer difficulty of interpretation. The overlapping narrative threads (both graphic and textual) turn the page spread into a screen on which Sanyú's drawings are projected, as if they were the obsessions expressed by the protagonist. In other words, the text becomes the narrator's stream of consciousness, while the drawings make manifest his unconscious.

The mosaic—the fragmentation of large areas—is the second salient graphic technique. Once again, Sanyú and Cava shatter the comic medium's conventions by abandoning the sacrosanct principle of sequentiality that requires a logical progression from one panel to the next, from one strip to another, from one page to the next. However, chapter 14 states the obvious—there is no traditional sequential chain at work here. Only by distancing him/herself from the panel, strip and page, and by striving to forget the text and focus on the drawings alone, can the reader fully appreciate the change in scale. Ultimately, the panels are a *trompe l'oeil* intended to maintain the illusion of narrative action, that is to say, the illusion of sequentiality.[29]

The double-page spread in chapter 20 (59–60), entitled "Maupassant y la mariposa de su sueño," is the exact opposite of the one in chapter 14 (fig. 26). Although it also plays on the monumentality of the mosaic, there are two notable differences. The first is rather obvious: the double-page is silent. The second is subtler: a sequential action unfolds across this double-page despite the fact that it is also a drawing fragmented into twelve panels, with the butterfly fluttering from frame to frame. It is, therefore, no longer a question of semiotics and narrative disjunction (text and drawing are no longer opposed), but a simple opposition between animate and inanimate. By the same token, it is no longer possible to speak of the illusion of sequentiality, but, rather, of the illusion of non-sequentiality.

Indeed, the reader is first struck by the fixity, the lack of animation in this fragmented representation of Maupassant that stretches over nine panels, where the author appears belly-down, inert, more dead than alive, arms tied behind his back in his straitjacket, legs spread and then folded like a frog or a butterfly with open wings. At first, we get the impression that this scene

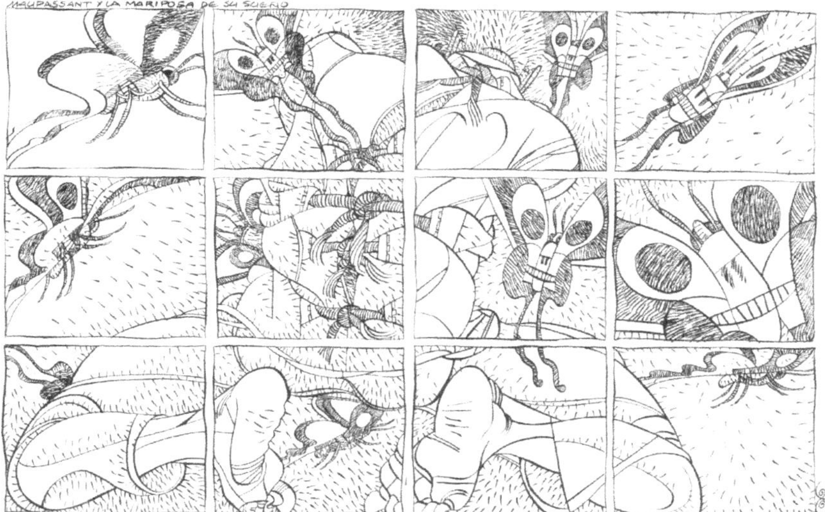

Fig. 26: *El hombre descuadernado* (Cava and Sanyú, 2009): "Maupassant and the Dream Butterfly," the insect fluttering from frame to frame.

is devoid of movement, as if we were looking at a painting or photograph. However, when we finally realize that this is not a butterfly colony twirling around the author, but the same insect reappearing in each panel, the illusion of a-sequentiality vanishes. This butterfly, displaying its death's head pattern, in no way resembles the "flower that flies" mentioned in the diary entry of August 19 in "The Horla." It only adds to the scene's morbidness, and rather than a flitting butterfly, it evokes the blowfly attracted by the stench of death. Furthermore, the seemingly lifeless and gagged body on the ground foreshadows the one in the next chapter, with Maupassant lying in his coffin, wrapped in a shroud.

These three main graphic and narrative strategies do more than just generate an effective aesthetics of madness. They also put *El hombre descuadernado* at the forefront of recent works characterized "by a poetics of reticence, ambiguity, and indeterminacy" (Groensteen, *Comics* 30). As Thierry Groensteen suggests, some authors are reluctant to stay on "the narrow path of 'narrative and nothing but,'" opting instead for "gray areas, images that are cut adrift, message-jamming strategies of all kinds" (*Comics* 30). Sanyú and Cava clearly belong to this category.

Conclusion

Jan Baetens recently observed that, "in essence, the cultural prestige of literature prevents comics from being conscious of their own strengths," while "the obsession with *fidelity* to the original text" remains the most controversial issue in comics adaptations to date (208). This opinion is shared by Benoît Peeters, who deems that "the main threat is academicism" (Ferniot 50), which only results in dull, illustrative works whose sole purpose is to make the "classics" palatable to a generation of young readers in the hopes that one day they will read the original. This view of adaptation relegates comics to functioning as a "cultural stage" in the child's development. All grown-up, s/he will eventually read "real literature without images," suggesting that comics remains an "auxiliary" medium to literature (Baetens 206). On this view, it becomes clear that, as far as adaptation is concerned, servility does not pay off and freedom (or betrayal) is the only thing worth striving for.

By freeing itself of fidelity and negating the fame of the text and its author (who acts as a gravitational point preventing critical distance), *El hombre descuadernado* goes far beyond straightforward adaptation and proves that, fortunately, comics can sometimes take advantage of their intrinsic narrative qualities. Although undeniable, intertextual debt is ultimately of little importance. *El hombre descuadernado* is a work geared towards creativity and originality, which explains why the authors preferred not to keep Maupassant's original title in order to assert that they are the authors of an altogether different work.

In short, the work's quality cannot be ascribed to its intertextual complexity or Maupassant's tutelage. Rather, it derives from the authors' perfect combination of languages that are normally "untranslatable," to borrow Oscar Steimberg's words: "[C]omics is a great medium. Precisely because it is the symbiosis of two languages which, in reality, are untranslatable; and the result is the artistic work. That's what makes comics so strong: they are impossible!"[30] (Berone and Reggiani 2010). Perhaps, *El hombre descuadernado* is a *tour de force* for that very reason: because it makes the impossible possible.

Notes

1. The original text reads: "Como Eisenstein en su día, sigo defendiendo que la mejor forma de acercarse a la realidad es trascender el realism."

2. The author of maupassantiana.fr lists thirty-five theatrical adaptations made between 1968 and 2013, including twelve of "The Horla." Between 1908 and 2013, there were no fewer

than 101 film adaptations. The titles most frequently adapted for the theatre are "Dumpling" (10 adaptations), *Bel Ami* (9), and "The Necklace" (9). As for television, the author identifies eighty-one adaptations produced between 1949 and 2011. Finally, in the comics medium, at least seven adaptations were published between 1952 and 1973 (apparently never reissued in album format), and twenty-five comics albums were released between 1983 and 2013. Not all of these twenty-five comics are exclusively dedicated to Maupassant. They are often thematic collections featuring only one of Maupassant's short stories. In addition, *El hombre descuadernado* is not included in the 249 adaptations listed on maupassantiana.fr. It is therefore very likely that the list of adaptations (except perhaps for film) is even more impressive. See http://www.maupassantiana.fr/Adaptations. Accessed on May 24, 2013.

3. The (poorly received) film adaptation of *Bel Ami* (2012) by English directors Declan Donnellan and Nick Ormerod comes to mind, as well as the comics adaptation of "The Horla" (with its abhorrent graphics) by Frederick Bertocchini and Eric Puech (Ajaccio: Éditions du Quinquet, 2012).

4. The issue of an author's celebrity is even more significant in the case of a comic adaptation, as the novella (like the novel) is traditionally seen as superior to comics in the hierarchy of the arts. The thesis that symbolic capital differs from one art form to another (and from one author to another) is raised by Groensteen ("Fictions" 11), and defended by Monique Carcaud-Macaire and Jeanne-Marie Clerc (17–18), as well as Hutcheon (34, 91–92).

5. Examples include *Maupassant : Contes et nouvelles de guerre* by Dino Battaglia (Saint Egrève, Mosquito, 2002), whose short stories were first published between 1976 and 1977 in the Italian magazine *Linus*. Counterexamples to the argument favoring the short form over the long story in comics adaptation are *Bel-ami* by René Detire, which was published in the daily *France-Soir* throughout 1952, or the work studied in the present volume by Thomas Faye, *El Cid* by Antonio Hernández Palacios, published in serial form in the Spanish magazine *Trinca* from 1971 onwards.

6. Despite the harsh judgements made by some critics (see note 1 of this article) on Stéphane Heuet's adaptation of Proust, the work was a great commercial success and was translated into fourteen different languages (http://www.stephane-heuet.fr/).

7. As Cava notes in the preface, the title is derived from Colombian poet Raúl Gómez Jattin (1945–97). The adjective *descuadernado*, though rare in Spain, is used quite commonly in Colombia as a synonym for *décousu*, "incoherent." In this case, "Flayed Alive" would be a fitting translation.

8. The advantage of adapting classics, as Keko (one of the authors of the *El cuarto oscuro* collection) confirms in a letter dated December 27, 2011, is that the copyright has expired. Because they are public domain, they are cheaper to adapt.

9. For additional context about the origin of this collection, I provide the following excerpt from my correspondence with Keko: "The idea came about during one of the convivial lunches Ana [Juan], Felipe [del Barrio] and myself often organized at the time [. . .] when Felipe was going through a very rough patch. We discussed the idea of a collection of frightful tales Ana and I love so much and which only Felipe could edit, and he threw in the idea of working on classics of the genre, whose copyrights had recently expired. I think he suggested the name, which was the source of many jokes since 'El cuarto oscuro' also refers to places where sexual encounters take place in gay bars." Original text: "La idea surgió en una de las fraternales comidas que habitualmente celebramos Ana, Felipe y yo, en un momento [. . .] muy difícil en la vida de Felipe. Hablamos de una colección de género terrorífico, algo a lo que Ana y yo somos muy aficionados, y que sólo podía dirigir Felipe, al que se le ocurrió la idea de trabajar sobre

clásicos del género que habían perdido los derechos de autor en fechas recientes. El nombre creo que también lo sugirió él y fue motivo de muchas bromas porque 'El cuarto oscuro' es también un lugar donde tienen lugar los encuentros sexuales en ciertos bares de ambiente gay."

10. Original text: "Era como si algo extraño se hubiera adueñado de él y se alimentase de todos sus conocimientos hasta irlo dejando inmaculado de recuerdos."

11. Original text: "un buen pretexto [. . .] para hablar de lo que me estaba sucediendo."

12. Original text: "Yo sería el protagonista de ese relato y, al mismo tiempo, el escritor que lo urdió cuando ya estaba amenazado por la pérdida de la cordura."

13. Original text: "Tenía que dar rienda suelta a los miedos que me corroían a través del cauce en el que más he creído a la fecha: el tebeo."

14. Original text: "Yo quería hacer toda una declaración de principios sobre una manera de abordar un drama personal que huyese de la moda, tan en boga, de apelar a enfermedades desde presupuestos presumiblemente realistas. Como Eisenstein en su día, sigo defendiendo que la mejor forma de acercarse a la realidad es trascender el realismo." This is an excerpt from my personal correspondence with Felipe Hernández Cava, dated January 12, 2012. To provide context for the quote, I would like to point out that Paco Roca had already tackled Alzheimer's disease in a realistic style in his comic *Arrugas* (Astiberri, 2007). The work was a huge success and won the 2008 Premio Nacional de Cómic in Spain. Hence, Cava's desire to go against the grain of everything that had been done on the subject and his desire not to be accused of opportunism.

15. Chapter 1 = May 8; chapter 2 = May 12; chapter 3 = May 18 and 24; chapter 4 = May 25; chapter 5 = May 8, June 2, and July 2; chapter 6 = July 2 and 3; chapter 7 = June 2, 4, and 5, and July 14; chapter 8 = August 2, 4, and 6, and July 4; chapter 9 = August 7; chapter 10 = August 7 and 8; chapter 11 = August 14; chapter 12 = August 17; chapter 13 = July 2; chapter 14 = August 19; chapter 15 = August 19; chapter 16 = August 19 and 21; chapter 18 = September 10 and 17; chapter 19 = July 16 and September 10; chapter 20 = September 10; chapter 21 = Ø.

16. Original text: "yo también, como el personaje de vuestro relato, veía desplazarse por el Sena las negras gabarras de carbón hacia Rouen . . . / . . . y el ir y venir de los barcos de tres mástiles que parecían deslizarse por mi jardín, arrastrados por un pequeño remolcador que zumbaba como una mosca entre el humo."

17. Original text: "Hablo mucho y a menudo con los muertos."

18. All these graphic details are rigorously accurate. Maupassant's attempted suicide was a hot topic in the press at the time, and his arrival at the mental hospital was also reported in the dailies (Satiat 574).

19. Original text: "Hoy he anunciado que he muerto. Aunque esto no sucederá hasta dentro de unos meses." Most of Maupassant's comments in *El hombre descuadernado* can be considered authentic. In this case, Maupassant's correspondence attests to several statements of this kind. They are very similar to what he wrote to Lulia Cahen, for example, on December 2, 1891: "Madam, I'll be dead in a few days" (Satiat 559).

20. Original text: "Pero, el, en cambio, no está muerto. Tendido está sobre la hierba, delante su casa."

21. Original text: "Duerme dos o tres horas hasta se renueva la crisis. Quiere gritar, pero no puede. Quiere moverse, tampoco puede. Se despierta bañado en sudor . . ."

22. Original text: "el escritor no siempre elige sus temas, sino que son los temas los que le eligen a él."

23. This is, perhaps, an allusion to another tale by Maupassant, "The Flayed Hand" (1875).

24. *El hombre descuadernado*: "What torments me is not knowing whether my hallucinations, my split personality, or persecution mania [. . .] / are the result of that stigma that love

put in my blood or that dark something that already took possession of another Maupassant [. . .] that thing that killed my brother Hervé" (Cava and Sanyu 12, C5–6). Original text: "lo que me tortura es no conocer si mis alucinaciones, mis desdoblamientos de personalidad, o mi manía persecutoria [. . .] / son fruto de ese estigma que el amor puso en mi sangre o de ese algo oscuro que se apoderó ya de algún Maupassant [. . .] eso que se llevó a mi hermano Hervé."

25. The multiframe designates the panels that make up a page.

26. The titles of the chapters point to this interpretation: "Flaubert and Maupassant" (chapter 3); "Maupassant and Dr. Landolt" (chapter 4); "Maupassant and Maupassant" (chapter 5); "Maupassant and his brother Hervé" (chapter 6); "Maupassant and his servant François Tossart" (chapter 7); "Maupassant and Baron, warden of Dr. Blanche's insane asylum" (chapter 10).

27. Pierre Borel reports in *True Maupassant* that, from 1883 on, the author began to suffer from hallucinations (133). But it was not until 1891 that he descended into a world of suffering and hallucination (Satiat 532–602).

28. Sanyú confirmed this in a letter dated February 11, 2012.

29. Thierry Groensteen has noticed this specific case in *System of Comics* (67).

30. Original text: "La historieta es un gran lenguaje. Porque, justamente, es la puesta en fase de dos lenguajes que, en realidad, son intraducibles; y el resultado es la obra artística. ¡Lo que tiene de bueno la historieta es que es imposible!"

Works Cited

Bachelard, Gaston. *Water and Dreams: An Essay on the Imagination of Matter*. Trans. Edith R. Farrell. Dallas: Pegasus Foundation, Dallas Institute of Humanities and Culture, 1999 [1941].

Baetens, Jan. "Le Roman graphique." *La Bande dessinée : une médiaculture*. Eds. Éric Maigret and Matteo Stefanelli. Paris: Armand Colin, 2012. 200–216.

Berone, Lucas, and Federico Reggiani. "Entrevista a Oscar Steimberg : 'Lo que tiene de bueno la historieta es que es imposible.'" *Estudios y Crítica de la Historieta Argentina* 36 (May 2010). http://historietasargentinas.files.wordpress.com/2010/05/entrevistaaoscarsteimberg_versionfinal.pdf. Accessed on May 10, 2013.

Borel, Pierre. *Le Vrai Maupassant*. Genève: Pierre Cailler éditeur, 1951.

Carcaud-Macaire, Monique and Jeanne-Marie Clerc. *L'Adaptation cinématographique et littéraire*. Paris: Klincksieck, 2004.

Cava Hernández, Felipe, and Sanyú. *El hombre descuadernado*. Alicante: Edicions de Ponent, 2009.

Ferniot, Christine. "Une belle trahison du roman." *Télérama* 3176 (24 October 2010): 50–52.

Gabilliet, Jean-Paul. "Introduction." *Otrante* 13 (April 2003): 5–10.

Gaudreault, André. "Variations sur une problématique." *La Transécriture : Pour une théorie de l'adaptation*. Eds. André Gaudreault and Thierry Groensteen. Montréal and Angoulême: Editions Nota Bene / CNBDI, 1998. 267–71.

Genette, Gérard. *Palimpsests: Literature in the Second Degree*. Trans. Channa Newman and Claude Doubinsky. Lincoln: University of Nebraska Press, 1997 [1982].

Groensteen, Thierry. *Comics and Narration*. Trans. Ann Miller. Jackson: University Press of Mississippi, 2013 [2011].

Groensteen, Thierry. "Fictions sans frontières." *La Transécriture : Pour une théorie de l'adaptation*. Eds. André Gaudreault and Thierry Groensteen. Montréal and Angoulême: Editions Nota Bene / CNBDI, 1998. 9–29.

Groensteen, Thierry. *The System of Comics*. Trans. Bart Beaty and Nick Nguyen. Jackson: University Press of Mississippi, 2007 [1999].

Hachet, Pascal. *Cryptes et fantômes en psychanalyse : Essais autour de l'œuvre de Nicolas Abraham et de Maria Torok*. Paris: L'Harmattan, 2000.

Hutcheon, Linda. *A Theory of Adaptation*. New York and London: Routledge, 2006.

Maupassant, Guy de. "Le Horla (*deuxième version*)" (1887). *Contes fantastiques complets*. Paris: Marabout, 1997.

Maupassant, Guy de. "The Horla." *The Necklace and Other Short Stories*. New York: Dover Publications, 1992. 100–126.

Marion, Philippe. "La guerre prise de vue : De *Shooting War* au *Photographe*." *Lignes de front : Guerre et totalitarisme dans la bande dessinée*. Eds. Viviane Alary and Benoît Mitaine. Genève: Georg, 2011. 287–312.

Peeters, Benoît, and Jan Baetens. "Je suis mon rêve: Les Impressions nouvelles." *Les Impressions Nouvelles*. 2012. http://www.lesimpressionsnouvelles.com/catalogue/je-suis-mon-reve. Accessed on May 10, 2013.

Satiat, Nadine. *Maupassant*. Paris: Flammarion, 2003.

Schlanger, Judith. *La Mémoire des œuvres*. Lagrasse: Verdier, 2008 [1992].

PART II

From Panel to Screen and Back Again

The Comic Book Effect in the Age of CGI: When Film Adaptations of Comic Books Evoke the Fixity of Their Model

ALAIN BOILLAT

My introductory essay to the collection *De la page à l'écran* proposed a typology of the "dialogues" between cinema and comics in terms of their practices and discourses. From an intermedial perspective, the question of film adaptation may seem a little narrow. However, films adapted from comics are marked by a set of sociocultural, technological, economic, and aesthetic determinations, the implications of which go beyond a simple comparison between the original work and its adaptation. For the purpose of this analysis, I will examine the works themselves rather than their context of production and reception, and consider the semiotic transfers in the transposition of an original comic to a film. Technology provides the overall frame ensuring the consistency and relevance of the films I will discuss, since I focus on productions from the last decade that exploit the resources of computer-generated imagery. My aim is not to examine the narrative structure of these films—an approach that can prove very productive[1]—but to study the modes of representation in these adaptations in relation to the specificities of both media within a broader reflection on intermediality. In order to limit the number of variables, I will situate the images in the framework of the apparatuses [*dispositifs*] currently associated with these media, i.e., comic books and theater projection. It goes without saying that other means of consumption, such as reading comics on a tablet or watching movies on DVD or Blu-ray on a TV screen—two interfaces capable of accommodating both media, and thus capable of exacerbating or obliterating differences between them—would further blur or complicate some of my lines of inquiry. This is even truer when taking into account the interaction by the user, who, by pressing a button on a remote control or touching a screen, can change the format, create a slow-motion effect or a freeze-frame, or even move a virtual "camera" on the screen. The existence of these devices nonetheless underlies my approach insofar as the intermedial character of contemporary audiovisual culture constitutes the condition of possibility for the formal choices

I examine. Indeed, the circulation between media with different modes of representation is so common today that the viewer-reader is used to viewing them on one device, like a computer screen for example.

The Other Within Itself: The Comics Effect

The sweeping development of commercial synergies between Hollywood studios and comic book publishers, which goes back to the first film in the *X-Men* series (Bryan Singer, 2000), is characterized by the maximization of the principle of horizontal integration within the mass-culture industry;[2] we sometimes no longer know which work is "derived" and which is the original.[3] With this in mind, one can rightfully question how films adapted from comics treat the means of expression they borrow from their narrative material. Indeed, the explicit reference to the original medium contains the potential for a specific use of film language. In such cases, the film gives rise to what I call a "comics effect," with the film incorporating elements commonly associated with comics, including the sequencing of still images, the inclusion of word balloons, changes in format, captions, and so on. Displaced to another semiotic environment, these elements disrupt the conventions of the host medium and introduce a reflexive dimension.

Over the course of film history, comics adaptations have rarely given us films that retain, in the language of cinema, traces of the medium of origin. In general, the heroes celebrated in magazines and their stereotypical actions are governed by genre film conventions. In the 1930s and 1940s, for instance, science fiction films exploited the narrative and figurative material of the *Flash Gordon* and *Buck Rogers* comics,[4] while various episodes from Chester Gould's *Dick Tracy* series were turned into B movies in the gangster genre by Republic and RKO studios.[5] These motion pictures, either in full-episode format or following a soap-opera logic, shared with their comics counterparts the innumerable twists and almost unbearable suspense of their incredible storylines. Other Hollywood movies like *Prince Valiant* (20th Century Fox, Henry Hathaway, 1954), adapted from the comic strip by Harold Forster, shifted the narrative towards a grander style, erasing all formal links with the original. Similarly, the *Superman* film series, starting with Richard Donner's 1978 film, adhered more to the conventions of the disaster and action movies of the period than to the tone of the 1940s comic books.

It is only in the recent adaptations that self-conscious play with the intermedial context occurs. This is partly due to the increase in legitimacy and popularity of comics in Europe and the US, as the label "graphic novel" proves. This recognition reflects the public's interest in films that play with the codes of comics—*American Splendor* (Shari Springer Berman and Robert Pulcini, 2003) comes to mind—as well as the possibility for comics artists to express themselves through the medium of film. Although his career might be the exception to the rule, Frank Miller is emblematic in his innovative approach to cinema linking the seventh and ninth arts. In Hollywood, his status changed from that of screenwriter to director of two films, *Sin City* (2005), co-directed with Robert Rodriguez, and *The Spirit* (2008), whose visuals are clearly inspired by his own graphic style. It is no longer just a matter of drawing visual motifs from the comics; it is the very materiality of the film that is now affected by the model. In these mass-market films, representation is foregrounded in all its artificiality, sometimes bordering on graphic abstraction. During postproduction, designers fill the green screens, which the actors had previously performed against, almost as freely as the comics artist creating a world out of a blank page. The image is called "synthetic," as an especially paradoxical form of synthesis between two media occurs.

This type of production could be studied from many angles, including the treatment of color and the staging (acting, stage design, lighting, etc.). In the following case studies, I will focus on one aspect of the identifying features of the two media under discussion, the opposition between fixity and movement, which I will consider as a continuum depending on the various speeds of the images. This is fundamental since, while comics generally *suggest* movement both inside the panel (signs and conventional postures, the composition of the image, and so on) and when switching from one panel to the other, film *reproduces* the movement of physical actions. Thus, when a shot is "frozen" or slowed down in a movie whose motifs are borrowed from a comic, the spectator is liable to view these processes that break the continuity of the cinematographic representation as formal references to the means of expression of the original work.[6] In the bonus features on the Blu-ray edition of the film *Dredd* (Pete Travis, 2012), which brings the hero of the British comic *Judge Dredd* (created in 1977 by writer John Wagner and artist Carlos Ezquerra) to the screen, a member of the production team explains that the slowed down sequences of the film produce "almost [. . .] the effect of a comic panel,"[7] a process diegetically motivated by the use of a drug called "slo-mo" (short for slow motion) altering the perception of its consumer (and temporarily that of the film's viewer) through temporal dilation. In this type of film shot in 3D,[8] the link to the language of comics is rather tenuous; with its puffs of smoke slowly unfurling and spatters of blood and water suspended in midair, it is more reminiscent of the photographic experiments by scientist Etienne-Jules Marey in his research on fluid dynamics,[9] than of comic book panels. However, evoking its origin as a comics narrative lends greater aesthetic value to the movie. In *Dredd*, as in other contemporary adaptations,[10] the intrusion of this reference to comics is like a graft and occurs only occasionally—otherwise it would no longer be a "film." As a specific characteristic of the language of comics, fixity, like speech balloons, conventional signs suggesting movement, the co-presence of successive images in the same reading space, and so on, ultimately resists transposition; it plays a part, along with other parameters, in the inalienable "mediativity" [*médiativité*] of comics, as defined by Philippe Marion (80–82). Or rather, comics create different effects in the new medium and denaturalize both the codes of comics and those of cinema, a perspective that highlights intermedial transfers rather than an underlying semiotic ontology.

Theorists of film adaptations (or translations) of literary works have underlined the richness of practices of "rewriting" by developing a methodology free from prescriptive and reverential attitudes towards the original, instead paying attention to the contribution of the adaptation to the original. The adaptation (or translation) is thus not seen as a smoothing over of differences, but as a means to emphasize semiotic (or linguistic) otherness and as a renewal of our relation to the source.[11] The films I have mentioned also take up a certain stance compared to the original comics, which is indicated by an intensification of the heterogeneity of new forms. The "split experience," which, in Thierry Groensteen's view, is characteristic of comics readers and film viewers, who "are simultaneously involved in the fiction while exposed to a specific medium" (28), is reinforced by an additional rift—the medium is "specific" to the extent that it imitates another one. Indeed, the film apparatus imposes a system of constraints that generates a fundamental break between the position of the comic book reader and that of the spectator; the source must find expression in the other medium, and not just be reproduced in the latter. Accordingly, intermediation can be seen as an encounter in a given discursive space shaped by the specificities of the host medium.

In an essay on Robert Pulcini and Shari Springer Berman's 2003 adaptation of the autobiographical comic book series *American Splendor*, Richard Bégin defines intermediality as "the fruit [. . .] of a discourse that, prior to expressing [. . .] a relation between media, must necessarily see these same media as mutually adapting to each other, thereby losing part of their identity and rules in favor of the single narrative and symbolic system now imposed by their encounter and composition" (121). This kind of sharing between media should not be considered in terms of loss but as an aesthetic contribution. One form of the comics effect is particularly explicit and literal: the presentation of the materiality of printed media (newspaper, booklet, album) on screen, usually in a diegetic guise. One example of this can be found in a shot from *Unbreakable* (M. Night Shyamalan, 2000). The camera pans to center on the comic book the child has just received as a gift, and which will continue to feed his fantasies as an adult trapped in a fragile body. Initially shown backwards, the magazine cover reappears after a visual pirouette that makes it legible [23:07–23:30]. However, the reading activity occurs offscreen, since we will never see more than the emblematic, non-sequential cover image. The camera ostensibly distances itself from the diegetic reader's gaze, thereby increasing the gap between reading a comic and viewing a film by making the coercive orientation of the spectator's viewpoint conspicuous. In this case, the reference to the comics medium has little effect on the filmic representation.

Nevertheless, the tabularity of the page can be simulated on the screen more concretely through digital special effects to give the impression that the camera is scanning a surface composed of panels, just like the eye of the reader moving across a comics panel, although the film viewer has no other choice than to follow the movement of the virtual camera. A film like *Hulk* (Ang Lee, 2003) makes use of this technique in its transitions, which, in terms of narrative tempo, correspond to the type of "narrative speed" Gérard Genette describes as "summary" (94). The latter allows for temporal flexibility in depicting a situation from multiple sides. This is the case in the scene where the captured superhero is transported to a secret base by helicopter [68:19–70:09]. Not only does the line traced by the whirl of the blades of the helicopter filmed in profile draw a line between two images (like the edge of a comics panel), but the camera moves parallel to the shot, creating a scrolling effect, juxtaposing images like a reader with his/her finger on a touchscreen. At the beginning of the film, a scientific experiment is shown on a computer screen, as if to help viewers get used to the spatialization produced by montage: the frequent use of split screens is rooted in an intermedial practice (Boillat, "Style et intermédialité" 389). The results of the experiment conducted by Bruce Banner and Betty Ross are made visible through a camera setup that multiplies the number of screens within screens [13:20–15:25]. The film thus depends on computer-literate viewers who are accustomed to reading multiple, often quite divergent types of documents simultaneously on the same screen. The monitors are juxtaposed like panels in a sequence, except that each contains a moving image, which is what happens when the frames leave the diegetic level to enter the filmic image itself in the form of a split screen. From the comic book, the film's creators retained the fragmentation of the surface of the page-screen as the "comics effect" (which does not exclude the simultaneous invocation of other media types or interfaces), and not the fixity of each panel.

These aesthetics, which in *Hulk* (2003) aimed at partially and selectively assimilating the film screen to a comic book page,[12] call attention to two related aspects that are usually associated with comics rather than film, precisely because the latter tries to obscure them; it pertains to the flatness of the image and the discontinuity of representation. Indeed, the split screen spatializes fragmentation between shots, obeying an aesthetic that, as Lev Manovich (136–45) has demonstrated, is a consequence of the ubiquity of the digital.

As comics are associated with publishing, any written trace can be used to connote the adaptation's origin in comics, especially when the graphic layout on the screen exhibits comics conventions. In *American Splendor*, for instance, captions are shown in the corner of the frames, while the background mimics the graininess of paper and the comic's color scheme; to the same effect, text bubbles are superimposed onto the shots of *Who Wants to Kill Jessie? / Kdo chce zabit Jessii?* (Vaclav Vorlicek, 1966).

By resorting to comics effects, the movie puts itself on display as a composite artifact. It is therefore hardly surprising that this type of practice is rare in Hollywood movies, which are so reluctant to break the illusion of verisimilitude required to create moments of attraction usually subordinated to the narrative and to conceal certain representations in order to ensure the maximum immersion in the story universe. Like the storyboard or any other phase in the production process of a film, the (sequences of) fixed and drawn images that predate the actual shooting tend to be disavowed in the final product. At best, they are confined to the first few images in the credits. These marginal references to the comics medium deserve more attention in that they are emblematic of the paradoxical status of the comics effect, which refers to an Other while at the same time having to conform to the semiotic specificities of the Same.

Comics and Credits: A Fixation

In his semiotic and pragmatic investigation of how film audiences gradually enter a fictional universe, film theorist Roger Odin points to the key role of opening credits. He calls the latter the site of "explicit inscription, in the film itself, of a certain number of enunciative markers of the film" ("L'entrée du spectateur" 204), often characterized, at least in "classical" cinema, by a conflict between the legible and the visible, leading to the victory of the former over the latter. From an intermedial perspective, credit sequences function as gateways to other media that present written accounts. Countless film adaptations, during the credits, feature a book that refers to the original work with pages listing all of the cast and crew members turning before our eyes. This undoubtedly derives from the credits' inherent reflexivity, as they point to the film's production rather than its fictional universe. Thus, in film adaptations, opening credits often contain the most explicit references to the language of comics (also in the sense of enunciative marking); because their location on the periphery of the film's diegesis make them autonomous, credits easily accommodate techniques that would jeopardize the transparency of representation elsewhere in the film. It is not uncommon for fixed or at least drawn images to appear in title sequences, in line with the tradition initiated by Saul Bass for Hitchcock's movies or James Bond title sequences, which were designed as showpieces reveling in their elaborate visuals.

The Adventures of Tintin: The Secret of the Unicorn (Steven Spielberg, 2011) is typical of this kind of standardization of the graphic and rhythmic virtuosity of film title design. Spielberg's crew reprised the style of *Catch Me If You Can* (Spielberg, 2002), developed by designers Olivier Kuntzel and Florence Deygas, accompanied by a score by John Williams. The title sequence of *The Adventures of Tintin* thus refers to the filmmaker's works while asserting a strong link to Hergé's albums due to the sheer presence of the drawings on the screen. The legacy of shadow puppet shows (Caran d'Ache, Steinlen, Christophe, and so on), common to the prehistory of both comics and cinema, is invoked in the opening credits, with black silhouettes set against a colored background, their flatness contrasting sharply with the 3D animation that is about to begin. More precisely, it is at odds with the expectations associated with this technology, as Spielberg, perhaps "against his will" (or at least against that of his hero), recalls certain effects of the clear line of Franco-Belgian comics. At the end of the title sequence, which explicitly refers to the materiality of the original work (Hergé's panels haphazardly crossing the screen, speech balloons enclosing onomatopoeia, the visual citation of the *Secret of the Unicorn* album cover in the form of a poster, etc.), the transition to computer animation is thematized through a reflexive effect; the crossfade that introduces the fictional world reveals, after an insert with shimmering lights reflected by an optical prism—a reference to photography, sandwiched between drawing and the digital image—a painter's palette. It belongs to none other than Georges Rémi, sketching a portrait of Tintin (an "image in the image" drawn in the style of Hergé) whom he addresses—first in a voice-over that takes over from the extradiegetic music, providing the transition from the credits to the film proper—not as his creation, but as if he were addressing the "real" reporter whose face he says he has already seen in the newspaper [3:55–4:07]. Moreover, the visualization of the hero is delayed and mediated through the drawing. Tintin's face is revealed only when it is time to point out how closely he resembles the drawn figure, the epitome of a self-reflexive moment highlighting the process of adaptation. Despite the allusion to the famous comics artist, we are now fully immersed in the diegesis. Perhaps unintentionally, the representation of the "birth" of Tintin transposes the creation scene of another famous hero of the Franco-Belgian comics drawn by Rob-Vel (Robert Velter), Spirou, to the medium of 3D animation. Indeed, the first page of the *Spirou* series depicts a painter drawing the young bellboy and then spraying *eau de vie* on the canvas, after which the boy steps out of the image, exclaiming, "Spirou, at your service!"[13] Spielberg's opening in the style of Sacha Guitry—we are reminded of Utrillo taking his easel to paint in the middle of a public square in *If Paris Were Told to Us* (1956)—conjures up a European atmosphere not only owing to the place of the story action, but also to the origin of the adapted work. It is symptomatic of the detours that frequently refer to comics, expressed through a third medium (in this case, painting). Intermediality frequently involves a network of relations between means of expression; it would be reductive to merely stick to the original medium and that of the adaptation. Incidentally, it is also in the margin of a text typed on a sheet of paper slipped into a typewriter that the figure of Tintin appears in the film, suggesting that it, too, owes its existence to the scenario.

The importance of credits in generating the comics effect is also based on their generally approaching the writing from a visual angle, with an often tenuous distinction between linguistic and iconic signs. In a recent book on film credits, Laurence Moinereau defines the specifics of her subject matter from a figural perspective:

> What characterizes the space of the credits is, first and foremost, the split, the disparity, or, conversely, the constitutive hybridization—writing+figuration—which is like the shadow cast in the representation of the discursive divide between enunciation and diegesis. Its most manifest, conspicuous and immediately identifiable effect is a phenomenon of contamination, of transfer of one element's properties to the other. (11)

A similar phenomenon of cross-contamination in film adaptations of comics can be observed, this time not just between word and image, but between comics and cinema. It is found primarily in the credits and has as its corollary the marking of the enunciative level of the film. For instance, the animated logo of Marvel films has ritually opened almost every Hollywood superhero production for the last fifteen years by taking the form of a comic book, whose pages are flipped through, surreptitiously (though long enough for us to recognize the hero) disclosing some of the drawings of the adapted work. Even though the principle of the flipbook constitutes the foundation of animation, with flickering drawn images appearing in full screen, the suggestion of movement remains minimal, as if it were limited to the cinematographic image that follows. The flickering of drawn images—intensifying the discontinuity associated with the comics gutter by referencing the perceptual effects characteristic of the optical devices that heralded the birth of cinema—gives way, little by little, to the stability of the word "Marvel," which gradually sets itself apart from the superimposed layers of drawings. The DC Comics logo, as it appears in, for example, *Superman Returns* (Bryan Singer, 2006), mimics Marvel's "gesture," but leaves less room for the drawn image and presents a dotted surface underlying the drawing, thereby invoking the pixels of the digital image. In both cases, the label that emphasizes the marketing of the comics gradually asserts itself on the screen at the expense of the reproduction of panels, the drawings relegated to the preproduction stage, at the threshold of the actual film. The nature of the viewer's involvement is literally "fixed" when fixity is literally rejected; we start from a comic book series to become the viewers of a film that, in most cases, preserves no trace of the transfer other than this inaugural symbolic identifier.

Film adaptations—especially those based on comics, which are ranked lower in terms of cultural legitimacy and are deprived of the reverence usually reserved for canonical literary works[14]—are generally subjected to the same double movement as the remake, as Harvey Roy Greenberg (169–70) observed when pointing to the similarities between *Always* (Spielberg, 1989) and *A Guy Named Joe* (MGM, Victor Fleming, 1943): the double gesture of the homage to the original and its repudiation or the rejection of its semiotic specificity. Without embracing an Oedipal reading, since auteurism hardly plays a role in the films I discuss—excepting for Frank Miller, who vampirizes Will Eisner's graphic style in *The Spirit* (2008)—it seems that the credits in Hollywood superhero adaptations acknowledge their origin in the medium of comics and initially exploit their fame only to discard them in the end.

The same holds for fixity. One of the stylistic hallmarks of one of the most celebrated artists in the superhero genre, Jack Kirby, is the splash panel, which became prevalent with the *Thor* series, according to Morgan and Hirtz (47–52). These panels often depict urban masses petrified against an apocalyptic decor, the image seemingly "fixated" and frozen in the awe expressed on contorted faces and inspired by the contemplation of spectacular vistas

(Boillat, "Le statut paradoxal" 420–23). The transfer of the artist's mythological universe to film usually ignores these hieratic visions, which, admittedly, appear intrinsically opposed to the standards of Hollywood action movies. Paradoxically, it is the contemporary technological practices at the heart of the filmic representation of action scenes that allow the repressed fixed image to resurface.

The Reactivation of the Chronophotographic Model by Computer Graphics

Still images—or rather, "frozen" images, since the traditional intermittent movement of the film image never gives the impression of being interrupted and provokes, through the succession of photograms, "imperceptible variations of light, palpitations [of] dust microparticles" that counter absolute stasis (Odin, "Le film de fiction" 149)—are one of the main forces behind the comics effect in film. Roger Odin described what he calls "the slide effect" in Chris Marker's short film *La Jetée* (1962) in a way that is applicable to the medium of comics, except that he discusses the photographic and not the drawn image:[15] "[N]othing moves, everything is frozen in an unusual stillness. Yet the representations are not particularly static; planes are presumed to fly, characters are walking [. . .], but this is indicated in a series of snapshots. In *La Jetée*, movement is represented, figured and not reproduced" ("Le film de fiction" 149). While, according to Odin, the destabilizing effect blocks the illusion of reality and the film's fiction—the blockage is obviously not as strong in animation, which does not comply as strictly with the need for photorealism, compared to films shot on location or with partly computer-generated images that deliberately confuse the boundary between real and imaginary[16]—it is, of course, not the same in comics where these characteristics are expected, as movement is inferred by readers conversant with its conventions. The reference to comics often penetrates film adaptations via an intermediary, as in the snapshots mentioned by Odin. The motif of the photographic image is, in effect, introduced in the film's diegesis as a bridge between comics and animated representation, or even to briefly suspend the hegemony of the moving image. In *Spider-Man 2* (Sam Raimi, 2004), whose hero, Peter Parker, works as a press photographer, the passage from the credits to the first images of the film occurs through a shift from drawn to photographic image at first without movement: the face of Mary Jane is revealed as both image and object of the male gaze in a track-out shot [2:55–3:18]. Later in the film, the vertiginous reiteration of the same advertising poster on a façade where Peter is "hanging by a thread" is presented like a "visual sequence" in comics, at the same time indicating the impossibility of actualizing the latter [29:26–29:46]. The series of still images fails to generate succession.

This is the case because the historical point of convergence between comics and cinema is chronophotography: in comics as well as in the photographic work of French physiologist Etienne-Jules Marey, the individual phases of the same movement are put in a sequence. Today's motion capture technology (mocap), used in the majority of the films discussed here, is part of the historical lineage of chronophotography and, therefore, confronts the creators with the fixity of points and posture, and with a form of movement that is envisaged as a succession of representational spaces rather than in its temporal development. As the "making-of" of the film *Hulk* (2003)—where, as often in this type of parafilmic production, the discourse is completely subordinated to an auteurist construction of the filmmaker—informs us, Ang Lee himself served as the motion capture model. The outfit dotted with sensors he wore during the filming of these scenes is reminiscent of the outfits conceived in the 1880s for Marey's experiments at the Physiological Station in the Parc des Princes (see Frizot; Mannoni 187–91). The analogy is even more striking when reading the description of a device used in a hospital for the experiments on pathological locomotion (i.e., the movement of people with a limp) carried out by Marey's assistant, Georges Demenÿ:

> We used incandescent electric lamps as light sources. [. . .] We placed these lamps on the patient at specific points to obtain the trajectory, such as the top of the head, the shoulder, the hip, the knee and the ankle. [. . .] We used red light so that the photographic plate would only be exposed to the very bright points of the lamps. We thus have a very clear print of the trajectories of the top of the head, shoulder, hip, knee and ankle. These trajectories are punctuated since the images are taken every 1/20 of a second. (Quénu and Demenÿ, "Etude de la locomotion humaine dans les cas pathologiques" [1888], cited in Braun, "Les limites," 87–88)

This method reveals obvious kinship with current optical motion capture systems. Once the images are loaded into the computer, the first step is to "isolate the markers, separating them from the rest of the environment. [. . .] The most basic approach is to separate all the groups of pixels that exceed a predetermined luminosity threshold" (Menache 19). Of course, when applying his "graphic method," Marey only cared about the visual representations he obtained through chronophotography insofar as they provided a schematization. For him, photography was just a convenience in case "the phenomenon of which we study the successive phases has no action on the inscription stylet" (Marey 31). Marta Braun, however, has shown that the approach of Marey's American contemporary Eadweard Muybridge was somewhat different, focused more on the attraction of the spectacle (and voyeuristic, phallocentric pleasure) than on scientific rigor. Thus, when Muybridge published his results in *Animal Locomotion* (1888), he did not use all the images, but introduced variations in the intervals between views, while rearranging the material to heighten the visual attraction of the image sequences (Braun, *Picturing Time* 238–54; Braun, "Muybridge le magnifique"). The distinction between Marey's and Muybridge's approaches can be related to each of the two media we have been discussing. Whereas film is defined by the mechanical regularity of the interval (a twenty-fourth of a second for each image) specific to Marey's scientific approach, one could say that Muybridge's principle of selection is close to comics, even if the rare cases exploiting a so-called "stroboscopic" effect (in the work of Carmine Infantino, for example) borrow more directly from the model of the multiplication of phases on the same plate that distinguishes Marey's research and Harold Edgerton's work. Indeed, as Thierry Smolderen (2014) has illustrated, Muybridge's publications greatly influenced some comics pioneers, including A. B. Frost and Winsor McCay (119–36, 149–61); in the *Little Sammy Sneeze* series (1904–1906), McCay skillfully combines the chronophotographic model with other principles of temporal arrangement, so that the actions in the same image sequence are not represented in the same way, as far as the "speed" inferred by the reader is concerned (Boillat, "Le récit minimal en bande dessinée"; Boillat and Revaz).

Comics radicalize the principle of extracting part of the action from a supposed but unrepresented continuum (Eisner 30, 80). Film, by contrast, participates in what Gilles Deleuze, in his commentary on Bergson's theses on movement, describes as "[t]he modern scientific revolution [that] consisted in relating movement not to privileged instants, but to any-instant-whatever. Although movement was still recomposed, *it was no longer recomposed from formal transcendental elements (poses), but from immanent material elements (sections)*" (*Cinema 1* 4, emphasis in original). Thus, to insert a still image in a film is to highlight a photogrammatic unity that is generally negated (except in experimental films such as those of Werner Nekes); it introduces the "pose" in a system defined by the principle of the cut (or the "section"). In comics adaptations, this results in the contamination of the filmic representation by a process typical of comics. Nonetheless, this disruptive effect reveals a certain kinship between media. The technique of the capture of movement by the filmic image has, for instance, led to the generalization of a new paradigm for conceptualizing movement and to a reconfiguration of the categories defined by Lessing. In an article on the recent *Spider-Man* series, Giusy Pisano elaborates on this change:

> The collage, the series, the hundreds of digital images of multiple instants brought together in one shot [. . .] are more akin to the "pregnant instant" in painting, depicting the poses that best correspond to the drawing of movement [. . .], the selection of the *most fecund moment* Lessing demanded of painting. The capture of movement, through construction, is a purely spatial composition [. . .]; time becomes accessible only in the metaphorical form of a *frozen time*, as Eisner conceived it for comics. (585)

I will now examine the issue of the frozen image in film representation by focusing on two contemporary adaptations of famous comics: *Watchmen* (2009), based on Alan Moore and Dave Gibbons's graphic novel, published by DC Comics in twelve monthly episodes between September 1986 and October 1987; and *300* (2006), adapted from Frank Miller's comic, often referred to as a "graphic novel" by analogy with other contemporary productions made in a different format. Both films were directed by Zack Snyder, probably one of the Hollywood directors most sensitive to intermediality in big budget films.[17]

Watchmen (2009): The Guardians of a Time Frozen in Photography

Watchmen the film is especially interesting because of its credit sequence, a place that is conducive to graphic treatment of the cinematic image. Interestingly enough, the film does not relegate the intermedial confrontation to the opening logo, but exploits it in a five-minute segment that, preceded by a pre-credit sequence,[18] combines writing with the presentation of the comic book universe. To begin, I will give a summary of the specificities of the adapted work to shed light on the choices underlying the filmic practices of the segment immediately following the prologue.

Gibbons and Moore's approach to superheroes is resolutely self-reflexive. In imagining how the history of the United States would have changed had the costumed vigilante imaginary come true, the famous British scriptwriter created a work that does not entirely belong to the superhero genre. While it was initially conceived as a way to recycle archetypal figures from the Charlton Comics catalog on behalf of DC Comics, *Watchmen* topicalizes a genre whose conventions it carefully deconstructs. The protagonists are fallen, aging, and disillusioned heroes, rejected by a society that has become aware of the fascist drive of their superhuman actions, and thus of the reactionary ideology of the superhero genre itself. The complexity of the interactions between the captions and the story's temporal levels is reinforced by the intrusion of full pages of text (for example, "Under the Hood," the fictitious memoirs of one of the Watchmen) and the drawn meta-narrative, *Tales of the Black Freighter*, an allegorical counterpoint to the main story. This "comic within the comic," inspired by one of the tunes of Brecht and Weill's *Threepenny Opera*, appears in the form of a pirate story, a genre that was popular in the 1950s (for example, in the comics of the magazine *Piracy* published by EC Comics, which featured the work of Bernard Krigstein); it often had a dash of the fantastic, the macabre, or even the horrifying. Recognizable from their garish colors and crude plots influenced by pulp fiction, the panels of this pirate narrative are inserted in the pages of *Watchmen*, their appearance motivated in the diegetic framework by the presence of a teenager reading the adventure story near a newsstand where news about the superheroes is discussed. In order to transpose this second narrative to cinema, Snyder chose an approach testifying to his interest in the material heterogeneity of filmic representation; for the director's cut on the DVD, he created an animated film (*Tales of the Black Freighter*) that he intended to transpose in "real" shots into fragments in the film. In this edition, in which the segment appears most often as a supplement, the animation takes on a "peritextual" role similar to that of the autobiography "Under the Hood," which, like other pseudo-factual documents, was featured in the final pages of each issue of Gibbons and Moore's comic.

Another narrative peculiarity of the graphic novel concerns the exceptional powers of atomic energy granted to Dr. Manhattan, who secures US control over the situation in Vietnam and guarantees the country's strategic superiority on the world stage, while simultaneously justifying the narrative's organization with its particular conception of temporality. In his recent monograph, *Alan Moore: Storyteller*, Gary Spencer Millidge describes Dr. Manhattan's capability and its astonishing narratological consequences: "The transcendent Dr. Manhattan perceives chronological time as a fixed state, able to experience past, present and future simultaneously" (127). This superposition of temporal strata, thereby intensifying the construction of "*alternatives* between sheets of past" envisaged by Deleuze (*Cinema 2* 117, emphasis in original), leads up to this fixed moment, which is one of the mainstays of the language of comics. In the graphic novel's diegetic universe, Moore reverses the opposition between fixity and movement by repeatedly appealing to photography. Not only are there group photos, traces of the past that prompt flashbacks from different points of view, but also photos that remind Dr. Manhattan that those closest to him are torn by the ravages of time, while he remains the same in all the spaces and times he can travel to simultaneously. His power is also a curse. During his self-exile on Mars, he decides to get rid of the photo whose indexical function is brought home on the cover image of the fourth issue, lying next to a footprint in the sand of the red planet; somehow the photo always ends up in Dr. Manhattan's hand again. The cover image with the photo in the sand is repeated twice on the issue's first page. Its first occurrence is framed by two panels with an identical sentence in an interior monologue: "the photograph is in my hand." The text of the panel reads: "In twelve seconds' time, I drop the photograph to the sand at my feet, walking away. It's already lying there, twelve seconds into the future." In the course of this expanded action (the authors already devoted the last page of the previous issue to it, giving it the enigmatic character of narrative suspension pertaining to serial logic), we realize that it is in the still image that the temporal layers converge, allowing Moore and Gibbons to play with the specificities of their medium, torn between the autonomy of the panel and its sequential arrangement, between the fixity of the drawing and the convention of suggested movement. Dr. Manhattan's superhuman powers highlight the activity of reading the comic book: unlike the film viewer who does not know which shots will follow, the reader cannot help but notice the subsequent panels on the same double-page, even in a strictly linear reading. This is further intensified through the numerous repetitions and echoes that lead the reader to return to the previous issues.

The *Watchmen* credit sequence skillfully transfers this issue by invoking the photographic model as well. The scenes are juxtaposed and punctuated by dissolves, unfolding in slow motion on a continuous visual plane. The spectator is thus made to experience the temporal unwinding of moments that correspond to key stages in the Watchmen's history. These moments are both suspended in the present of our viewing and rejected in the past of the fiction, as if the spectators, like Dr. Manhattan, were travelling through different temporal layers. The expansion of these gestures over time is all the more striking as it contrasts with the normal speed of the simulated movements of the camera. This anisochromia between staging and framing, in a sense, simulates the experience of reading a comic book, adding the trajectory of the reader's gaze scanning the page to the temporality of the text-image. The tracking shots impart their regular cadence to the representation, indirectly placing the observer in the position of a reader leafing through a picture book. Moreover, the slow motion is almost always punctuated by a flash from a photo camera, allowing the credits to interweave the personal

Fig. 27: *Watchmen* (Snyder, 2009): a slow-motion shot of the superheroes posing for a family portrait during their glory days.

experience of the superheroes with their collective history (the gunman assassinating Kennedy and Dr. Manhattan reflected in Neil Armstrong's visor). Visual documentation is reinserted into the fiction as it is literally grafted onto archival footage thanks to a technique famously used in *Forrest Gump* (Robert Zemeckis, 1994). The photographic image is ubiquitous because it is part of various stagings (group photos, press photos, images of crime scenes) (fig. 27). Indeed, in this postmodern maelstrom, the fictional world is staged from the outset as a representation, negating and subverting a host of easily recognizable iconographic motifs. For instance, the scene of the Last Supper is cited, suddenly bathed in an almost divine light at the very instant the press photographer's camera flash goes off.[19] Having a pregnant woman occupy the position traditionally reserved for Christ turns the shot into a pastiche comparable to (more radical) re-appropriations of Christian iconography by contemporary artists such as Elisabeth Ohlson and Renee Cox (Dietschy 2008). The reference to the Passion of Christ is emblematic of the credit sequence's intermedial self-awareness. In the West, the Passion has become part of mass culture, with images appearing in sequentialized form across different media (Boillat and Robert 2010), including the magic lantern, *tableaux vivants*, illustrated Bibles, and in early films that were to be decisive for the evolution of film narrative (Burch 1990). Art historian François Boespflug stresses how the stages of the life of Jesus were considered pregnant moments: "The figure and main scenes of Christ's life were illustrated first, especially those scenes which could be condensed in a pose or a gesture. The frontal Christ is like a frozen movement, a gesture immobilized by art" (9).

This is also true in film (see Walsh 2003), notably in the representation of the Watchmen's own "Way of the Cross," where each stage is presented through the filter of a double mediation; the action is served up to the photo lenses of journalists standing in the foreground, but the photographed object itself refers, given the composition of the image, to photographs that marked the second half of the twentieth century, here transposed into color and cinemascope format. The film evokes André Burri's portraits of Che Guevara (1963) and Marc Riboud's "The Girl with the Flower" (1967), which became emblematic of the hippie protest movement, an impression reinforced by the use of Bob Dylan's song in the credits.[20] Alfred Eisenstaedt's photo is also featured, depicting Times Square during the victory parade of the marines on August 14, 1945, with the famous kiss reframed in a lesbian context. The camera angle of each cited photograph is altered through a decentering of the axis connecting the photographer with the scene, while the constant modifications of the framing during the tracking shots re-appropriate the original composition, which is reconfigured by focusing on an element of the decor and narrativized by initiating an action. In the credits, everything is recycled, including the subversive practices of Pop Art figured through its star, Andy Warhol. The adaptation digests and reconfigures a whole tradition of fixed images, thereby inserting the original work in a network of intermedial relations. The film image and the viewer's temporal experience are thus extensively shaped by the references to the still image. However, as this representation is subject to the codes of cinema, nothing is absolutely fixed, except in certain shots where a character strikes a pose (or except when the body depicted is lifeless). The signified of fixity passes through a pictorial and photographic intertext the spectator is encouraged to recognize, while variations in speed affect the actions within, and the scrolling of, the images. It is against the backdrop of a series of banal instances that the pregnant moment emerges.

300 (2006): The Multiple Speeds of the Image

In films reflecting (on) contemporary intermediality, the opposition between fixity and animation is approached along a continuum marked by multiple speeds. *300* (2006) is a film that, like *Dredd* (2012), exploits this aspect. One shot in particular seems ideal for formulating some concluding remarks on the influence of comics in the representation of movement in film by computer images.

Frank Miller's *300* plunges us into the bloody battle of Thermopylae, where the Greeks of Sparta confronted Xerxes's imperial Persian troops. Herodotus's account is, above all, a pretext for a spectacular and graphic depiction of the virile doggedness of Leonidas and his men, the clash of battle, and the

Fig. 28: *300* (Snyder, 2006): speed and shot size vary as King Leonidas advances on his Persian adversaries with his spear.

invasion of the battlefield by a mass of soldiers. In the first part of the film's battle scene, a slow-motion shot stands out from the others because of its duration (it lasts more than a minute), whereas the previous shots unfolded over just two or three seconds. The shot shows us the unstoppable Leonidas, bravely pushing forward through a horde of enemies, dismembering all who cross his path (fig. 28) [46:07–47:14]. As in the *Watchmen* credit sequence, this shot mixes strong continuity editing (in the classic sense of the term, since the "seams" between various shots are invisible)[21] with variations in speed of the image sequence.

These sudden changes, underlined by the soundtrack, are synchronized with fast zoom-ins and zoom-outs that, like the slow motion, brutally enhance the shot and isolate specific actions that appear "pregnant," projecting the chaos of intertwined bodies into the flow of the choreographed battle. The changes in focal length result in constant variations in the composition of the image, organized around three main shot sizes. The exclusively lateral point of view, as well as the figure of Leonidas draped in his scarlet toga, stand out against a uniform, light beige background. This evokes Marey's use of chronophotography in his study of movement, an archeology shared by cinema and comics,[22] as we have seen. In the preceding shots, the camera did not occupy a specific position on the battlefield; here, the chosen locations adhere quite strictly to the axis of the performance. Although the technology is similar, it is actually the opposite of *The Matrix*'s bullet time (Lana and Lilly Wachowski, 1999). The latter is characterized by a movement around the protagonist, while the hero of *300* is constantly shown in profile in the course of a horizontal translation vectorized to the right (a trajectory highlighted by that of the arrow), just as Marey studied the way his test subjects walked. The military (and even militaristic) context of *300* is not unrelated to the work of the physiologist, and especially that of his assistant, Demenÿ, who in 1902 took charge of the laboratory at the Joinville military school (Guido 292–300). Marey also solicited the Ministry of War to support his studies of physical education:

> All these experiments on the physiological laws of human labor are officially intended for the army: after all, it determines the length of the soldier's step, the pace of his march, the load he must bear, the shape of his shoes, and even the rhythm of the bugle that regulates his step so as to maximize the use of his strength. (Mannoni 191)

In *300*, the spectacle of muscular strength so dear to Demenÿ is put to the service of a patriotic and sacrificial ideal, magnified by the glorification of the Spartans and the aestheticization of combat, both in Miller's large panels and the film shots that intensify the actors' gestures.

The graphic novel also presents the action on a horizontal axis, which, as in the film, is intensified by staging parallel actions on the same visual plane. However, Miller can take advantage of the unity of the page, which at times instills a sense of closure, especially in a chaptered work such as *300*. Due to the emphasis of the tabular dimension through the large format and the reduction of the number of panels per page, the graphic novel's vectorization tends to shift toward the interior of the image rather than occur through the movement from one panel to the next, with the distinct phases of the action distributed among multiple characters. It is the eye of the reader that virtually "animates" the image in scanning the page, an effect Snyder achieves through the movements created through computer graphics.

The violence depicted in *300* innervates the image itself: the characters' endless battle seems to parallel the movie's effort to break with the conventions of the comic and adapt them to film. The *Watchmen* and *300* credits are rather isolated cases in the mass of Hollywood comics adaptations. They testify to an aesthetic treatment of the reference to the medium of the original work, proving that contemporary cinema, with all its digital effects, does not always emerge unscathed from its confrontation with comics, which it tends to invoke via a detour through a common ancestor: chronophotography. From an intermedial perspective, film adaptations of comics (and similar observations could be made for films derived from video games) involve a self-reflexive treatment of filmic expression with contemporary digital technologies, beyond the transfer of diegetic or narrative content and the reimagining of iconographic motifs. Unsurprisingly, it is the very variations in the image's speed that affect the gestures of the superheroes' colossal bodies, of these quasi-mythological figures ready to be frozen in the resin of merchandising figurines. They are the perfect embodiment in American popular culture of what Philippe Hamon calls "referential characters," figures that "unambiguously refer to a full and set meaning immobilized by a certain culture and its stereotyped roles, programs and jobs, and their legibility depends directly on the degree of the reader's participation in that culture (they must be learned and recognized)" (122). This immobilization, conceived in *Watchmen* as a parodic intensification of the genre's conventions, is emblematized in *300*'s slow motion and delays, with the hero becoming an icon abstracted from diegetic duration through a series of narrative pauses and sculptural poses. The fixity of certain shots in these films isolate the movements' phases and generate traces of an Other, allowing the comics medium to inscribe itself in the film adaptation.

Notes

1. See, for example, Danielle Chaperon's study, which compares the ideological messages in *V for Vendetta* by Alan Moore and David Lloyd (1982–90) and in James McTeigue's 2005 film adaptation.

2. See Thomas Schatz, who discusses the Spider-Man adaptations and explains how the contemporary Hollywood industry is governed by the franchise principle, in which derivatives are made readily available across a host of media as early as the preproduction stage.

3. Consider, for instance, *Battleship* (Peter Berg, 2012), the *Transformers* series (2007–), and *GI Joe* (2009–), co-produced by Hasbro, and the links between the film and toy industries, which have been reinforced considerably as a result of the merchandising around the Star Wars franchise (see Boillat 2006).

4. *Flash Gordon* (Universal, Frederick Stephani, 1936, 13 episodes); *Flash Gordon's Trip to Mars* (Universal, Ford Beebe and Robert F. Hill, 1938, 15 episodes); *Flash Gordon Conquers the Universe* (Universal, Ford Beebe and Ray Taylor, 1940, 12 episodes); *Buck Rogers* (Universal, Ford Beebe, Saul A. Goodking, 1939, 12 episodes).

5. More specifically, *Dick Tracy* (Republic, Alan James and Ray Taylor, 1937, 15 episodes), followed by *Dick Tracy Returns* (Republic, John English and William Witney, 1938, 15 episodes). As we shall see below, *Dick Tracy, Detective* (RKO, William Berke, 1945) makes explicit references to the Gould comics through drawings in its title cards, thus becoming a specific means of invoking the original work.

6. The discontinuity of the film medium (segmentation in film strips) and projection (a regular frame rate of twenty-four per second) is erased by the perceptual effects induced by the flicker frequency (Bordwell and Thompson 11–12).

7. The comment accompanies in voice-over an image, which, by showing multiple excerpts simultaneously, reinforces the reference to the comic through a split-screen technique that is not even used in the film.

8. One should nonetheless refrain from making too strict a distinction between stereoscopy and the flatness of a comics page, given that 3D movies have revived the tiering of action in multiple shots so frequently used by comics artists. Despite the argument of enhanced immersion

in Hollywood's promotional discourse, one may wonder if this technology is not closer to the superimposition of representations of certain pre-cinematographic devices, as the credits of the film *Oz the Great and Powerful* (Sam Raimi, 2013) seem to suggest.

9. See Georges Didi-Huberman and Laurent Mannoni.

10. The slow motion in Pete Travis's film takes advantage of the technological possibilities of the latest digital cameras. Incidentally, this technique was not used in the previous adaptation of the comic book, *Judge Dredd* (Danny Cannon, 1995).

11. For more on adaptation theories, see Thomas Leitch's critical assessment (1–16). For details about the translation studies of literary texts, see Hans-Jost Frey, who considers intertextual relationships as new texts (or rather as fragments in a large network that is continually expanding). The obstacle of "fidelity" to the source is less of a problem in comics since, despite a growing legitimization, the medium does not yet have a canon that can rival that established by centuries of literary criticism.

12. This approach was completely abandoned in the new adaptation, *The Incredible Hulk* (Louis Leterrier, 2008), also produced by Universal and Marvel Enterprises. The film is not a sequel but was intended to replace Ang Lee's commercially unsuccessful version by offering a product more in line with mainstream blockbuster expectations.

13. *Journal de Spirou* 1, April 21, 1938, reprinted in Rob-Vel 2013, 45. For more on the authorship of this first panel, which was drawn by Luc Lafnet (the painter sharing his traits), see Christelle and Bertrand Pissavy-Yvernault 72–74.

14. I will discuss *Watchmen* as an exception, since it is the first graphic novel to have won a Hugo Award (a literary prize for science fiction).

15. One could say the same of the non-narrative short film *Salut les Cubains* (1971), made the same year by Agnès Varda, who thanks Chris Marker in the credits; it is mainly composed of photographs taken in Cuba by the filmmaker. In the dance sequence with Benny Moré, the "king of rhythm," still images scroll past in a series and are repeated in a loop with identical centering, the singer successively occupying different parts of the image (as in comics using the regular "waffle iron" layout), allowing the viewer to infer the dancer's movements from the juxtaposition of poses. The duration of the projection of each image generates a specific rhythm. Varda even places balloons with texts attached to the mouth of the singer, thereby simultaneously evoking the photo novel and the comic book.

16. Animation films, which are often more self-reflexive, regularly contain many forms of allusion to the still image. Think of Winsor McCay explaining the genesis of the film *Little Nemo* (1911), or of *Band of Ninja* (1967), in which Nagisa Oshima "animates" the panels by manga artist Sampei Shirato through sound and the movements of a rostrum camera. The same can be said of the experimental period of television—for example, when Leblanc, director of the Lombard publishing house, created the subsidiary Belvision and began producing animated films for Belgian television in the mid-1950s: "These productions were like soundtracks, filmed storyboards and radio serials to which pictures would be added" (Capart and Dejasse 98). In cases such as these, film is openly involved in its filiation with the magic lantern, a medium that mainly used non-photographic images (i.e., images painted on glass plates, at times partly mechanically animated). It is worth recalling that Hergé's *Tintin* series was also marketed as a "film fixe," in which each image projected by the home user corresponded to a panel in the comic.

17. In *Sucker Punch* (Snyder, 2011), other means of expression converge; the film obscures the choreographic performances—the young woman dances to distract her enemies, as Scheherazade does with her stories-by foregrounding a universe inspired by video games, which are equally indebted to motion capture and the stylization of gestures.

18. This structure, as well as the form of the credits (a synthetic representation of the fictional universe through artificial archival documents), recalls another adaptation of a superhero comic, *Hellboy* (Guillermo del Toro, 2004).

19. The shot alludes to the photo shoot, which, in the scene from Luis Buñuel's *Viridiana* (1961) where all the beggars pose, was irreverently replaced by the exhibition of the female sex.

20. Of course, the song "The Times They Are a-Changin'" (1964), like so many other references to American popular culture, also thematizes the passage of time, which is so crucial to the movie's narrative and opening credits.

21. On the DVD commentary, Snyder remarks that the scene was shot simultaneously with three lenses (long, medium, and wide) before adding that, "physically, it is one and the same take." The relationship with Muybridge's capture of movement through multiple devices is obvious.

22. Caroline Renouard emphasizes the relationship between certain tracking shots in Snyder's film and the "sliding of plates in the magic lantern" (100); I have discussed the use of "sliding patterns" to suggest movement in a series of drawings as a meeting point between pre-cinema and comics ("La figuration du mouvement" 35–36).

Works Cited

Bégin, Richard. "L'appareil symbolique intermédial : autour de *American Splendor*." *Bédé, ciné, pub et art*. Eds. Philippe Kaenel and Gilles Lugrin. Gollion: Infolio, 2007. 117–40.

Bœspflug, François. *Le Christ dans l'art : des catacombes au XXe siècle*. Paris: Bayard, 2000.

Boillat, Alain. "Du personnage à la figurine : les produits dérivés de *Star Wars* comme expansion d'un univers." *Décadrages* 8–9 (2006): 106–36.

Boillat, Alain. "La figuration du mouvement dans les dessins de presse et albums illustrés signés « O'Galop » : des images en séries (culturelles)." *1895. Revue de l'association française de recherche sur l'histoire du cinéma* 59 (2009): 22–45.

Boillat, Alain. "Prolégomènes à une réflexion sur les formes et les enjeux d'un dialogue intermédial. Essais sur quelques rencontres entre la bande dessinée et le cinéma." *Les Cases à l'écran : Bande dessinée et cinéma en dialogue*. Ed. Alain Boillat. Genève: Georg, 2007. 25–121.

Boillat, Alain. "Le récit minimal en bande dessinée : L'histoire constamment réitérée d'un éternuement dans la série *Little Sammy Sneeze* de Winsor McCay." *Le Récit minimal : Du minime au minimalisme. Littérature, arts, médias*. Eds. Sabrinelle Bedrane, Françoise Revaz, and Michel Viegnes. Paris: Presses Sorbonne Nouvelle, 2012. 103–17.

Boillat, Alain. "Le statut paradoxal du référent de la fixité dans la bande dessinée." *Fixe/animé. Croisements de la photographie et du cinéma au XXe siècle*. Eds. Laurent Guido and Olivier Lugon. Lausanne: L'Age d'Homme, 2010. 413–34.

Boillat, Alain. "Style et intermédialité dans *Hulk* : le *split screen*, la planche des comics et l'écran d'ordinateur." *Film style/Cinema and Contemporary Visual Arts*. Eds. Enrico Biasin, Giulio Bursi, and Leonardo Quaresima. Udine: Forum, 2007. 385–93.

Boillat, Alain, and Françoise Revaz. "Intrigue, Suspense, and Sequentiality in Comic Strips: Reading *Little Sammy Sneeze*." *Narrative Sequence in Contemporary Narratologies*. Eds. Raphaël Baroni and Françoise Revaz. Columbus: Ohio State University Press. 2015.

Boillat, Alain, and Valentine Robert. "*Vie et Passion de Jésus-Christ* (Pathé, 1902–1905) : hétérogénéité des « tableaux », déclinaison des motifs." *1895. Revue de l'association française de recherche sur l'histoire du cinéma* 60 (2010): 33–64.

Bordwell, David, and Kristin Thompson. *Film Art: An Introduction*. 8th ed. New York: McGraw-Hill, 2008.
Braun, Marta. "Muybridge le magnifique." Études photographiques 10 (2001): http://etudes photographiques.revues.org/index262.html. Accessed on April 28, 2013.
Braun, Marta. "Les limites de la photographie instantanée dans le domaine médical." *Cahiers de Marey* 2 (2011): 82–89.
Braun, Marta. *Picturing Time: The Work of Etienne-Jules Marey (1830–1904)*. Chicago and London: University of Chicago Press, 1992.
Burch, Noël. "Passions, poursuites : d'une certaine linéarisation." *La Lucarne de l'infini : Naissance du langage cinématographique*. Paris: Nathan, 1990. 137–54.
Capart, Philippe, and Erwin Dejasse. *Morris, Franquin, Peyo et le dessin animé*. Angoulême: Editions de l'An 2, 2005.
Chaperon, Danielle. "Maladaptation ! (autour de *V pour Vendetta* de David Lloyd et Alan Moore)." *Les Cases à l'écran*. Ed. Alain Boillat. Genève: Georg, 2007. 303–28.
Deleuze, Gilles. *Cinema 1: The Movement-Image*. Trans. Hugh Tomlinson and Barbara Habberjam. London: Athlone Press, 1986.
Deleuze, Gilles. *Cinema 2: The Time-Image*. Trans. Hugh Tomlinson and Robert Galeta. London: Athlone Press, 1989.
Didi-Huberman, Georges, and Laurent Mannoni. *Mouvements de l'air : Etienne-Jules Marey, photographe des fluides*. Paris: Gallimard, 2004.
Dietschy, Nathalie. "L'autoportrait en Christ de Renée Cox : Étude d'un scandale." *Points de vue sur Jésus au XXe siècle*. Eds. Alain Boillat, Jean Kaempfer, Philippe Kaenel, and Pierre Gisel. Lausanne: Etudes de Lettres, 2008.
Eisner, Will. *Comics and Sequential Art*. Expanded edition. Tamarac, FL: Poorhouse Press, 2000.
Frey, Hans-Jost. *Der Unendliche Text*. Frankfurt am Main: Suhrkamp, 1990.
Frizot, Michel. "E. J. Marey, chronophotographiste." *La Passion du mouvement au XXème siècle : Hommage à Etienne-Jules Marey*. Ed. Franck Gautherot. Beaune: Musée Marey, 1991. 51–62.
Genette, Gérard. *Narrative Discourse: An Essay in Method*. Trans. Jane E Lewin. Ithaca: Cornell University Press, 1980.
Greenberg, Harvey Roy. "Riders of the Lost Text: Remaking as Contested Homage in *Always*." *Journal of Popular Film and Television* 18.4 (1991): 164–71.
Groensteeen, Thierry. "Fictions sans frontières." *La Transécriture : Pour une théorie de l'adaptation*. Eds. André Gaudreault and Thierry Groensteen. Montréal and Angoulème: Nota Bene and CNBDI, 1998. 9–30.
Guido, Laurent. *L'Âge du rythme : Cinéma, musicalité et culture du corps dans les théories françaises des années 1910–1930*. Lausanne: Payot, 2007.
Hamon, Philippe. "Pour un statut sémiologique du personnage." *Poétique du récit*. Eds. Roland Barthes, Wolfgang Kayser, Wayne C. Booth, and Philippe Hamon. Paris: Seuil, 1977. 115–80.
Leitch, Thomas. *Film Adaptation and its Discontents*. Baltimore, MD: Johns Hopkins University Press, 2007.
Mannoni, Laurent. *Etienne-Jules Marey, la mémoire de l'œil*. Paris and Milan: Cinémathèque française and Mazzotta, 1999.
Mannovich, Lev. *The Language of New Media*. Cambridge, MA: MIT Press, 2000.
Marey, Etienne-Jules. *Le Mouvement*. Nîmes: Jacqueline Chambon, 1994.
Marion, Philippe. *Movement*. Trans. Eric Pritchard. New York: D. Appleton and Company, 1895. *Internet Archive*. Accessed on April 8, 2017.
Marion, Philippe. "Narratologie médiatique et médiagénie des récits." *Recherches en communication* 7 (1997): 61–87.

Menache, Alberto. *Understanding Motion Capture for Computer Animation*. Burlington: Morgan Kaufmann, 2011.

Miller, Frank. *300*. Milwaukie, OR: Dark Horse Comics, 1999.

Millidge, Gary Spencer. *Alan Moore, Storyteller.* New York: Universe, 2011.

Moinereau, Laurence. *Le Générique de film : De la lettre à la figure*. Rennes: PUR, 2009.

Moore, Alan, and Dave Gibbons. *Watchmen*. New York: DC Comics, 1986.

Morgan, Harry, and Manuel Hirtz. *Les Apocalypses de Jack Kirby*. Lyon: Les Moutons électriques, 2009.

Odin, Roger. "L'entrée du spectateur dans la fiction." *Théorie du film*. Eds. Jacques Aumont and Jean-Louis Leutrat. Paris: Albatros, 1980. 198–213.

Odin, Roger. "Le film de fiction menacé par la photographie et sauvé par la bande son (à propos de *La Jetée* de Chris Marker)." *Cinémas de la modernité : films, théories*. Eds. Dominique Chateau, André Gardies, and François Jost. Paris: Klincksieck, 1981. 147–71.

Pisano, Giusy. "Du papier à l'image en mouvement, de la chronophotographie à l'image numérique. L'exemple de *Spider-Man*." *Cinema and Comics*. Eds. Leonardo Quaresima, Laura Ester Sangalli, and Federico Zecca. Udine: Forum, 2009. 581–602.

Pissavy-Yvernault, Christelle, and Bertrand Pissavy-Yvernault. *La Véritable histoire de Spirou, 1937–1946*. Marcinelle: Dupuis, 2013.

Renouard, Caroline. "Incrustations et images composites. Quand le cinéma numérique adapte picturalement la bande dessinée." *Cinéma&Cie* 10.14–15 (2010): 95–103.

Rob-Vel. *Spirou, l'intégrale, 1938–1943*. Marcinelle: Dupuis, 2013.

Schatz, Thomas. "New Hollywood, New Millenium." *Film Theory and Contemporary Hollywood Movies*. Ed. Warren Buckland. New York and London: Routledge, 2009. 19–46.

Smolderen, Thierry. *The Origins of Comics: From William Hogarth to Winsor McCay*. Trans. Bart Beaty and Nick Nguyen. Jackson: University Press of Mississippi, 2014.

Walsh, Richard. *Reading the Gospels in the Dark: Portrayals of Jesus in Film*. London: Trinity Press International, 2003.

From Marvel Comics to Marvel Studios: Adaptation, Intermediality, and Contemporary Hollywood Strategies

DICK TOMASOVIC

Over the past few years, a host of new, original films have spurred an explosion of studies on the relationship between comics and cinema.[1] Inspired by the graphic arts, these films question the status of images, their translation from one medium into another, as well as their use of technological innovations. This chapter will focus on a specific contemporary corpus, namely, the superhero movies adapted from Marvel comics. In the 2000s, in search of expansion and new audiences, the publishing house went into film production,[2] proceeding to develop an original adaptation strategy characterized by its hybridity and intermediality.[3] By borrowing typical features from comics (seriality, crossover, shared universes, and so on), these films have ultimately revitalized the poetics of the Hollywood blockbuster. In turn, they have influenced the aesthetics of comics, inverting the usual hierarchy between the original and the adaptation. The issue of adaptation, or *transécriture* (Groensteen 9–29), which is made somewhat opaque given the reciprocal interactions between comics and films,[4] becomes even more complex given that comics and films are not the only media or practices in play: animation, toys, and video games must also be considered. To identify the stakes of Marvel's current adaptation strategy from an aesthetic as well as commercial point of view, this chapter will focus on three related issues. First, it examines the superhero film and the influence of comics on the renaissance of the action film. Secondly, it describes the production methods at Marvel Studios. Lastly, it identifies what makes Marvel adaptations so unique through a case study of the iconic film *The Avengers* (Joss Whedon, 2012).

The Superhero Film: Comics to the Rescue of Action Movies

Over the last twenty years, Hollywood seems to have rediscovered the colorful world of comics, finding new sources, subject matter, visuals, and, above all, new characters.[5] Film's renewed interest in comics follows a change in its target audience (the increasing importance of adolescents since the late 1970s), the revival of special effects (digital technology making possible what had previously been unimaginable onscreen), the consecration of pop culture (what some refer to today as "ludic art"; Kriegk, 11–124), the resurgence of paranoid narratives,[6] and, of course, the obsession with the moving body as the defining feature of what was hitherto the most profitable Hollywood genre: the action movie.[7]

A quick overview shows that most of these superhero action films are adaptations of comics published by Marvel,[8] one of the two largest comics publishers, which owns the rights to popular individual characters such as Spider-Man and the Hulk, as well as the X-Men and Avengers franchises. These blockbusters belong to a veritable subgenre with a clear commercial logic, while sharing a series of narrative, referential, and cinematographic codes.

These films have sometimes been discussed as examples of the formal renewal of the action movie genre. In terms of poetics, certain characteristics are particularly conspicuous. The camera appears free from its usual technical and physical constraints, as if it were liberated—unleashed, even, with its frantic, mostly virtual movements made possible by digital imagery. Scenes from *Spider-Man* (Sam Raimi, 2002, 2004, and 2007) show the hero swinging from web line to web line, closely followed in the air by a camera that no crew member, crane, or helicopter could ever operate. These fully digital scenes allow the camera to move in the sky with the same ease as the hero, creating a spectacle that revives the attractions of fairground films. When the franchise was relaunched, the trend was even more pronounced. *The Amazing Spider-Man* (Mark Webb, 2012) uses 3D depth of field, which is especially striking in the character's motion sequences. If this type of filming, with its spectacle of swirling bodies, is now shared by many other action movies, it remains specific to superhero films, as the shots in *The Avengers* (2012) illustrate.

Other recurrent figures remind us, directly or indirectly, of how these films have adapted the comics medium. This is especially true of the temporal changes and use of slow motion in the final images of a shot. The slowing down of the shot seems intended to create a parallel between film montage and the reading of comics with its successive panels, compelling the gaze to linger on the individual image. The films (of Sam Raimi, Zack Snyder, Steven Johnson, Stephen Norrington, Guillermo del Toro, and Jon Favreau) freeze the actions of the characters as a way to anchor them and reproduce the efficacy of comics panels. These variations of speed are supported by an overall intensification of the characters' poses, further reinforced by perspective and background lighting, which, in the absence or suspension of movement, seemingly evokes the dynamism of the drawings in typical action comic books. In this respect, *Hulk* (Ang Lee, 2003) is probably the most extreme example, going so far as to reproduce the split panels and simultaneity found in comics pages.

The intrusiveness of the images,[9] the organization of action scenes into a series of snapshots, and the graphic treatment of shots make the genre easily recognizable, even though these films are, of course, governed by multiple generic codes. Some are narrative (for example, the genesis of the superhero, accompanied by what are often alternatively amusing or belabored scenes detailing the discovery of superpowers or the invention of gadgets such as costumes, armor, and weapons, the crisis of faith and doubt haunting the superhero, the final battle against the villain, and so forth). Others are referential, including the appearance of writers, artists, or creators of comics characters (Stan Lee being the most prominent, but also Kevin Smith or J. M. Straczynski, for example) or references to objects or characters from Marvel's extended diegetic universe. Finally, the Marvel Studios logo, a kind of flipbook leafing through the most famous of their comics panels (now imitated by their main rival, DC), emphasizes the provenance of the motifs and the process of adaptation itself (to put the comic into moving images) by branding the film as belonging to the superhero genre from the start.

It seems that the superhero film has become sufficiently homogeneous to become a genre distinct from that of the 1980s–90s action movie. This process, which took about a decade, was spearheaded by two producers who played a major role in the renewal of the Hollywood industry[10]: Avi Arad and Kevin Feige. Their main business asset was the catalog of Marvel characters. However, a study of the close ties between film and comics must also pay attention to the cross-media approach at the core of their production practices.[11]

Producing to Adapt: Marvel Studios

Among today's most influential Hollywood producers, Avi Arad first worked in the toy business (he led Toybiz in the early 1990s), later in television (especially cartoons), and then in comics publishing (merging the toy industry with children's and teenager's literature,, both in crisis at the time).[12] After a series of events too elaborate to be recounted here (Raviv 18–44), Arad, a majority shareholder of the Marvel publishing house, became head of Marvel Studios in 1993; he founded the division to make film adaptations, produced first in partnership with large companies (mainly Sony Pictures and 20th Century Fox) before becoming independent in 2008. Independence was short-lived as Disney purchased Marvel in 2009. Today, Marvel Studios is part of Walt Disney Studios, where it enjoys relative artistic freedom and a status similar to that of Pixar. Arad left Marvel in 1998 and continued to work as an independent producer and consultant during the 2000s on numerous film adaptations from the Marvel back catalog—not just for Marvel Studios, but also for Sony Pictures, 20th Century Fox, and Columbia Pictures.

The businessman has always been closely involved with his productions, overseeing preproduction (choosing directors, writers, cast) and being quite active on the set (possibly delegating some of his authority to close associates).[13] The producer developed the genre thanks to three trilogies, all of which testify both to the intentions and nuances foundational to the genre. The first, the *X-Men* series (2000–2006), explores paranoid allegorical motifs while being partly consistent with 1990s action film tropes. The *Spider-Man* series brought more spectacle, color, pop culture, and sheer entertainment, and was explicitly targeted at teenagers. Finally, the *Blade* trilogy (1998–2004) is more violent, openly flirting with horror and B movies. Each of these series was aimed at specific audiences and involved a differentiated merchandising strategy. These trilogies still stand as the canonical reference points for every new superhero film.

Avi Arad has created numerous interactions between comics and films, each benefiting from the success of the other.[14] Examples are legion, but the most famous involve the casting of the films. In the *Ultimates*[15] series, whose editing purposely evokes Hollywood action movies, Mark Millar and artist Bryan Hitch decided to draw Nick Fury in the likeness of actor Samuel L. Jackson in the comics, though he did not exactly correspond to the traditional representation of the character. A few years later, the same actor made a brief appearance at the end of the screen version of *Iron Man* (Jon Favreau, 2008). Since then, the character associated with the actor has become an important figure in several films and publications.[16] Conversely, certain films (especially *X-Men*) have changed the print series.[17] Arad's policy has consistently encouraged the interaction between comics and film, transforming the meaning of "tie-in," as the production of toys and figurines is, from the start, integrated into the conception stage of the film.[18]

Thus, behind the relatively interchangeable roles of the directors and writers lies a shrewd producer who targets teen audiences while combining three major media: comics, action films, and animation.[19] What the three have in common is the fantastic and phantasmagorical image of the body of the protagonists. Indeed, the superhero film systematizes a link with the extraordinary body—latent in the action movies of the late 1980s—and seduces its audience with the promise of the spectacular exploits accomplished by this amazing body. Of course, such an image of the body predates cinema, but its appearance in moving pictures points to a significant displacement: the story of the exploits matters less than the representation of the bodily performance itself (unlike the comics, which recount the superhuman epics through serialization and cliffhangers).[20] In other words, the body becomes the site of adventure, and the spectacle of the body becomes the crux of the film. Transformation scenes are crucial; think, for example, of the change in Flint Marko's cellular structure in *Spider-Man 3* (Raimi, 2007), which endows him with the dynamogenic power of quicksand and, incidentally, evokes the medium of animation. In these films, the characters exhibit extraordinary bodily properties.

Given Avi Arad's expertise in the toy industry, merchandising, and spinoff business, it should come as no surprise that the producer was quick to capitalize on the characters by imposing a commercial logic that crosses multiple platforms; one need only compare the film characters' trademark poses to those of the toy figures.[21] Animated TV series, movies for the big screen, video games, and toy design echo one another. Whether it is Webb's *Spider-Man* (Marc Webb, 2012), *Iron Man 2* (Jon Favreau, 2010), or *The Avengers* (2012), the characters not only appear in films, comics, television series, toys, and video games, but they do so with a high degree of similarity. Their visual identities show such uniformity that it is practically impossible to distinguish the cinematic image from comic book covers or the video game avatars. The superhero movie is part of a commercial transmedia chain and must adapt to various extra-cinematic factors and changes in product design. It has become an essential link in the current development of convergence and hybridization strategies across different modes of expression and entertainment sectors.

This transmedial aspect is, of course, also at the heart of the work of producer Kevin Feige. Unlike Arad, Feige's career has always centered on Hollywood. A graduate in film studies, he began his career at Richard Donner's production company at Warner Bros. (Donner famously directed the *Lethal Weapon* trilogy of the late 1980s and the *Superman* film of 1978), before being hired as an associate producer for *X-Men* (Bryan Singer, 2000). He quickly became a close associate of Avi Arad and participated in the development of numerous Marvel films (the *X-Men* saga, the *Spider-Man* trilogy, *Daredevil* in 2003, *The Punisher* in 2004, *Elektra* and *Fantastic Four* in 2005, and so on), before being hired to head Marvel Studios in 2007. A self-proclaimed fan of the Marvel universe and especially its tie-ins (toys, figurines, and so on),

Feige intensified the convergent strategies and enlisted film in the crossover logic so essential to the world of comics. The diegetic universe is shared by multiple films, allowing the most popular Marvel characters (or at least the licensed characters) to meet or clash.[22] The construction of this "Marvel Cinematic Universe" (the diegetic world these works share), as the producer himself calls it (Salard 54), became reality in 2008 after the studio obtained autonomy and produced the first installment of *Iron Man*. The films are the basis of a dizzying game of references from one film to the next, thereby contributing to the creation of the shared universe.[23]

First, there are the more or less explicit allusions and references in the films. Costumes, props, names, and quotes appear from one film to another. These include, for example, Captain America's shield in the background of the *Iron Man* films; the cosmic cube, the famous tesseract, is the MacGuffin shared by *Captain America* (Joe Johnston, 2011), *Iron Man 2* (Favreau, 2010), *Thor* (2011), and *The Avengers* (2012); Odin's treasure chamber in Thor holds several talismans referring to upcoming Marvel movies. Certain musical themes are also repeated, including that of the Stark Expo in *Captain America* and *Iron Man 2*. These references are primarily intended for fans and those familiar with the Marvel universe, and can be read as knowing clues, just like the cameos by the creator of all these characters, Stan Lee, who never fails to make an appearance in each film.

Secondly, the final scenes after the credits have, ever since the first films produced by Arad (*Blade* and *X-Men*), invited the viewer to the follow-ups of the superhero adventure, with the implication that the stories are never-ending. Originally, this form of cliffhanger marked the serialized nature of the stories. Under Feige, these sequences announce future crossovers in the character of Colonel Fury, who unites these heroes under the banner of the Avengers.

Third, an important role is given to spinoffs and additional plot lines through a series of sporadic short films (either as DVD bonuses or posted on the web) presented under the label Marvel One Shot. *The Consultant* (Leythum, 2011), *A Funny Thing Happened on the Way to Thor's Hammer* (Leythum, 2011), and *Item 47* (Louis Esposito, 2012) bring together other narratives by referring to S.H.I.E.L.D. Agent Phil Coulson, for example, a character designed for the "Marvel Cinematic Universe," who plays an increasingly important role in the Marvel stories (a recurring character appearing in different films, his sacrifice is central to the plot of *The Avengers*). Coulson also became a prominent character in the comics and is featured in the TV series *Agents of S.H.I.E.L.D.* (ABC, 2013–).[24]

To manage this crossover and its effects in cinema and comics, Feige relies on a creative team to maintain the cohesion of the project. This "Marvel committee" consists of four major names in the Marvel comics company: Joe Quesada, editor in chief of Marvel Comics from 2000 to 2011, who is now the creative director, having successfully overseen major crossovers these past few years[25]; Dan Buckley, Marvel's managing editor; Alan Fine, vice president and Marvel's chief marketing officer (before joining Marvel in 1996, Fine was head of the toy distributor Kay Bee Toys); and finally, Brian Michael Bendis, one of the main writers at Marvel Comics, who oversees several major series and crossovers. Other scriptwriters (Matt Fraction,[26] Ed Brubaker,[27] and J. Michael Straczynski)[28] are sometimes invited to the committee to discuss specific characters or outstanding issues. The comics artists and publishers thus play an important role as consultants.

The Avengers: Gatherings and Convergences

The focus of all this creative energy was directed at the launch of what quickly became one of the biggest blockbusters of all time—a "tent-pole"[29] for Disney, really, after *John Carter* had flopped (Andrew Stanton, 2012) a few months before—the film *The Avengers* (2012), conceived by Avi Arad in 2005, whose unique structure reflects the culmination of multiple crossover and transmedia strategies.

The production of the blockbuster was entrusted to Joss Whedon, an inexperienced director whose single previous film, *Serenity* (2005), is relatively unknown. However, Whedon is a legend among science fiction and comics fan communities. He owes this status to his work as screenwriter for *Toy Story* (John Lasseter, 1995) and *Alien Resurrection* (Jean-Pierre Jeunet, 1997), as creator of the cult series *Buffy the Vampire Slayer* series (WB, 1997–2003), *Angel* (WB, 1999–2004), *Firefly* (Fox, 2002–2003), and *Dollhouse* (Fox, 2009–2010), as well as author of the cult web series *Dr. Horrible's Sing-Along Blog* (2008).[30] He is also the scriptwriter of *Astonishing X-Men* (2005–2007), a series loved by many Marvel comics readers. Previously approached by Warner Bros. to direct an adaptation of *Wonder Woman*, Whedon, an expert dialogue writer and crossmedia enthusiast (his television series *Buffy* lives on today in comic book form), was eventually chosen by Marvel Studios to write and direct *The Avengers* (2012), on the condition that he conform to precise specifications based on the pre-established characters and narratives he was inheriting.

The film was announced with great fanfare at the San Diego Comic-Con, one of the world's largest comics events, which now includes television series, video games, manga, "Japanimation," toys, trading cards, and fantasy novels.[31] Though a film, *The Avengers* (2012) clearly follows a commercial and multi-platform logic.

Backed by a major marketing campaign on social media and inspired by the world of the comic book series *The Ultimates*, the film also draws on previous film adaptations featuring Marvel heroes. *The Avengers* taps into an episodic structure that recalls, if not the first superhero serials of the 1940s,[32] then at least the serialized writing of comics and television series, including those created by Whedon. Not only is each character allowed his or her time in the limelight to preserve narrative balance (and to avoid offending fans), but the film's iconography also plays on the world of toys and collectible figurines. In a remarkable metadiegetic gesture, the very idea of collecting superhero merchandise is integrated into the film: the fact that Agent Coulson collects Captain America cards has a substantial impact on the narrative. The film multiplies disguised references and allusions to create a sense of collusion with fans, enhancing the feeling of community to the point of momentarily breaking the logic of the story. This type of break is reminiscent of the vivid and complicit writing of Stan Lee, which set Marvel apart from its competitors in the 1960s.[33]

Moreover, many of the scenes are designed to evoke not only the comics panels, but also—perhaps even primarily—the Turbomedia panels, a type of interactive animation developed online by publishers striving to attract readers to the electronic comic book version.[34] With its spectacular metamorphoses[35] and cartoony moments,[36] animation film is another major source of inspiration, and undoubtedly refers to the many produced by Marvel Animation studio for the Disney XD channel among others.[37] Lastly, there are multiple cinematic sequences that suggest parallels with the video game universe: the use of overhead or over-the-shoulder shots, the fusing of character and background textures, the unique perspective provided by a virtual camera focusing on a specific part of the action—these techniques frequently appear in video games.

One particular sequence exemplifies this intermedial logic [116:38–117:19]. The amazing long sequence shot of the final battle scene in Manhattan, with its frenetic camera movement, unites all the protagonists. The camera, portraying a Homeric battle scene, moves from the Black Widow to Thor, and lingers on Iron Man, Captain America, Hawkeye, and the Hulk. The aim was to capture the heroes' titanic battle in just a single shot. More than an action scene, this is a moment where the characters are presented in all

Fig. 29: *The Avengers* (Whedon, 2012): the superheroes in their characteristic (and marketable) poses before the final battle.

their glory and celebrated in their characteristic poses. Obviously, integrating this type of shot in the middle of a heavily edited action scene makes it especially emblematic. The vision will not surprise gamers, who are accustomed to varying points of view and the impact of cut scenes that highlight characters or meaningful moments in the story. Overall, the film breaks with the prevailing imagery of recent action films (high speed editing of the action, elliptical montage, the fragmentation of the body, and so on). The reason is twofold. First, the conversion to 3D film imposes the need for a less hectic pace and the extension of shot lengths.[38] However, more important, perhaps, is Whedon's desire to make the body wholly legible, something that is characteristic both of his TV series and of mainstream comics in general. Moreover, throughout the film, the camera avoids getting too close to ensure figurative omnipotence, evincing a desire to abolish the offscreen by foregrounding omniscient, alternating montage. The long sequence with the attack on S.H.I.E.L.D.'s flying fortress is exemplary in this respect; the storm scatters the assembled heroes inside and outside the craft into different pairs, who either stick together or are at loggerheads (Iron Man and Captain America / Black Widow and Hulk / Hulk and Thor / Thor and Loki / Loki and Agent Coulson / Black Widow and Hawkeye, and so on) [72:20–89:10]. The camera seems ubiquitous, while its alternating perspectives allow the viewer to follow all characters and actions simultaneously; the film is an exploration of the dialectic between the heroes' scattering and regrouping. Whedon's directing preserves the integrity of the statuettes and aspires to create a large picture book (fig. 29).

The Avengers (2012) thus represents the culmination of a logic of film production inspired by characteristics of the comics industry.[39] This successful film[40] requires us to consider not only the forms and stakes of Hollywood structures and the aesthetics of the blockbuster, but also the question of film adaptations of comics that goes beyond a trans-semiotic perspective to account for interactions across various media. Of course, film has maintained intermedial relations since its beginning (Gaudreault 111–44). Winsor McCay, a comics and animation pioneer, had already adapted his *Little Nemo* from the page to the screen by bringing together other cultural and media practices.[41] The transfer of works from Marvel Comics to Marvel Studios thus fits into a long history of intermediality. Given the multi-platform strategies, the generalization of cross-media practices and changes in the culture industry, the adage that adaptation always involves more than two media or art practices is perhaps even more relevant today.

Notes

1. The 2009 international conference *Cinema e fumetto : Cinema and Comics* at the University of Udine was a highlight.

2. There is, however, little overlap between the comics and movie audience (Rae and Gray 86–100).

3. This is a process characterized by constant interaction between media concepts (Müller 113).

4. In their serial form, comics resist closure and reflect current cinematic trends. In fact, the influence of comics serialization on film merits a full examination that would consider film history as a whole (Oms 153).

5. The superhero has been adapted to numerous media throughout the twentieth century, especially in film (Misiroglu 17–20).

6. Once again, Hollywood cinema seems to reflect America's anxieties in the countless paranoid plots of contemporary films (Aknin 156; Bidaud 7; Guido 7–40; Letort 9–14; Tomasovic, *Le Palimpseste noir* 69–92).

7. The body is the structuring element of the superhero genre regardless of the media (Haver and Meyer 170).

8. Founded in 1939 by Martin Goodman under the name of Timely Comics.

9. Characters and landscapes surge at full speed before the spectators' eyes, harking back to the early cinema of attractions (Belloi 86–154).

10. The industry had to develop new business strategies within the constraints of a global market and complex industry model (Martel 97–119; Mingant 75–100).

11. I use the term "cross-media" to refer to the articulation of different target media responding to a global communication project (Azemard 232).

12. After years of struggle, Marvel filed for bankruptcy in 1996 (Picciau, "Marvel, superhéros de l'entertainment").

13. See the interview with Avi Arad (Pierce 32–34).

14. Here I am developing points made in a previous article entitled "Images dessinées / images animées."

15. Created by Mark Millar and Bryan Hitch and launched in 2002, the series chronicles the exploits of a superhero team similar to the Avengers in an alternate, modernized Marvel universe.

16. In comic books, the character appears in the series *Ultimate Origins*, *Ultimate X-Men*, *Ultimate Enemy*, and *Spider-Man*, and is featured in the films *Thor* (Kenneth Branagh, 2011) and *The Avengers* (2012). A film with the title *Nick Fury* is in development according to the website Comicbookmovie.com (accessed on April 9, 2013).

17. One example is the way the *New X-Men* series (2001–2004) by Grant Morrison and Frank Quitely adapts the costumes of the film to their characters.

18. Storyboards and studies of the characters' designs take into account the positions of the figures, as shown by the illustrated book *Art of Marvel Studios* (2012).

19. For more on Arad's career and vision, as well as details on these three intertexts, see my previous article, "Le masque et la menace."

20. Myths and the epic genre are central to comic books (Klock 19–25).

21. For example, the figure "Black Widow The Avengers" produced by Hot Toys in 2012 shows surprising similarities with the character played by Scarlett Johansson in *The Avengers* (2012).

22. At the time of writing, Fox has the rights to Daredevil, the X-Men (including Wolverine), and the Fantastic Four; Spider-Man and Ghost Rider are licensed to Sony. Disney has expressed its desire to obtain these licenses.

23. So far, six films take place in this universe: *Iron Man* 1 and 2, *The Incredible Hulk*, *Thor*, *Captain America: The First Avenger*, and Marvel's *The Avengers*.

24. In August 2012, Marvel Studios and ABC News announced they were developing the S.H.I.E.L.D. series with Joss Whedon and his brother Jed at the helm.

25. Comics like *House of M*, *Civil War*, *World War Hulk*, and *Secret Invasion*, just to name a few.

26. Fraction wrote numerous episodes of *The Invincible Iron Man*. He was recently put in charge of *Fear Itself*, one of the few crossovers not written by B. M. Bendis.

27. Brubaker is a prolific author best known for his contributions to the *Captain America* series.

28. Straczynski is a novelist and writer of TV series, including *Babylon 5* (PTEN, 1994–1998). He has been one of the key writers of the *Thor* series in recent years.

29. A huge, successful blockbuster's box-office revenue can offset the failure of other films as well as protect the producers.

30. Viewed 2,225,000 times in five days (Rose 187).

31. Comic-Con can be described as a space of transmedial convergence for popular cultures (Salkowitz 190–200).

32. *Batman* by Lambert Hillyer in 1943, *Captain America* by John English and Elmer Clifton in 1944, and *Superman* by Gordon Spencer Bennet and Thomas Carr in 1948.

33. According to Alain Boillat, most film adaptations of Marvel comics avoid audience complicity and reflexivity to facilitate immersion (35).

34. One example is the scene with the frozen image of Thor and the Hulk facing the audience when the green giant suddenly hurls his companion sideways into the background [117:31].

35. Examples include shots of Tony Stark putting on the Iron Man armor or of Bruce Banner transforming into the Hulk [74:30].

36. The scene where the Hulk grabs Loki by the feet and slings him to the floor repeatedly recalls the wild and sudden humor of Tex Avery's cartoons [120:20].

37. *The Avengers: Earth's Mightiest Heroes* has been on air since late 2010.

38. Whedon's unease with this technique is well-documented. After testing the 3D camera for the post-credit sequence of *Thor*, Joss Whedon abandoned it for *The Avengers* (2012) in favor of 3D conversion.

39. According to Kevin Feige, the film became even more successful in the following months (Salard 54).

40. Third in the list of the most profitable films of all time, *The Avengers* (2012) prompted Warner and DC entertainment to restructure (Delcroix 149).

41. In this case, the burlesque, vaudeville, and dance (Tomasovic, "Les Greffes du corps animé" 83–100).

Works Cited

Aknin, Laurent. *Mythes et idéologie du cinéma américain*. Paris: Vendémiaire, 2012.

The Avengers. Written and directed by Joss Whedon, based on a story by Zak Penn and Joss Whedon. With Robert Downey Jr. (Tony Stark / Iron Man), Chris Evans (Steve Rogers / Captain America), Mark Ruffalo (Bruce Banner / the Hulk), Chris Hemsworth (Thor), Scarlet Johansson (Natasha Romanoff / Black Widow), Jeremy Renner (Clint Barton / Hawkeye), Tom Hiddleston (Loki), and Samuel L. Jackson (Nick Fury). Marvel Studios / Paramount Pictures, 2012. DVD. Disney, 2012.

Azémard, Ghislaine. *100 notions pour le crossmédia et le transmédia*. Paris: Les Éditions de l'Immatériel, 2013.

Belloï, Livio. *Le Regard retourné : Aspects du cinéma des premiers temps*. Montréal and Paris: Nota bene / Méridiens Klincksieck, 2001.

Bidaud, Anne-Marie. *Hollywood et le Rêve américain : Cinéma et idéologie aux États-Unis*. Paris: Masson, 1994.

Boillat, Alain. "Prolégomènes à une réflexion sur les formes et enjeux d'un dialogue intermédial." *Les Cases à l'écran*. Ed. Alain Boillat. Genève: Georg, 2010. 25–121.

Daniels, Les. *Marvel: Five Fabulous Decades of the World's Greatest Comics*. New York: Abrams, 1993.

Delcroix, Olivier. *Les Super-héros au cinéma*. Paris: Hoëbeke, 2012.

Gaudreault, André. *Cinéma et attraction*. Paris: CNRS, 2008.

Groensteen, Thierry. "Fictions sans frontières." *La Transécriture, pour une théorie de l'adaptation*. Eds. André Gaudreault and Thierry Groensteen. Montréal and Angoulême: Nota bene / Centre national de la bande dessinée et de l'image, 1998. 9–29.

Guido, Laurent. "Entre cauchemar et paranoïa : une introduction aux représentations de la peur dans le cinéma fantastique hollywoodien." *Les Peurs de Hollywood*. Ed. Laurent Guido. Lausanne: Antipodes, 2006. 7–40.

Haver, Gianni, and Michaël Meyer. "Du papier au pixel : les balancements intermédiatiques du corps super héroïque." *Du héros aux super héros, Théorème*, vol. 13. Ed. Claude Forest. Paris: Presses de la Sorbonne Nouvelle, 2009. 159–71.

Klock, Geoff. *How to Read Superhero Comics and Why*. New York: Continuum, 2003.

Kriegk, Jean-Samuel, and Jean-Jacques Launier. *Art ludique*. Paris: Sonatine, 2011.

Letort, Delphine. *Du Film noir au néo-noir : mythes et stéréotypes de l'Amérique (1941–2008)*. Paris: L'Harmattan, 2010.

Manning, Matthew, John Barber, and John Rhett Thomas. *Art of Marvel Studios*. New York: Marvel Comics, 2012.

Martel, Frédéric. *Mainstream : Enquête sur la guerre globale de la culture et des médias*. Paris: Flammarion, 2012.

Mingant, Nolwenn. *Hollywood à la conquête du monde : marchés, stratégies, influences*. Paris: CNRS, 2010.

Misiroglu, Gina. *The Superhero Book: The Ultimate Encyclopedia of Comic-Book Icons and Hollywood Heroes*. Detroit: Visible Ink, 2012.

Müller, Jürgen. "L'intermédialité, une nouvelle approche interdisciplinaire : perspectives théoriques et pratiques à l'exemple de la vision de la télévision." *Cinémas : revue d'études cinématographiques / Cinémas: Journal of Film Studies* 10.2–3 (2000): 105–34.

Oms, Marcel. "Un âge d'or sans innocence." *Cinéma et bande dessinée*. Ed. Gilles Ciment. Courbevoie: Corlet, 1990. 145–53.

Picciau, Kevin. "Marvel, super-héros de l'entertainment ?" *InaGlobal: La Revue des industries créatives et des médias*. Aug. 8, 2011. http://www.inaglobal.fr/edition/article/marvel-super-heros-de-lentertainment. Accessed on May 11, 2013.

Pierce, Scott. "Marvel Movie Magic." *Cinefantastique* 32.6 (2001): 32–34.

Rae Neil, and Jonathan Gray. "When Gen-X met the X-Men: Recontextualizing Comic Book Film Reception." *Film and Comic Books*. Eds. Ian Gordon, Mark Jancovich, and Matthew P. McAllister. Jackson: University Press of Mississippi, 2007. 86–100.

Quaresima, Léonardo, Laura Ester Stangalli, and Federico Zecca, eds. *Cinema e fumetto / Cinema and Comics*. Udine: Forum, 2009.

Raviv, Dan. *Comic War: Marvel's Battle for Survival*. New York: Broadway Books, 2002.

Rose, Frank. *Buzz*. Paris: Sonatine, 2012.

Salard, Pierre-Eric. "La seconde phase de l'univers Marvel au cinéma." *L'écran fantastique* 338 (2013): 54–59.

Salkowitz, Rob. *Comic-Con and the Business of Pop Culture*. Columbus, OH: McGraw-Hill, 2012.

Tomasovic, Dick. *Le Palimpseste noir : Notes sur l'impétigo, la terreur et le cinéma américain contemporain*. Crisnée: Yellow Now, 2002.

Tomasovic, Dick. "Images dessinées / images animées : stratégies et convergences de la firme Marvel." *Cinéma&Cie, International Film Studies Journal* 10.14–15 (Spring-Fall 2010): 55–61.

Tomasovic, Dick. "Le masque et la menace. Constitutions et crises identitaires de la figure super héroïque contemporaine." *Du héros au super héros : mutations cinématographiques*. Ed. Claude Forest, *Théorème*. Vol. 13. Presses de la Sorbonne Nouvelle, 2009. 173–84.

Tomasovic, Dick. "Les Greffes du corps animé : Winsor McCay, de la bande dessinée au film d'animation." *La Decima musa. The Tenth Muse. Le cinéma et les autres arts*. Eds. Leonardo Quaresima and Laura Vichi. Udine: Forum, 2001. 83–100.

Fritz the Cat (1972): From Crumb to Bakshi, Betraying the Author and Translating the Zeitgeist

JEAN-PAUL GABILLIET

In October 1969, the New York publisher Ballantine released a 10x13 collection of three stories featuring Fritz the Cat (fig. 30). The tabby was one of the main characters created by Robert Crumb, then a rising star of American underground comics. When TV producer Steve Krantz and animator Ralph Bakshi discovered the book, they hit on the idea of turning it into an animated feature film not designed for children.

In February 1970, negotiations to get Crumb to sign off on the adaptation rights started and proved extremely complicated because of the cartoonist's reluctance to authorize the making of a movie on which he would have no creative control. The film finally came out on April 12, 1972, after two chaotic years during which Bakshi and a team of animators, sometimes reduced to a minimum whenever production was running short on money, produced seventy-eight minutes of unprecedented animation (fig. 31). The $850,000 movie received an X rating at its release as some of its scenes were deemed "pornographic," but it ultimately grossed over a hundred million dollars. The positive reception of the public and most critics were not, however, entirely unanimous: Crumb repudiated the film even before it hit the theaters, even going so far as to have his name removed on all promotional material.

The artist had mixed feelings about the overall quality of the animation, but he mostly blamed Bakshi for what he regarded as the unacceptable distortion of his comics' original meaning and for adding elements he thought contrary to the spirit of his work. He was so appalled by the enthusiastic reception of the film that he soon published *Fritz the Cat "Superstar,"* a fifteen-page story recounting how the cat became cynical and obnoxious as a result of Hollywood celebrity culture and was eventually stabbed to death by one of his many ex-girlfriends (Gabilliet 93–97).

■ ■ ■

Fig. 30: cover of R. Crumb's *Fritz the Cat: 3 Big Stories!* (1969).

Fig. 31: original US poster of *Fritz the Cat* (Bakshi, 1972).

Ralph Bakshi's *Fritz the Cat* is a textbook example of the potential hurdles that arise in adapting a comic book to film, when the complexity of the adapting process matches the complexity of the source material and far exceeds the simple switch from black-and-white to color. Before discussing a number of issues relating to the transposition of Crumb's comic to the screen, it is important to underline some characteristics of the book published in October 1969. As its title suggests, *Fritz the Cat: 3 Big Stories!* did not contain a unified narrative but three separate stories featuring one character . . . of a sort. The stories were actually never intended to be published in a single volume in the first place. The collection was a marketing ploy designed by Ballantine to replicate the success of Viking Press's *Head Comix*, the anthology of Crumb comics that had unexpectedly become a runaway bestseller in the fall of 1968. At this early stage in Crumb's career, Fritz was the only one of his characters that had already appeared in a relatively large number of stories longer than the one- to three-page format that represented most of his comics output at the time. The first two stories of the Ballantine book were old material: the twenty-two-page "Fritz Bugs Out" had been published in the men's magazine *Cavalier* between February and October 1968, but actually drawn during the winter of 1964–65; the fifteen-page "Fritz the Cat: Special Agent for the CIA" had been unpublished since the magazine's creation in the spring of 1965. To expand the volume and stretch it to sixty-four pages, Crumb completed the sixteen pages of "Fritz the No-Good" in the fall of 1968, publishing it as the third story. In the film, Bakshi used the first and third stories, as well as the ten-page "Fritz the Cat" Crumb finished in the summer of 1965, first published in Viking Press's *Head Comix* in 1968. The animated film is thus based on two stories from 1964–65 ("Fritz Bugs Out" and "Fritz the Cat") and one from 1968 ("Fritz the No-Good").

This gap in chronology could be merely incidental had the cat been a "classic" character, i.e., one inscribed in the dynamic of a traditional serial narrative, like the protagonists of long-running, mass-audience newspaper strips or comic books, or European *bande dessinée* album series. But this was not so. Fritz was descended from one of the many animals, including Brombo the Panda and Fuzzy the Rabbit, that featured in the several dozen stories Robert and his older brother Charles drew in their notebooks throughout the fifties (Gabilliet 24–27). As Crumb became older, he continued to draw some of his characters in his sketchbooks and comics, hoping that one day they would get published. From 1964, Fritz became the recurring protagonist of several stories of various lengths, although he did not function as a character with a stable identity. Over eight years, Crumb successively cast him as a penniless musician returning to his old mother's shack in the countryside before fornicating with his little sister ("R. Crumb Comics and Stories"), a pop star assailed by groupies ("Fred the Teen-age Girl Pigeon"), a student-*poète maudit* beatnik rebel ("Fritz Bugs Out"), a secret agent on a mission to China ("Special Agent for the CIA"), an illusionist ("Fritz the Cat Magician"), yet another student more interested in bohemian life than in university ("Fritz the Cat"), a jobless slacker that gets kicked out of his home by his wife and ends up with various dropouts almost as clueless as himself ("Fritz the No-Good"), and finally a Hollywood star ("Fritz the Cat 'Superstar'").

The psychological and narrative continuity uniting all these stories was tenuous. Like many of Crumb's subsequent characters, Fritz was primarily one of his doubles, an embodiment of the alternately adolescent, cynical, sarcastic, and disillusioned views he cast on his own life and American society at the time. The cat rarely functioned in an autobiographical way however. Only in "Fritz the No-Good," a comic drawn in the autumn and winter of 1968, did clear allusions to his life show through: fatherhood, financial aid, the profligate life outside of home, and the encounter with radical political ideas refer to specific biographical elements of 1968. Similarly, a number of images of the final Fritz story bore the marks of the latent depression he suffered from 1971 onwards.

In other words, Fritz the Cat was not a classic character as they appeared in mainstream comics of the time, but rather a kind of Everyman constantly reshaped according to the whim of Crumb's narrative desires. All this highlights the artificiality of the marketing ploy that had given birth to Ballantine's Fritz collection; the three stories gathered there did, indeed, feature one protagonist, but one that changed radically from one story to the next. This fact alone foreshadows the great complexity of the process that marked the film adaptation.

■ ■ ■

The creative encounter between Crumb and Bakshi was one between two individuals with huge egos. In 1969, Bakshi was in charge of the low-budget *Spider-Man* television cartoon series (ABC, 1967–1970), which to him was the rock bottom of what could be done in animation. His pet project was to create a feature-length animated cartoon for grown-ups that would break with all traditional audience expectations regarding the genre. He had begun to jot down rough ideas for a film entitled *Heavy Traffic*, about an animation artist trying to live from his art in a deprived urban area. However, his producer Steve Krantz warned him that such an unorthodox project would never find financing (in fact, an ill-inspired prediction, since *Heavy Traffic* was the film he was able to make in 1973 following the success of *Fritz the*

Cat). Bakshi discovered the R. Crumb book shortly after its release in the fall of 1969 during a visit to Greenwich Village's East Side Book Store. He showed it to Steve Kranz shortly after and told him that Crumb had accomplished in comics what he wanted to do in film. He would later summarize his opinion succinctly with the phrase: "They were animals fucking" (Gibson and McDonnell 62). The producer was amenable to the arguments of the animation artist (to the point that he later claimed that he, not Bakshi, had fathered the project), especially since he knew he could sell the film on the strength of Crumb's name and persona. Bakshi then rushed in headlong to make hundreds of preparatory drawings for Crumb to see when the filmmakers flew him over to New York in February 1970. The rest of the story is a series of misunderstandings between the two illustrators, which has never been cleared up. Essentially, it boils down to a simple notion: Crumb has never forgiven Bakshi for making a Bakshi movie instead of a Crumb movie. What crime did the animator commit?

■ ■ ■

I will not go into the chaotic conditions in which the film was made and its erratic financing. The project was rejected by Warner Bros., then picked up by Cinemation Industries, a company specializing in low-budget, independent, and exploitation movies (Gibson and McDonnell 72). Adding to the chaos was Bakshi's impulsive decision to relocate his New York studio to Los Angeles in April and May 1971 (Gibson and McDonnell 77). The organization of the production labor was just as unusual as the film itself: Bakshi never provided a detailed storyboard; his team would discover overnight what sequences they would be working on next; and, because of budget constraints, he checked the timing of the animation simply by flipping each animator's drawings in his hand instead of relying on pencil tests to spot issues before the animation was inked, painted, and photographed against the background paintings (Barrier, "Filming, Part One").[1] However, the film's technical weaknesses were not the main sources of Crumb's dissatisfaction.

As far as the writing was concerned, Bakshi was forced to base his script on heterogeneous material—four stories connected by no continuity. He immediately dismissed "Secret Agent for the CIA," a somewhat heavy-handed parody of James Bond films, to retain the three stories focused on bohemian life and marginality. Even with this main thread, they were still too distinct to be simply juxtaposed, since they were part of a creative process in which consistency and the continuity of the story's main character were secondary in the first place. Bakshi added to this his own artistic take by working adult humor into an animated film and satirizing contemporary society, while using the naturalistic imagery and situations reminiscent of the early twentieth century's Ashcan School painters (Culhane D13; Gibson and McDonnell 77).

Predictably enough, Bakshi's adaptation intertwines fidelity to, and deviation from, its source material. After the pre-title sequence and the credits where three workers are having a discussion during lunch on top of a skyscraper under construction, with one of the three urinating on the head of a hippie passing by on the sidewalk (pure Bakshi!), the first fifteen minutes is a relatively faithful transposition of the story "Fritz the Cat" with four added scenes [3:13–16.54]. The first depicts the discussion between three coeds explaining their fascination with African American culture to a crow, and the other three scenes feature two police officers drawn as pigs, which in the original comics are anonymous characters that appear only on the final page. The next sequence, where Fritz takes refuge in a synagogue with the police officers in pursuit, is Bakshi's brainchild [16:55–22:15].

After the image fades to black, we find Fritz at New York University, where he is a student. For forty minutes, the film follows the storyline of "Fritz Bugs Out," from the sixth page onwards, and expands on it considerably [22:16–63:09]. The scenes that are not in Crumb's comic are the following: the crows' conversation in a Harlem bar [27:21–29:59], the row between the bartender and Duke the raven [33:25–34:52], a dialogue between two pig policemen and a car chase [36:42–38:23], an extended riot scene and the subsequent police and army intervention [48:10–52:26], and the hillbilly who slaughters chickens in his truck [60:40–61:10], just to name a few. Bakshi also chose to expand certain scenes; for example, page eleven of "Fritz Bugs Out" becomes a four-and-a-half-minute-long scene during which Fritz and Duke enter a nightclub, Bertha the boa-clad female raven makes Fritz smoke several joints until he loses all self-control and ends up chasing her to make love to her [41:21–45:49]. In addition to diegetic expansion, Bakshi added psychedelic background color and music the moment Fritz feels the effects (quite spectacular in his case) of marijuana [42:30].

The final narrative sequence consists of a two-minute introductory scene in which the heroin addict, Blue the rabbit, and his girlfriend, Harriet the mare, are introduced [56:56–58:50], followed by a ten-minute sequence in which Fritz meets a group of sadistic and disturbing revolutionaries and reluctantly participates in a terrorist attack [63:10–72:42]. The latter is a dark reinterpretation of pages 9–12 of "Fritz the No-Good," in which the cat latches on to an underground cell of no-account radicals.

The final sequence of the film, where we see Fritz about to die in a hospital before regaining his energy for a bit of nooky, does not appear in Crumb's comic [72:43–76:08].

▪ ▪ ▪

As adaptations go, Bakshi's *Fritz the Cat* can be considered as a middle-of-the-road product. It is not an example of a film that is perfectly faithful to a comic, as *Sin City* (2005) is to Frank Miller's original material. Neither can it be put at the other end of the spectrum, where comic characters are cast in scenarios that amalgamate multiple source stories and dilute them into a script that conforms to a cinematic rather than a comics intertext. One need only think of the numerous Marvel and DC superheroes, whose transposition to the big screen is somehow "facilitated" by the narrative plasticity of franchised characters that are meant to appear in an infinite number of stories with narrative formulas evolving over a long period of time.

Bakshi implements four principal adaptation strategies—subtraction, expansion, addition, and modification—which are sometimes used simultaneously.[2] I will just mention *subtraction* in passing, a term referring to the disappearance of sequences of variable length from the source comic. Of the three stories used to make the film, almost all of "Fritz the Cat" (nine pages and the first panel of page 10), and half of "Fritz Bugs Out" (eleven pages out of twenty-two; essentially pages 7 to 13 and 16 to 20) are preserved; of the 16 pages of "Fritz the No-Good," only the dialogues remain of the last four panels on page 9, page 10 in its entirety minus the last frame, and two panels on page 12.

As far as *expansion* is concerned, several scenes retain entire sections of Crumb's original dialogue, although they occur in situations that differ from the comics. When Fritz, having returned to college, gives a monologue on the futility of wasting his life away while studying [22:16–25:37], the film's dialogue reproduces the text on pages 6 and 7 of "Fritz Bugs Out" almost word for word. However, the passage in the comic where the cat thinks out loud at his desk and sets fire to his books (p. 6, strips 3 and 4; p. 7, strips 1 and 2) becomes a dream sequence in the animation film and lasts more than three minutes. Against a black background, Fritz walks through an open door, finds himself wrapped head to foot in paper, runs to the window, opens it, sees the image of Honeybunch Kaminsky, whom he screws before returning to take the papers to Heinz the pig's office; he then rushes into a tunnel of female breasts and piles up sheets of paper which he then ignites by spitting fire before waking up and returning to the reality of his dorm room [22:16–25:37]. The expansion of Crumb's original diegesis is a recurrent strategy implemented throughout the film; it allows for the adaptation of static scenes in the source comic book to the temporality of animation, that is to say, the sustained rhythm of film editing. Other examples include the wild chase of Fritz and Duke in the car they stole [34:53–38:44], which corresponds to page 10 of "Fritz Bugs Out," as well as the following sequence, from the moment the pair enter the crows' nightclub to the time Fritz makes love to Bertha [41:21–45:49], which corresponds to page 11.

The *addition* of scenes not in Crumb's comic is somewhat artificial. The discussion between the three coeds and the crow on Washington Square at the beginning of the film [4:54–06:00] is part of the comic, though wordless ("Fritz the Cat," page 2, panels 5 and 6; page 3, panel 2). This is the only time Bakshi fills in an ellipsis in the source narrative, changing a character's persona in the process. In the comic (page 3, panels 3 to 5), Fritz makes the crow leave by giving him a tip on a drug deal; but in the film, the crow leaves by himself after the viewer has understood that he is a queen with no interest whatsoever in the three girls [5:45–6:00]. Otherwise, the added scenes correspond to moments that do not exist in the comic: the pre-credits with three workers sitting on top of a skyscraper under construction, all the scenes with the two pig policemen, the scene at the synagogue, the discussion between the three crows in a Harlem bar, the game of pool and the row with the bartender, the riot in the ghetto, the death of Duke the crow, the police intervention and air raids on the ghetto, the scene with the junkie rabbit biker and the mare in the desert, the hillbilly who slaughters his chickens, and the last five minutes of the film, from the moment when Fritz sabotages the power plant until his recovery in the hospital room. None of these scenes are to be found in Crumb's original material.

The final strategy, *modification*, concerns what happens when elements from the source comic are inserted in a context that changes their implicit or explicit original meaning. Bakshi mainly used it in the second part of the film. After ditching his companion Winston in the middle of the desert, Fritz follows the rabbit biker Blue and Harriet the mare to a sinister cemetery that houses the secret lair of a terrorist cell whose members are John, a snake in a red monk's robe with an overly affected lisp, and a cruel and sadistic female lizard. They inform Fritz and Blue that they are about to commit a series of attacks in the neighboring town in order to take control of it. The scene turns to chaos. When Harriet tells Blue she wants to leave, he lashes out and whips her with his chain. Fritz tries to defend her, to no avail. Eventually, she is chained to a bed under the sadistic gaze of the rabbit, snake, and lizard lady. In the next scene, the viewers see her half-naked (seemingly raped) outside, with Fritz trying to comfort her. Without much enthusiasm, he then prepares to carry out the attack. Once he has set up the dynamite, he changes his mind, but the lizard lady triggers the explosion that sends him to the hospital.

This whole scene crystallizes Crumb's resentment toward Bakshi. In the original story, Fritz runs into his old buddy, Fuz the rabbit, who then introduces him to a radical far-left cell jointly led by Spick the lion (inspired by artist Spain Rodriguez) and a nameless bird; the attack Fritz and Fuz were to carry out turns into a fiasco when they realize they forgot the matches to light the fuse of their dynamite. Crumb created this story at the end of 1968 as a satire of revolutionary action, yet without calling into question the radical ideology in which he sincerely believed at the time. That was why he never forgave Bakshi for changing his original story into a conservative critique of late 1960s radicalism and featuring far-right revolutionaries with ambiguous sexual proclivities (John and the lizard lady are obviously gay), prompting Fritz to say: "You're full of shit. All you care about is a reason to hurt, to destroy, and to blow up!" [70:47]; "You don't know what a real revolution is, none of you sons of bitches do!" [71:02]. Notwithstanding Crumb's criticisms, Bakshi made Fritz look a lot more likeable in this passage than in the original scene. In the comic, the cat passively smokes a joint, while the conspirators plan their attack; he is the first to rape Harriet the mare, who is tied on the floor, and he finally participates in the terrorist attack not out of conviction, but because he has nothing better to do.

■ ■ ■

Bakshi's adaptation strategies led to a result that differs significantly from what Crumb had put in his Fritz the Cat stories, both in form and substance. However, the difference in chronology is a factor that significantly widens the gap between the *comix* and the movie. The film, released on April 12, 1972, opens with a shot of Times Square; in the middle of the screen, the words "the 1960s" appear with a voice-over saying: "Hey, yeah. The 1960s? Happy times, heavy times." *Fritz the Cat* is first and foremost a movie of the early 1970s that looks back at what was then already the previous decade.[3] The only specific historical reference in the film is the Six-Day War (June 5–10, 1967) in the synagogue scene [20:58]. This allusion establishes the action in June 1967 and therefore implies that Fritz and his girlfriend Winston travel to California to take part in the Summer of Love in San Francisco. Even though, over forty years later, Bakshi's film may convey a 1960s feel to most early twenty-first-century viewers, one should keep in mind that it was fundamentally a product of the 1970s.

In a column published in the *New York Times* in July 1972, Lee Beaupre commented in extremely harsh terms on the critical success of the film at the time of its release three months earlier. For him, the critical enthusiasm around Bakshi's film reflected a *zeitgeist* that delighted in the failure of the utopian projects of the counterculture of the 1960s: "Now, with most youths having abandoned violent activism, with the drug scene receding and with Watts and Kent State only a memory, our reviewers would seem back in their own Nixonerous element" (Beaupre D7). As Beaupre noted, the satire practiced by Crumb from inside the countercultural movement between 1964 and 1968 was reused a few years later to proclaim the superficiality of the counterculture and the political illegitimacy of radical activism. While the film was appreciated by critics who were not familiar with Crumb's comics in the first place, such as Vincent Canby in *The New York Times* (Canby D3), reviews by those who had been closer to the countercultural movement were mixed. A case in point was *Rolling Stone* film critic Thomas Albright, who wrote a laudatory piece after watching a thirty-minute cut several months before the film's release, but radically changed his mind when he saw the final theatrical version ("Crumb's Cat" 14; "Fritz" 74).

Its *succès de scandale* was, of course, largely due to its X rating, promising viewers an animated counterpart to the then nascent "mainstream" porn film.[4] Yet several critics pointed out the relative paucity of sex in the film; in the *New York Times* of April 29, 1972, Roger Greenspun argued that only the bathroom orgy scene warranted the X rating, while Michael Barrier, in a 1973 issue of his prozine *Funnyworld*, deemed that "as a pornographic film, the movie is a dud, because there isn't very much sex in it" ("Filming, Part Two"). In fact, the film does not contain any realistic or explicit representations of male or female genitalia, and the passages where characters are shown having sex barely add up to ten minutes of a seventy-minute film. Indeed, by early twenty-first-century standards, *Fritz the Cat* is not very pornographic.

An additional feature warranting closer scrutiny in light of the main film genres at the time is the emphasis on crows, that is to say, African Americans. Fritz appears on screen next to or among crows for over a third of the film in scenes that are extensive elaborations of the original story [27:58–52:26], as I have indicated above. Bakshi never explained why he made this choice, but several elements suggest that the process of adaptation and its resulting scenes steered the film in the direction of *blaxploitation*, B films featuring black lead actors (Koven 2010). This genre, which reached its peak in the first half of the 1970s, was one of the main niches of Cinemation, *Fritz*'s distributor. The long central sequence staged in Harlem—at least until the riot during which Duke the crow is killed by a stray bullet and the subsequent intervention of military aircraft dropping napalm on the ghetto [48:10–52:26]—can be read as a succession of stereotypical blaxploitation scenes: the exclusively

African American bar where a white man shows up, with the black bartender expressing his contempt for white people and the ensuing row between the bartender and the black customer who protects the white man; the road trip in a stolen car; the African American nightclub where a white guy (or cat ...) samples marijuana, succumbs to hallucinations, and eventually pursues a voluptuous and licentious black lady who makes fun of the size of his penis before finally agreeing to have sex with him. The advertising campaign for the general public was distinct from the one targeted at black audiences, highlighting the film's "90 minutes of violence, excitement and SEX" with posters featuring crows next to Fritz (Gibson and McDonnell 72).

The contemporary sociocultural context also provides clues as to the overwhelmingly positive reception of the film. In the early 1970s, the momentum of social change that had run through the previous decade collapsed with the gradual withdrawal of US troops from Vietnam and the mutation of the utopian, countercultural agendas into "lifestyles" advocating free love and soft drug use. By then, these movements were largely disconnected from their ideological roots and had ceased to be alternatives to the social conformism of the postwar period. But doing away with conformism did not mean the same thing for Crumb as it did for Bakshi.

Robert Crumb broke with his social milieu, the white lower middle-class, by representing in comics the urban bohemianism of the 1960s, the hippie lifestyle that he experienced firsthand and whose value system was diametrically opposed to his family's culture of consumerism and materialism. Bakshi's background was significantly different. Born in Haifa in 1938, a son of Jewish immigrants, he arrived in the United States when he was only a few months old and grew up in working-class Brooklyn. For him, breaking with his parents' desire to fit into American society never took the form of a generalized rejection of consumer society, but of an aesthetic project: the weaving of naturalism into animated cartoons, which, historically, had been the genre most constrained by social convention, both in film and television. This was the reason why several scenes added by Bakshi were deliberately designed to stage "real" people. The pre-credit discussion between the three workers [0:27–2:31], the scene with the three old rabbis inside the synagogue [16:57–18:15]—not really spontaneous, as the voices are those of Bakshi's father and two of his uncles—and the scene with the three crows that opens the sequence at the Harlem bar [27:21–29:59] correspond to "authentic," preexisting dialogues with which the director constructed scenes he intended to be naturalistic (Gibson and McDonnell 67, 77). In this case, the three scenes have nothing in common except that they endow the story with a certain atmosphere. The strategy works reasonably well for the Harlem bar sequence, but mainly produces a slice-of-life effect in the other two.

Crumb was no stranger to naturalism due to his longtime obsession with 1920s and 1930s American popular culture, especially its cartoons and music. One of his first assignments as a professional artist was a series of drawings depicting Harlem street life that appeared in Harvey Kurtzman's magazine *Help!* (Crumb, *Sketchbook Reports*) in January 1965. Later on, the naturalistic bent of his work became more obvious, particularly in his contributions to Harvey Pekar's yearly magazine *American Splendor* from 1976 onward (Pekar and Crumb, *Harv & Bob*). However, the Fritz the Cat stories corresponded to an earlier stage of his career where comics were a means to express his deep aspirations for individual emancipation, while his experiments with naturalism at the time were confined to the hundreds of drawings with which he would fill his sketchbooks.[5]

If naturalism was the aesthetic point of contact between the two men, it was their disagreement over the work's political meaning that caused the divide. Whereas Crumb's comic satirized the counterculture without calling into question its basic principles, Bakshi turned it into an animated cartoon that conveyed a counter-nostalgic message resonant with the post-utopian disenchantment that permeated the seventies (Schulman 14–16; Friedman 24–47). The movie, therefore, staged the moral and ideological bankruptcy of the sixties counterculture, while cashing in on two contemporary film genres, pornography and blaxploitation. If his adaptation was indeed a "betrayal" of Crumb's ideological horizon in the stories starring his feline double, it "translated" at the same time the middle-class' co-opting of the sixties' hedonistic values and practices after they were irremediably purged of their utopian and reformist aspirations.

Notes

1. Michael Barrier conducted a detailed and uncompromising investigation of the making of the film based on interviews with Bakshi and several members of his team in the two long articles he published in his professional magazine *Funnyworld* in 1972 and 1973. Jon M. Gibson and Chris McDonnell's version in their authorized biography *Unfiltered: The Complete Ralph Bakshi* is a more hagiographic account of the animator's career. A third source offering insight into the material aspects of Bakshi's work is the thirty-minute documentary by Georg Stefan Troller, *Robert Crumb: Comics und Katerideen*, broadcast by ZDF (Germany's second TV network) as part of the 1972 *Personenschreibung* broadcast. The latter is specifically devoted to the film adaptation of Crumb's comic and contains several scenes showing the artist and his family on their farm in Potter Valley, California, as well as Ralph Bakshi and Steve Kranz

working on the feature film in New York, with several scenes where the animator photographs and records passers-by on the street.

2. These are strategies identified by Robert Stam (34) and other theorists of adaptation.

3. The historiography of the 1970s is distinct from that dealing with the sixties. For a general historical approach, see, for example, Bruce J. Schulman's *The Seventies: The Great Shift in American Culture, Society, and Politics* (2001). For film, see Lester D. Friedman (ed.), *American Cinema of the 1970s: Themes and Variations* (2007) or, in French, *Le Cinéma américain des années 70* by Jean-Baptiste Thoret—although both authors, regardless of their comprehensive agendas, never mention Bakshi's movie.

4. *Deep Throat* (Gerard Damiano) and *Behind the Green Door* (Artie and Jim Mitchell), the first two US box-office-hit porn films, were released in the wake of *Fritz*, in June and December 1972, respectively.

5. For a bibliography of Crumb's sketchbooks, see Gabilliet 213.

Works Cited

Albright, Thomas. "Crumb's Cat Fritz Comes to Screen." *Rolling Stone* 97 (December 9, 1971): 14.

Albright, Thomas. "Fritz the Cat." *Rolling Stone* 109 (May 25, 1972): 74.

Barrier, Michael. "The Filming of *Fritz the Cat*, Part One." *Funnyworld* 14 (Spring 1972). http://www.michaelbarrier.com/Funnyworld/FritzPartOne/FritzOne.htm. Accessed on March 15, 2013.

Barrier, Michael. "The Filming of *Fritz the Cat*, Part Two." *Funnyworld* 15 (Fall 1973). http://www.michaelbarrier.com/Funnyworld/FritzPartTwo/FritzFour.htm. Accessed on March 15, 2013.

Beaupre, Lee. "Phooey on *Fritz the Cat*." *New York Times* (July 2, 1972): D7.

Canby, Vincent. "'Fritz' Is A Far Cry from Disney." *New York Times* (April 30, 1972): D1, D3.

Crumb, Robert. *The Complete Fritz the Cat*. New York: Belier Press, 1979.

Crumb, Robert. *Fritz the Cat*. Paris: Cornélius, 2013.

Crumb, Robert. *R. Crumb's Fritz the Cat. 3 Big Stories!* New York: Ballantine, 1969. Includes "Fritz Bugs Out" (1964–65), "Special Agent for the C.I.A." (1965) and "Fritz the No-Good" (1968).

Crumb, Robert. *R. Crumb's Head Comix*. New York: Viking Press, 1968. Includes "Fritz the Cat" (1965).

Crumb, Robert. *Sketchbook Reports*. Paris: Cornélius, 2000.

Culhane, John. "Ralph Bakshi: Iconoclast of Animation." *New York Times* (March 22, 1981): D13.

Friedman, Lester D., ed. *American Cinema of the 1970s: Themes and Variations*. New Brunswick, NJ: Rutgers University Press, 2007.

Fritz the Cat. Dir. Ralph Bakshi. With the voices of Skip Hinnant (Fritz), Rosetta LeNoire (Bertha, other voices), John McCurry (Blue, John, other voices), Judy Engles (Winston Schwartz, Lizard Leader), and Phil Seuling (Pig Cop #2). Steve Krantz, 1972. DVD. MGM Home Entertainment, 2002.

Gabilliet, Jean-Paul. *R. Crumb*. Pessac: PU de Bordeaux, 2012.

Gibson, Jon M., and Chris McDonnell. *Unfiltered: The Complete Ralph Bakshi*. New York: Universe, 2008.

Greenspun, Roger. "An X-Rated Cartoon." *New York Times* (April 29, 1972): 19.

Koven, Mikel J. *Blaxploitation Films*. Harpenden: Kamera Books, 2010.

Pekar, Harvey, and Robert Crumb. *Harv & Bob*. Paris: Cornélius, 2010.

Personenbeschreibung: Robert Crumb. Comics und Katerideen. Dir. Georg Stefan Troller. Zweites Deutsches Fernsehen, 1972. DVD.

Schulman, Bruce J. *The Seventies: The Great Shift in American Culture, Society, and Politics*. New York: Free Press, 2001.

Stam, Robert. "Introduction: The Theory and Practice of Adaptation." *Literature and Film: A Guide to the Theory and Practice of Film Adaptation*. Eds. Robert Stam and Alessandra Raengo. Malden, MA, Oxford, and Carlton, Australia: Blackwell, 2005. 1–52.

Thoret, Jean-Baptiste. *Le Cinéma américain des années 70*. Paris: Cahiers du cinéma, 2009.

Adapting a Graphic Novel into Film: Historicity and the Play of Signs in *Corto Maltese : La cour secrète des arcanes* (Pascal Morelli, 2002), an Adaptation of *Corto Maltese in Siberia* by Hugo Pratt

PHILIPPE BOURDIER

In his "Commentaries on Art," Jean-Antoine Dominique Ingres argued that "to draw does not mean simply to reproduce contours; drawing does not consist merely of lines: drawing is also expression, the inner form, the plane, the modeling" (112). Expressing what was not a common aesthetic view at the time, Ingres emphasized how the visual dimension could not be reduced to the figurative content immediately perceptible to the eye. He also underscored how underlying the creative act of drawing are more enigmatic operations requiring the artist's attention and talent. This discourse also holds for comics, whose storytelling potential appeared early on as a supplement to the image, with narrative seen as fundamental to the very definition of this mode of artistic creation (Blanchard 1969; Lacassin 1982). This discourse is also pertinent when approaching cinematography from a genetic point of view, as "an experimental space of the visible and of forms" (Rancière 89). As such, from a semiotic perspective, the complexity of film lends itself to an investigation of signification and to analyses.[1] The need to broaden perspectives on comics and film is especially useful when considering a form of filmmaking that claims it originates not only in the writing of a literary work, but even more so in those visual and narrative discursive creations we call comics. Is the film marked by the forms and choices characteristic of comics? To what extent does the film version lay claim to, reveal, or betray its roots?

I will address some of these questions by examining an adaptation of a comic by Hugo Pratt, *Corto Maltese in Siberia*, published in France in 1979 and previously as a serial in the monthly comics magazine *Linus*, from January 1974 to July 1977. What is peculiar about this adaptation is that Corto Maltese's twenty-fourth adventure was brought to the screen not as a feature film, but as an animated film by Pascal Morelli in 2002. This adaptation raises several questions: what form does this crossing of genres take, this transfer from comics to animation, from the icono-verbal to the visual, narrative, and sonic space of film? And how does a film portraying a comics hero adored by an often expert adult readership offer semiotic equivalences between the comics characterized by Pratt's "clear line" and the animated film intended for an audience not limited to children?

These questions may find some theoretical answers if we consider film adaptations of comics as the result of economic contingencies: technical choices based on production costs, the choice of actors, identification of the target audience, editing that conforms to TV formats, and so on. There are many constraints, as with any film. Reconstructing the historicity of these aspects to gauge their significance is thus of paramount importance. However, the specificity of this adaptation, which establishes a contiguity between two iconic spaces, also invites us to revisit the residual issue of fidelity in film adaptation from a semiotic perspective. I will argue that this adaptation is marked by the economic and cultural context in which it is embedded. It also seems that the animated film adaptation of a comic offers a play of shifting signs that enhances the meanings of, and responses to, this type of film. Focusing on both the visual characteristics and the actors' voices should enable us to broach, from a semiotic perspective, the theoretical issues raised by adapting a comic into animated film.

Adaptation and Historicity

When Morelli, at the request of Robert Rhea, producer at Ellipsanime Studios, launched the project of adapting Pratt's comic into an animated feature, he knew he would have to overcome difficulties and make choices that derived from the translation of comics to film, as well as from the specificity of Pratt's work.[2] A few years before the production began in 1997, Pratt had agreed to what was to become the first animated film based on his *Corto Maltese* series. As a challenge, he offered a rather vague condition: "I'd like you to do *Corto,* if you do him better than *Tintin*."[3] The condition addressed to the film director and to producer Robert Rea, both fans of Pratt's work, does not seem to have governed the visual contiguity adopted for the film (from comics drawings to animation), since the project for this mode of adaptation existed before Pratt's comment, and since the artist, who died in 1995, would know very little about the project.

Prior to this project, Morelli had worked on a series of animated films for television, including *Sophie et Virginie* (TF1, 1990–92), *Gadget Boy and Heather* (Disney, 1995–96), and *Les Exploits d'Arsène Lupin* (YTV, 1996). His personal interest in the work of *Corto Maltese* dates back to a unique bond forged in childhood: "Like so many boys of my generation, I discovered Corto Maltese in *Pif Gadget* when I was about twelve. I did not like it at first, but I had, of course, never really tried to read it. [. . .] Pratt opened the door to a confusing, at times illogical and contradictory, but always fascinating world: the world of adults."[4]

The project was initially rejected in 1997 due to the complexity of its production in the two proposed forms: a television series accompanied by a TV movie for RAI. However, from 1989 onward, a climate favorable to French animation films allowed the production of the film to take on greater momentum, eventually leading to a feature-length animation. *La Cour secrète des arcanes*, *The Triplets of Belleville* (Sylvain Chomet, 2003), *Raining Cats and Frogs* (Jacques-Rémy Girerd, 2003), and *The Rain Children* (Philippe Leclerc, 2003) received significant support from the CNC (Centre national du cinéma et de l'image animée) and advances on earnings. The awareness of the emerging importance of what in animation became known as the "French touch," as well as the successful ratings[5] of the French-Canadian television series produced by Robert Rhea, *The Adventures of Tintin* (FR3 / The Family Channel / HBO, 1991–92),[6] adapting the canonical work by Hergé, facilitated considerable investment in Morelli's film project: 400 employees for five years, for over 1,000 shots requiring 500,000 drawings.

Like *The Adventures of Tintin*, the project was intended for a wide audience. It was embedded in a specific historical context of French production, characterized by the adaptation of comic books held in high esteem. The support for animated film was an important factor in the adaptation of a comic with an ambitious narrative, novelistic complexity, and, above all, a paradoxical view of adventure.

Corto Maltese is an enigmatic character, an adventurer whom the panels nonetheless depict as rather static. Although caught in violent situations, he appears serene in this particular adventure set in an Asian continent in chaos, as he does in the other adventures related in the series. Indeed, the Russia, Siberia, and Manchuria of 1919 are traversed by armored trains carrying the gold of deposed tsars. Held by a counterrevolutionary government, this gold arouses greed—that of a perverse duchess and a cruel general—and the interest of other characters whose motives are more ambiguous and violent than political. Secret societies are at the heart of the action; adventurers, driven by the desire to lay their hands on a huge treasure, seem to act on a whim, without any plan, sometimes even going against their previous actions.

The hero himself is no exception in this universe populated by shady characters. His complicity with Rasputin, an elusive figure who does not obey the rules of sincere friendship, challenges readers accustomed to more schematic

Fig. 32: *Corto Maltese : La cour secrète des Arcanes* (Morelli, 2002): Corto meets Rasputin.

characters (fig. 32). In adventure stories, the faithful sidekick does not constantly threaten the hero: "I could kill you, Corto Maltese / Oh! You will kill me again" [6:30]. Pratt's creative freedom gives rise to a fictional world where there is confusion between characters, and where reactions are sometimes illogical or unexpected. The characters often disregard the conventional bonds uniting the hero to the other characters. The hero, Corto Maltese, responding to the call of adventure and traveling far from his safe haven, does not find in Rasputin a mentor who would guide him to a more "spiritual" world and whom he would ultimately surpass; this runs counter to the archetypal character of the adventurer, as defined by Joseph Campbell (1949).

These complex and unexplained relationships, which have fascinated generations of young readers, function like an entry into a sometimes bitter and paradoxical adult world marked by nostalgia, which the hero overcomes through adventure. However, would the audiences of the animated film rediscover the original quality that struck them when reading the 126-page-long *Corto Maltese in Siberia*?[7] What are the forms of equivalence between the two, given that the adaptation was conceived from the outset as a film intent on reaching the widest possible audience and achieving box-office success? According to Morelli, the freedom and uniqueness of this comic, "the digression of the characters, where the enigmas remain unresolved, [are] part of the charm of the stories of Corto Maltese" (2). However, can this freedom be a source of cinematic creativity and be greeted favorably by a broad audience, and not just by a few passionate and loyal readers? The questions informing Morelli's directorial decisions give rise to a more general reflection on the adaptation of comics to animation and the notorious question of fidelity.

Theoretical Problems When Adapting a Comic into an Animated Film

The characteristics of the adaptation process will be approached from a semiotic perspective. In its definition of the iconic sign, Groupe μ offers a conceptual framework that has renewed the conception of the visual sign by complexifying it. Indeed, it is because the "referent is not an object of reality, but at the same time and always, a culturalized object" that it is a complex object (141). Groupe μ considers the iconic sign to be the result of a relationship between three elements: the iconic signifier, the type, and the referent. Signifier and referent are marked by the fact that both have "commensurable" spatial characteristics that require transformation (Groupe μ 141). If we extend this view of the iconic sign to the regime of film images derived from comics, it is this kind of relationship that can play a role in the appreciation of film adaptations. The question as to whether the film depicts the same places, characters, and world can then be raised, as well as the issue of fidelity to the source. Generally present in the discourses that comprise a film's reception, the question of an adaptation's fidelity has often been subject to sweeping generalizations, as Robert Stam points out: "When we say an adaptation has been 'unfaithful' to the original, the very violence of the term gives expression to the intense sense of betrayal we feel when a film adaptation fails to capture what we see as the fundamental narrative, thematic, or aesthetic features of its literary source" (Stam 14). In *Traité du signe visuel*, this feeling and discourse are dubbed the "power" of the visual channel; they lead to "the elaboration of constructs that appear self-evident (such as line, surface, contour, shape, content)" (Groupe μ 63). Accordingly, Morelli's film can be appreciated in a diametrically opposite way, depending on whether the viewers are old or new readers of *Corto Maltese in Siberia*.

Originally published in black-and-white on thick paper, which further highlighted the black ink of the drawings, the album was reprinted in color several times from 1982 onward with different covers, as was common practice for the publisher (Casterman) at the time. In the first color edition, prefaced by Oreste Del Buono, a film critic and friend of Pratt's, color was added using watercolors by Pratt; this was repeated in the 2000 reprint. These editorial characteristics may have inspired the color choices for the film images, which were designed to be faithful to the original album so as not to upset *Corto Maltese* fans. A different relationship between the cognitive constructions arising from the reception of the film images and those of the source comic, whose images are anchored in memory, is established depending on whether one has read the comic in its black-and-white or color editions. These responses are part of a network of endless comparisons between comic and film insofar as, for Groupe μ, the film's énoncé establishes systems based on the play of oppositions.

This is equally true of the lines of the drawings or, in semiotic terminology, the combination of "texture" and the "formeme position." (The "formeme" refers to the three parameters—position, dimension, orientation—that define form.) Pratt's rough line is deliberately sketchy; drawn by a steady hand, the outlines turn back on themselves and thicken, evolving into sharp contours which paradoxically approximate the clear line. Without giving in to the temptation of making a feature film, which demands a different reflection on the choice of images for adaptation (from the image drawn for the panel to the storyboard image designed for the shot) as was the case with other French films produced shortly after,[8] Morelli seems to have conceived his film by combining fidelity to, and emancipation from, the original comic. These choices show how the animated film responds differently to the question of the relation between film and drawn or painted work, a problem formulated in more general terms by Joëlle Moulin: "Where does this familiar yet unknown *jouissance* of the gaze come from that overcomes us in front of a film screen, as if the projected image exposed another image, exalted another presence?" (1)

The other presence the film image celebrates is that of the first image, easily recognizable, since the character is well-known. The film can also be seen as the result of the tension between the gridded image and the moving image, between the original story and the story created for film. In an adaptation, the latter would constitute the "anchor of meaning," while the cinematic text would be "the movement of production-dismissal of the signifier,"[9] to use Marie-Claire Ropars-Wuilleumier's phrase (67). This tension can be clarified through the second semiotic relationship of the iconic sign; it concerns the link between the referent and type. A type is defined as "a category of percepts grouped in a movement that neglects certain characteristics judged as non-pertinent" (Groupe μ 143). This is a process that functions as a means for stabilization and abstraction, and makes it possible to single out characteristics from a plurality of images that are then taken as a paradigm. When the type is confronted with the referent, the main issue concerns the level of conformity of the detail to the whole, which, in the case of an adaptation, applies to the relation between the film and the comic.

For instance, consider the hero. From the project's beginning, the audience's familiarity with Corto Maltese made fidelity requisite for the director and his team.[10] The screenplay's author, Thierry Thomas, understood from the outset that animating the romantic sailor required a certain amount of respect so as not to offend first-time viewers of the adaptation. To a certain extent, the animated film character must be in accordance with its model, whose visual details undeniably constitute a paradigm: the same shape, silhouette, dominant color, and brightness. Color saturation is more pronounced in the film because of the change in medium. This is the case for most of the film, though not always.

In terms of content (what the Groupe μ calls "expressiveness"), the film sometimes differs significantly from the comic. In the comic, the hero rarely intervenes in violent action scenes requiring hectic line work that could endanger Corto Maltese's lofty demeanor. By contrast, in the film, from the scene on the junk onward, the hero displays energy in the fierce fight scenes on the junk, in the snow, and on the train. The visual type of the adventurer participating in violent actions is thus set against its referent, the comics' hero, who is more a witness of than a participant in the fights. This may have been a response to the criticism of having erased the physical violence in Hergé's work, directed at the *Tintin* series (also produced by Robert Rhea) a few years before. But it may also just stem from the influence of similar action scenes that were omnipresent in early 1990s children's animation. Either way, it suggests that the adapters somewhat fell into the trap of conformism.

Indeed, the third relationship defining the iconic sign sheds some light on the form of aesthetic recuperation evinced in comics adaptations. The signifier is also related to the type insomuch as the iconic sign leads to a confrontation between a "singular object" (the set of traits that define the hero) and a "general model," namely, that of the belligerent adventurer. Fight scenes and the expansion of their visual representations in filmic time differ from how they appear in comics. This changes the image of the hero who becomes more like the type of adventurer more in vogue at the time of the film's production. However, this does not represent a radical break, since these sequences are framed by others where we can find the conventional iconic signs associated with the Corto comics. Indeed, the elegant sailor is modeled on an old figure of Western literature. An avatar of Odysseus, Corto is the modern incarnation of a mythic hero who has renounced all glorifying trials held in great esteem by others, animated by an individualistic form of energy, without any other ideal than the one he sets for himself and achieves thanks to the characters he encounters in his travels through a chaotic world. Perhaps it is this strength of character embodying the wanderings of humanity and providing a reassuring representation that makes possible the transposition of the comic to film. The transfer requires a subtle adaptation of the images; it should not be too obvious to keep the viewer aware of the underlying myth, yet also not too muted either to avoid reducing the character to the usual myth adapted in so many guises in other stories.

Artistic Choices When Adapting: "A strong line can be changed into a frail line and a frail line can be changed into a strong line."[11]

The visual component of the animated film rests on a semiotic function that oscillates between fidelity and invention, which constitutes the film's plastic signature from the beginning of the narrative, in close relation to the artistic choices Pratt made in his albums. While the author's style transpires through his masterful integration of the hero's silhouette in carefully composed panels, the animation underlines the importance of the movement of film images, thus creating a certain tension with the source work. This is immediately apparent in the film's opening minutes, especially since the action starts after the comic's prologue: "There are several ways to start a story. That of Corto Maltese and Baron Roman Von Sternberg-Ungerne, who, by the way, was crazy, can start with a broken line signifying 'no' in the game of 'I Ching,' the Book of Changes" (Pratt 30).

This quote highlights the extent to which the story is related to the visual dimension of the album, which has disappeared in the film, replaced with a simple caption announcing "Hong Kong, February 15, 1919" [2:20]. However, it serves to foreground the text of the other speech balloon of the comic in the following shot: "Through change, the S becomes a highly agile line." The voice then utters these enigmatic words, which correspond to the text in the speech balloon of the following panel: "A strong line changes into a frail line and a frail line changes into a strong line." These sentences provide a metaphorical commentary on Corto Maltese's wanderings in the story; they can also be interpreted as an aesthetic manifesto for the adaptation of the drawn to the moving image. Placed in another visual context, the sinuous line of the S becomes an animated path. What better and more refined definition of adaptation of the still to the moving image could the director of an animated film provide in the opening words of the story?

The film thereby announces the visual choice for the first mode of transposition in the adaptation of the comic: the movement emanating from the still image itself. In the sequence, the ink, diluting into clear water, gradually creates a new image in a kind of gentle rush flowing from the still to the moving image (fig. 33) [2:28]. Beginning the story with a shot that shows an animated image borne of stillness, following the movement of dilution, gradually—and reflexively—transforms the trajectory mapped by the panels fixed in print for the comics reader into the flow of animated film. At the opening of the film narrative, this process suggesting movement through slow long shots resembling still images is the preferred way of treating the transfer from comics to animation.

Fig. 33: *Corto Maltese : La cour secrète des Arcanes* (Morelli, 2002): Long Life the calligrapher's ink diluted in water.

Clearly, the adaptation of a comic to animated film upsets the "spatio-topical system"[12] of the image, even if the opening sequence seems to provide a bridge between the two. The animated version, of course, does away with typical comics features, such as the gutter, the page spread, and the additional space taken up by speech balloons. On the other hand, animation benefits from characteristics of the film medium. In Morelli's version, the typical order of the comics grid, "the moment of *taking possession* of the original space" (Groensteen 144, emphasis in original), is supplanted by the potential of the stage scenery of the comics albums. Pratt reduced sets to a few details, characters, and iconic objects. In the film, however, they become important visual components. The addition of scenery, which inscribes the hero in a specific socio-historical reality, is quite common: shots of courtyards, populated streets with people bustling in the background, crowds with people just going about their business, and so on. The decors, I would argue, humanize the hero, providing him with an environment that situates him in a context that is even more precise than in the comics. Unlike the comic that centers on the hero, with his unique silhouette and the singular color of his outfit, the first shots of the film show him as part of the crowd, until he is gradually positioned at the center of the image.

The animation of lines in the film images also utilizes a process that seems indebted to Renaissance painting: *sfumato*.[13] This technique might seem inconsistent with Pratt's clear line. However, Morelli and his team apply it successfully to create a certain visual exoticism, especially for the decors. Morelli explains in *Paroles du réalisateur*: "As for the sets, there is no real precedent: Pratt did not create any, which suited the comics. For us, it became a task involving historical and graphic research, but it does not look anything like what he did."

The comic's dearth of scenery allows for invented landscapes to appear in a specific historical space in forms that may not be easily recognizable to the viewer. Thus, the port of Hong Kong in 1919 is enveloped in the haze of autumn light at the beginning of the film, softening the edges of the buildings [4:14]. At other times in the film, *sfumato* is used to generate background effects, such as rising smoke, twirling dust [4:12], dispersing fog or snowfall [43:42], magnified in slow panoramic shots. Together, these iconic signs loosen the links in the relationship between the iconic sign's semiotic components in the comics and in the animated film, and between referent and type. In other words, the profilmic, here, highlights the specificity of the medium. More precisely, it is the type associated with Pratt's watercolors, which serves as the junction with the film's referent. All these visual choices are part of an artistic adaptation that yields neither to the temptation of feature film clichés, nor even to the necessary fidelity of the film to the original work; instead, it adheres to Pratt's work as watercolorist.

Film, Comics, and Orality

With painstaking attention to detail, Morelli underscores the visual, cinematic choices that made it possible for him to adapt Pratt's work. However, he rarely mentions the narrative dimension of the film's dialogue and soundtrack in the interviews and promotional material on the DVD extras. Everything seems to indicate that the animated version of Pratt's work was geared towards the treatment of the visual dimension of the comic, so that one wonders whether any significant choices have been made regarding sound and voice.

The adaptation of the verbal layer of text in the speech balloons to film dialogue involves, in effect, an update of the hero's characteristics through language. When comparing the dialogue in the comics with those in the film, there seems, at first, to be few changes. But on closer inspection, the changes are twofold. First, the language has frequently been updated to contemporary usage. One speech balloon of the comic reads: "You always want to joke. But the Book of Changes is no joke."[14] In the film, this becomes: "You always want to joke around, Corto, but I'm not kidding"[15] [3:06]. The word change ("kidding" instead of "joking") makes the language sound more contemporary. On the other hand, the esoteric elements in the comics (the Book of Changes) disappear to lend visual support to an onscreen character, with Long Life saying, "I'm not kidding."

The differences between the two media—the written text in the speech balloons compared to the film's dialogue—are minimal. If some changes are informed by the need for concision, modernity, and the greater accessibility of Corto Maltese's language, they do not seem to be the most salient feature of how the film adapts the verbal layer of the comic.

Indeed, the adaptation is less concerned with the content of the characters' discourse than with the choice of particular actors who are strongly identified with the characters through contrast. Studies of the soundtrack have demonstrated the importance of voice-centered choices in film. Michel Chion's comprehensive research of sound in cinema has illustrated its diversity and insisted on how it establishes different relations with the visuals. He stresses the extent to which voices in film pose questions regarding reception; who is the voice addressed to, and to whom do they belong (Chion 1984)? Dominique Sipière (2011) has further described how film fixates faces in the memory of the audience through the double trace of the image and the voice of the actor. These theories apply to the dubbing of contemporary animated films; the grain of the actor's voice, the speech tempo, and verbal interactions all play a significant role in the transposition of the contents of speech balloons into film dialogues, as they breathe life into the text. In the case of *La Cour secrète des arcanes*, the voices of Richard Berry for Corto and Patrick Bouchitey for Rasputin not only turn the text into spoken dialogue; they also construct a recognizable acoustic identity that sounds unique to the viewer, thereby marking the difference between one character and the other in the image. In *Paroles du réalisateur*, Morelli stresses the importance of voices:

> Richard Berry is Corto. We needed someone with charm, a certain nonchalance and sense of humor and irony. Patrick Bouchitey is perfect as Rasputin because Rasputin is so elusive. You never know what he will say next, what he thinks; he always takes you by surprise. Bouchitey is a master of improvisation; he can be scary, funny, caustic; he has such range. Marie Trintignant is the Duchess, a character with weary charm, and an elegance of another era. (3)

The vocal characteristics of the actors' voices are based on their affinity with the traits of the comics characters as expressed in their actions, visual peculiarities, and dialogue. Rasputin, Corto's unpredictable and elusive ally, has a voice that is as surprising as his presence in the story action and images. He appears for the first time in the story as an isolated hand moving towards the hero [5:22]. He then frequently disappears from the story to inexplicably reappear later, having overcome great danger. Bouchitey's guttural voice, constantly shifting from low to high, is consistent with the character's unpredictability, making him both unique and surprising to the viewer. When the spectator recognizes the voice, it will be associated with the actor who lent his voice to numerous film dubbings and even humorous wildlife documentaries[16] of great fame.

From a semiotic perspective, Rasputin's voice provides a counterpoint to Corto Maltese's sensual, serious, and monotonous voice; it helps create, through visual and sound contrasts, a duo caught up in adventures. Thus, Sipière's distinction between character, *persona*, and person plays an important role in the adaptation of a famous comic book hero to film. The character of Corto Maltese, like that of Rasputin, is widely known both from an onomastic and a literary perspective. The voices of the main characters are familiar and have a strong identity owing to the *persona* of the actors in other films; it is hard to imagine Berry's voice without his charm and seriousness, while Bouchitey gives voice to every imaginable fantasy. Assuming the traits of the paper characters, the voices ultimately refer to the person, to the actor, since "everything seems possible in the writing of artifice. It is the diegesis and the story that enable the assemblage of these 'faces'" (Sipière 165). For the viewer, the movie's sounds and voices drown out the memory of the comics. They establish a distance between the comic and its film adaptation by imposing other referential systems (the familiarity of the voices, the personality, the memory of the actors' physical appearance) that counterbalance the importance of the memory of the albums.

■ ■ ■

In short, as with any other film, these aesthetic characteristics can be interpreted differently depending on the audience and especially the cultural context they are situated in (Altman 1999; Esquenazi 2007).[17] The values attributed to voices, sounds, and effects created by the images do not escape this rule. However, considering an adaptation from a semiotic perspective as "a transmutation of material torn from the conventions of a historically dated imagination in order to be reinterpreted, realigned with a mythic architecture and substance" (Serceau 93) makes it possible to see how Morelli's own adaptation alters the paradigm of the hero. The adaptation ties the figure of Corto Maltese to a specific period in contemporary history, recognizable by historical events, and especially through shots that contextualize his actions in space and society. Whereas Hugo Pratt's Corto Maltese appears as an independent, Rimbaud-like adventurer who, for mysterious reasons, links his individual fate to collective history for just a short time, the film presents him as less self-centered. Moving away from the enigmatic, mythical figure who arises from the comics through a few visual features (the sailor's outfit, a haughty demeanor intensified by the predominance of depictions in profile, his cap, upturned collar, cigarette), the film evokes a hero more involved in the setting by a more sustained interaction with other characters, which further humanizes him.

Generally speaking, the animated film as a form of comics adaptation raises with great acuity the issue of fidelity in the perception of iconic signs; the composition of the shot incites comparisons to the drawings and page layout. The semiotic study of the hero in Morelli's film has allowed us to identify the play of variations and reproductions between the shots in the film, and the composition and drawings on the page. It has also allowed us to see how this play revolves around the complex relationship between the iconic signifier, type, and referent, evincing a complexity that is even greater in the case of animated film since the close relationship of its images with those in the comic may disappoint the viewer. If reception connects a subject and an object of desire, then the subject engendered by the adventures of Corto Maltese can be rediscovered in the film adaptation as a particular instance of the mythical hero. However, in the adaptation of a comic to an animation film, the object of desire formed by the film image has changed. Even if the characters were the same, their actions similar, the découpage and *mise en scène* identical, the simple fact remains that the spatio-topical system is no longer the same: the panel, hyper-frame, gutter, the play with the functions of the panel, and layout are not to be found in the film. This means that for many readers of *Corto Maltese in Siberia*, the animated film *La Cour secrète des arcanes* is destined to be performed against a different semiotic background—namely, that of the comic. In the case of an adaptation of a comic into a feature film, the semiotic rupture is greater, allowing more distance from the original work, with the new version as a kind of authorized translation that may or may not be close to the original. However, in the case of animated film, the break appears to be more of an evolution of the sign system, which must leave traces of its iconic origin apparent and reveal their original stillness in the uninterrupted movement of the film's images. Hence, perhaps, the use of other forms of equivalence—namely, those of the recognizable and undistorted voices that are combined with the drawn characters. This contributes to the shattering of the film's referential illusion and brings out the arbitrariness of the choices in an adaptation of a comic to film, especially when the source work is famous.

Notes

1. See, for example, *Analyser un film* by Laurent Jullier.
2. DVD bonus feature.
3. DVD bonus feature.
4. DVD bonus feature.
5. The broadcast of the animated adaptation of *The Adventures of Tintin* was an important event for the French channel FR3. The first episode was shown on May 5, 1992, after which the network programmed the series in primetime on Tuesday evenings between May and November of 1992. Each episode was presented by the network's star host, Vincent Perrot. FR3 even organized a whole weekend of reruns, with journalists and leading hosts (C. Ockrent, E. Luce, Fabrice, etc.) situating the series in the collective experience of discovering Hergé's work as a child.
6. Followed by twenty-one forty-five-minute episodes, three of which were edited to fit the time format for television.
7. The album was reprinted five times between 1979 and 2009.
8. *Michel Vaillant* (Louis-Pascal Couvelaire, 2003) and *Largo Winch* (Jérôme Salle, 2008) are two such examples.
9. Original text: "point d'ancrage significatif" and "le mouvement de production-destitution signifiante."
10. DVD bonus feature.
11. The latest and readily available French version of *Corto Maltese en Sibérie* is the 2010 colored edition published by Casterman. A new English edition has been published by IDW (2017).
12. See the first chapter of Thierry Groensteen's *The System of Comics*.
13. In Renaissance painting, this technique refers to the hazy effect obtained by the superposition of delicate layers of paint, giving objects indeterminate, soft contours.
14. Original text: "Tu as toujours envie de blaguer. Mais le livre des mutations n'est pas une blague."
15. Original text: "Tu as toujours envie de plaisanter Corto, moi je ne plaisante pas."
16. In the series *La Vie privée des animaux* (Studio Lavabo / Sony BMG France 1990–) notably.
17. See chapter 3 in particular, as it deals with interpretation, description, and judgement (75–89).

Works Cited

Association Française des Cinémas d'Art et Essai. *Paroles du réalisateur Pascal Morelli*. Paris: AFCAE-CNC, 2002.

Campbell, Joseph. *The Hero with a Thousand Faces*. New York: Pantheon Books, 1949.

Chion, Michel. *Un Art sonore, le cinéma*. Paris: Cahiers du Cinéma, 2003.

Chion, Michel. *La Voix au cinéma*. Paris: Cahiers du Cinéma, 1984.

Corto Maltese : La Cour secrète des arcanes. Dir. Pascal Morelli. Written by Natalia Borodin, Pascal Morelli, and Thierry Thomas, based on Hugo Pratt. With the voices of Richard Berry (Corto Maltese), Patrick Bouchitey (Raspoutine), Barbara Schulz (Changaï Li), and Marie Trintignant (La Duchesse Marina Seminova). Canal+, 2002. DVD. Studio Canal, 2003.

Esquenazi, Jean-Pierre. *Sociologie des œuvres : De la production à l'interprétation*. Paris: Armand Colin, 2007.

Groensteen, Thierry. *The System of Comics*. Trans. Bart Beaty and Nick Nguyen. Jackson: University Press of Mississippi, 2007.

Groupe μ. *Traité du signe visuel : Pour une rhétorique de l'image*. Paris: Seuil, 1992.

Ingres, Jean-Antoine Dominique. "Commentaries on Art." *Nineteenth-Century Theories of Art*. Ed. Joshua C. Taylor. Berkeley: University of California Press, 1987. 105–28.

Jullier, Laurent. *Analyser un film : De l'émotion à l'interprétation*. Paris: Flammarion, 2012.

Moulin, Joëlle. *Cinéma et peinture*. Paris: Citadelles & Mazenod, 2011.

Pratt, Hugo. *Corto Maltese en Sibérie*. Paris: Casterman, 2010 [1974].

Pratt, Hugo. *Corto Maltese in Siberia*. Trans. Simone Castaldi and Dean Mullaney. San Diego: IDW Publishing, 2017.

Rancière, Jacques. *The Aesthetic Unconscious*. Trans. Debra Keates and James Swenson. Cambridge, UK: Polity Press, 2009.

Ropars-Wuilleumier, Marie-Claire. *Le Texte divisé*. Paris: PUF, 1981.

Serceau, Michel. *L'Adaptation cinématographique des textes littéraires*. Liège: Céfal, 1999.

Sipière, Dominique. "La voix au cinéma, divorce et retrouvailles." *Tropisme* 17 (2011): 159–72.

Stam, Robert, and Alessandra Raengo, eds. *Literature and Film*. Malden, MA: Blackwell Publishing, 2005.

Sin City (Frank Miller and Robert Rodriguez, 2005): Improbable Encounters between Embodied and Drawn Characters

PIERRE FLOQUET

> Cinema's first utopia was that it was a language—syntax, architecture, symphony—better equipped than the language of words to embrace bodies in movement. This utopia has always had to confront, during the silent and talking eras, the limits of its capacity to speak and all the returns of the "old" language.
>
> —JACQUES RANCIÈRE (167)

Two recent events that chance has ironically linked illustrate in their own way the issue I will explore in the following pages: the death of Ray Harryhausen on May 7, 2013, and the French release of *Iron Man 3* (Shane Black) on April 24. Critics presented the film as the most successful adaptation of the Marvel hero's adventures, the obligatory digital environment and special effects nonetheless leaving pride of place to the actors.[1] This description reminded me of the work of director, producer, and special effects creator Ray Harryhausen, and more specifically of the fight sequence between human "heroes" (played by the actors) and the skeletons (animated creatures) in *Jason and the Argonauts* (Don Chaffey, 1963), where the images mixed direct shots with animation scenes.[2] Fifty years separate *Jason and the Argonauts* and *Iron Man 3*, yet both, in their own way, are adaptations of existing stories with a high iconographic impact;[3] both adapt their filmic subject to technological developments and the possibilities of representation offered and favored by their contemporary contexts.

In *Sin City* (2005), the profilmic context resonates with these two films. First, like *Iron Man 3*, it is directly inspired by a comic; secondly, it uses both animation as well as scenes with live actors, like *Jason and the Argonauts*. But other than that, *Sin City* remains a special case. This chapter reflects on the screen treatment and the resilience of the *personae* of the actors in the film adaptations of comics and graphic novels, insofar as the film presents an aesthetic alternative that very faithfully reproduces the graphics, if not the panel layout, of the original works.

■ ■ ■

This respect for the initial format and content questions the view of adaptation as defined by Linda Hutcheon, that is to say, where adaptation is seen as a rereading and a deliberate prolongation borne out of a given work of art: "An adaptation is an extended, deliberate, announced revisitation of a particular work of art" (170). Because it is sufficiently wide-ranging to accommodate *Sin City* as an example, this definition will reframe the more detailed points made by Hutcheon in the first chapter of her book (8). According to her, the process of transposition in an adaptation must be recognizable; we must be able to identify an act of appropriation that is both creative and interpretive, while finding the intertextual interactions that inform the adapted work. While these three elements are present in Rodriguez and Miller's film, their project cannot be limited to this frame, which one could almost see as tantamount to defining adaptation as a genre for a number of reasons I will elucidate below.

Hutcheon briefly invokes *Sin City* in a short passage, using a very euphemistic "perhaps," only to dismiss it as a counterexample that illustrates the difficulty of the "performing" arts in transcoding writing: "Graphic novels are perhaps more adapted to film [. . .] *Sin City* was made into a visually spectacular surreal movie with live actors but digitally created settings that recall those of the comics" (43). The opposition between actors and sets, made explicit by the word "but," erases what constitutes the attraction and originality of the film. Certainly, this is an adaptation, but beyond that, it is also necessary to consider the mixing of techniques, hybridity, in the treatment of the original graphic novels, the filmic representation, and the appearance and performance of the actors. Thus, the images of the drawings are transposed, alternately and conjointly, in either animated images or live film.

Neither animation, nor live film, nor a movie with typical Hollywood blockbuster special effects, *Sin City* is an adaptation at the margins of diverse cinematic forms. The role that the cinematic treatment of the actors plays in setting the panels in motion is essential to the adaptation. To study it, attention will be paid to the color scheme, voice-over, the importance of drawings, and the recycling of original panels, and more generally, to the interplay between graphic novel and film.

The presence—in the sense of existence—of actors in a digital film such as *Sin City* exemplifies the growing hybridity of genres and techniques witnessed in recent films. When reviewing the graphic arts from the past twenty years, Alphonse Cugier points to the emergence of "a new body, or even a virtual body," in certain works; such a body "opens up a unique space or moves towards the crossroads of genres, through different paths and reflected echoes" (182). In *Sin City*, in particular, the performance of the actors, along with the aesthetic decision to stick to the source material's iconography, testifies to this evolution. Pascal Lefèvre's assertion that one can draw a parallel between adapted animations and films (2) highlights, in effect, the artistic and technical challenges of *Sin City*—integrating the actors within the iconography in order to create a coherent extension of the existing graphic novels.

■ ■ ■

Before analyzing *Sin City* in detail, a sampling of other films with animation or digital special effects—not necessarily adaptations—will allow us to gauge the special role given to the actors in the act of representation, and help us appreciate the film's breadth of range. It is from this creative substratum that the specificity of this film as adaptation unfolds.

Interactions between actors and animation, the intersections between static and moving images, between animated backgrounds and real filmed scenes, are ontologically linked to the rise and development of cinema, from Mélies to Tex Avery, Harryhausen, Robert Zemeckis (*Who Framed Roger Rabbit?*, 1988), and Spielberg (*The Adventures of Tintin*, 2011). In these works, bodies—whether actual bodies, drawn, modeled, or computer-generated—are transformed and recomposed so as to adapt to both the diegesis and aesthetics (burlesque, fantasy, horror, noir, etc.). As Caroline Renouard has emphasized, "the manipulated body, both the object of attraction and of unique experiences, has not ceased to be a source of inspiration for spectacular cinema" (249).

Thus, the phenomenon of the fusion between actor and animation diversified at the close of the late twentieth century, with many actors credited and lending their voices if not their appearance to animated characters. *Antz* (Eric Darnell and Tim Johnson, 1998) is the first feature film to really take up this approach. Before that, characters—drawn, puppets, or digital—were generally dubbed by actors who did not enjoy star status. Quite the contrary, this practice was perceived as secondary, especially in a film genre relegated to the children's film category. Moreover, *Antz* surprised everyone by showing monstrous creatures on screen: ants and other insects gifted with speech and emotion, talking in the easily recognizable voices of Woody Allen, Ann Bancroft, Danny Glover, Gene Hackman, Jennifer Lopez, Sylvester Stallone, Sharon Stone, and Christopher Walken. In *Antz*, the comic disjunction between famous voices and drawn creatures is no longer intended as it was in Avery's cartoons. On the contrary, the public can recognize voices and associate them with the personality of the actors. Intrinsically, they transplant onto the animated characters the psychological—even physical—depth of the roles they usually play in movies. This is a first step in filmic hybridization.

From a technical and artistic point of view, the characters in *Antz*, while they may have been spectacular in 1998,[4] are admittedly rough when compared to what technology and experience have given us ten years later (for instance, *Coraline*, directed by Henry Selick, won the Grand Prix at the Annecy Animation Film Festival in 2009). Beyond marketing considerations, providing characters with well-known voices was, at the time, also a way to overcome the limitations of digital animation and further their humanity. Peter Lord, co-founder of Aardman studios, which produced *Chicken Run* (Peter Lord and Nick Park, 2000) and *Wallace and Gromit: The Curse of the Were-Rabbit* (Steve Box and Nick Park, 2005), recently described the art of animation in these terms: "An animator will have a character move; a good animator will get a character to live; a great animator will enhance a character's thoughts." Obviously, the results rely largely on facial movement, especially the expressiveness of the eyes. In 1998, digital animation was not yet capable of satisfying such requirements in the quest for realism, no matter how creative and virtuoso the DreamWorks animators were.

However, there is only so much a famous voice can do, as proven by *Immortal (Ad Vitam)* (Enki Bilal, 2004) and *The Polar Express* (Robert Zemeckis, 2004). *Immortal* has clear parallels with Rodriguez and Miller's film. While *Sin City* is adapted from *The Hard Goodbye* (1991–92), *The Big Fat Kill* (1995), *That Yellow Bastard* (1996), and *Booze, Broads and Bullets* (1998), *Immortal* is taken from Enki Bilal's Nikopol trilogy (1980–93). The two authors, Miller and Bilal, were both involved in the filmic process and helped condense the narrative, which is common practice in the process of adapting several stories in one work. In theory, their involvement was meant to guarantee a smoother shift from one medium to the other in their capacity as scriptwriter. As Lefèvre suggests, "[f]ew adaptations faithfully follow the plot of a given comic. Any true cinematic author recognizes that this medium follows its own laws and rules. A direct adaptation will rarely turn out to be a good choice" (4). Miller and Bilal seemed well-placed to rewrite their own texts. This is also what Lefèvre thinks when he states that, in his view, the two films follow the style and atmosphere of the books with equal success (10).

Nevertheless, the resemblance between the two films ends the moment one focuses on the filmic representation and the expressiveness of the characters. In *Immortal (Ad Vitam)*, disjointed movements and the relatively limited digital images upset the bond between the characters played by actors and the animated characters. Indeed, it is as if the characters were utterly devoid of sensitivity. True to the original images, Bilal's aesthetics alone fail to overcome technical deficiencies. More specifically, the approximate synchronization between the words and the movements of the lips and faces paradoxically illustrates the chasm between the effects and what virtuosos of expressiveness, such as Jerry Lewis, were able to bring to the screen. Serge Cardinal notes that "certain actors make possible the invention of certain forms; this aesthetic and poetic invention is also the creation of a possibility of life" (66). It is precisely this possibility of life, which in some sense echoes the principle of realism so dear to Disney animation,[5] that is sought by filmmakers who combine real and virtual images.

In *Immortal,* the confrontation between actors and virtual characters accentuates the gap inherent in the actors' performances, while the diegetic reality reveals the result of the manipulation of the virtual to be clumsy. If the CGI gods are an adequate indication of the distance befitting their divine condition, their presence expresses at the same time a sleek, digital coldness with a rigidity that deprives their bodies of empathy. Their performances render hollow the embodiment of speech and its psychological and emotional verisimilitude, sometimes at the risk of becoming a cliché, if not a caricature. The relative box-office failure of the film in France and its limited distribution abroad can not only be explained through the elliptical scenario that combines elements of three separate albums into one story, but also through the weakness of its digital animation. In this respect, *Immortal* appears to be a significant counterexample to the successful *Sin City.*

The Polar Express, also released in 2004, was not enthusiastically received either. The conductor in the film is a digital clone of Tom Hanks. As a result of the rough and slow animated movements of his face, his character and expressiveness are but rigid reflections of the actor's digitally "botoxed" image. He keeps staring at sets and extras in a vain attempt to find meaning and emotion behind the transparency of the digital frame. And the actual voice of the "real" Tom Hanks brings meager consolation! Should the questionable aesthetic result be attributed to the desire to stay as close as possible to the illustrations in the children's book that served as the film's inspiration? Must the technique known as *imagemotion technology* (which consists in digitally recording the actors' movements before they are "dressed" up in their animated appearance) be seen as a deliberate aesthetic choice, or should we see it as evidence of its own limitations? In this type of film, the viewer remains, despite himself, the witness of the tension between the pre-filmic personality of the actor and the stuttering, even wretched attempts to convey emotions in the expressions and gestures of the actor's computer-generated clone.

Raymond Bellour's analysis of such attempts is highly critical, as his discussion of *Who Framed Roger Rabbit* shows:

> If *Who Framed Roger Rabbit* is a solid film, it is not because, like others before it, it combined cartoons (schematism) with traditional shots (the photographic analog); it is because it did so with such quickness and confidence in the procedure. Thanks to the rapidity that prevails in mixing the figures (the computer's contribution), the image reaches a level of blending that had been unimaginable before, with a "naturalness" that is immediately accepted and establishes a new wavering between levels of representation. But, above all, as in typical great Hollywood films, the power of the entangled screenplay lies in its having turned the wavering into its subject: can we distinguish between one image and another? Toontown and Hollywood? A toon and a man? Can we still conceive the function of a show that serves as a catharsis for the community? Or does it run the risk of dissolving, along with the images, in the "quick dip," the acid in which the true-false judge, a symbol of disorderly law, wants to plunge all the cartoon creatures that have been conceived in the history of (American) cinema? (187)

True, Bellour nuances his hypothesis by formulating it in a series of questions. We can, of course, consider cartoons as just a subset of animated film; in the end, however, his verdict remains negative. Yet his analysis from 2009 is based on a 1998 film. Admittedly, recent technological advances did not lead to the dissolution but rather to an effective aesthetic symbiosis between multiple kinds of representations on screen (that one is free to like or dislike).

In fact, these techniques can just as equally be seen as enriching the actor's creative repertoire. We have already mentioned Jerry Lewis's genius plasticity. In addition, voice, and with it, the entire body of the actor is going to adapt to deal with this "new frontier" in artistic expressiveness. In the quest for the "transformation of the actor into the character" (Chekhov 116), the actor will continue what playwright Michael Chekhov defined as "incorporation": "The actor imagines with his body. He cannot avoid gesturing or moving without responding to his own internal images. The more developed and stronger the image, the more it stimulates the actor to physically incorporate it with his body and voice. On this natural ability of the actor we base our principle of Incorporation" (95, capitalized in original).

To some extent, this is what the collaboration between the actors and directors of *Sin City* (2005) ultimately aims at by sticking closely to the panels of the graphic novels. Previously, technological limitations, marketing demands, and aesthetic alternatives prompted the use of flesh-and-blood actors in films that were predominantly, if not entirely designed, on computers with a host of special effects. Although it might not be directly relevant here, we

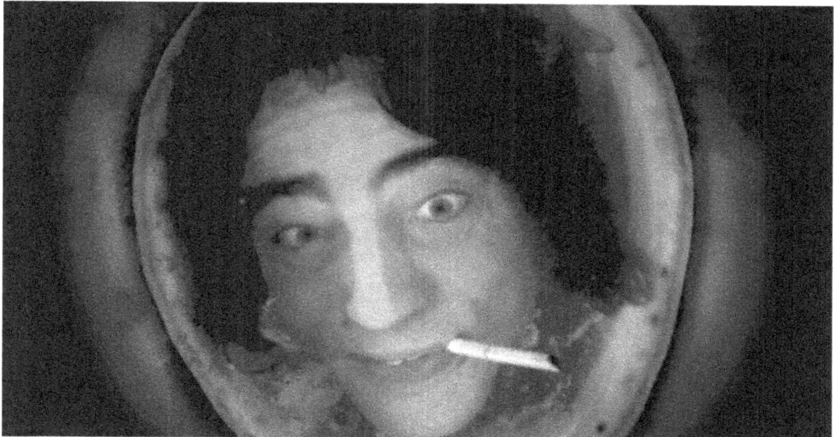

Fig. 34: *Sin City* (Miller and Rodriguez, 2005): Jackie Boy gets his face shoved in the toilet.

can think of the partial success or artistic impasses of productions such as *Hulk* (Ang Lee, 2003) or the *Matrix* trilogy (Lana and Lilly Wachowski, 1999–2003). Moreover, one can also think of directors who alternate, throughout their films, animated characters with their "fetish-actors"; *Corpse Bride* (Mike Johnson and Tim Burton, 2005), in which Helena Bonham Carter and Johnny Depp lend their physical appearance and voices, immediately comes to mind.

Having established this, we can now return to *Sin City*. The whole film was shot in a "digital backlot"; all the action was filmed before a green screen, and the setting was added during postproduction. Only a handful of scenes were filmed on actual sets, those that take place in Kadie's Bar, Shellie's apartment, and the hospital corridor in the epilogue, which, incidentally, does not appear in the graphic novels. Somehow, *Sin City* gathers all these components, both technical and artistic, in a *métissage* of direct film, special effects, animation, and comics.

I use the term "*métissage*" quite deliberately, not to deny the more formal sense of the term "adaptation" as developed by Hutcheon, but because the term evokes the creation of a hybrid film form. Bellour speaks of "the encounter and the possible fusion with the registration of human forms" (521). Robert Rodriguez describes his approach as a "translation," which explains the absence of a screenwriter in the credits. In fact, Miller is mentioned as the author of the graphic novel, and it is evident while watching the film that entire pages of the original graphic novels were used as a storyboard. Theme, action, point of view, lighting, layout—whole sections of the source text are transposed in moving image and sound. For example, the shot of Dwight drowning Jackie Boy in the toilet shows the corrupt cop's face being pushed down into a low-angle frontal close-up, eyes wide open, a cigarette still between his lips, framed by the rim of the toilet (fig. 34) [50:30]. This shot is a faithful transposition of three panels of *The Big Fat Kill* (25). In the same comic, a full-page drawing depicts a young woman in tight clothes, whose luscious figure standing before the headlights of a car is divided into black-and-white (34). Her earrings, necklaces, and cross-shaped pendants alone create sharp contrasts, casting implausibly clear shadows on the dark silhouette. The same effect is used in the film [54:20]. Compared to the graphic novel, the decor offers, no doubt, less of a playful caricature of white and black contrasts. However, never do the jewels glisten in the darkness in such an unexpected and uncanny way as when the crosses of white light announce the demonic character lurking underneath the young woman's apparent vulnerability.

These transitions from book to film are facilitated by the cinematic quality of the original panels. It is unlikely that Miller had conceived his stories as the storyboard of a possible film beforehand. Rather, like Will Eisner (43), he uses cinematic techniques of centering (angles, variations in focus, depth of field, etc.). The resultant fidelity to visual effects meets the criterion of persistence and variation identified by Hutcheon: adaptation "is repetition but without replication, bringing together the comfort of ritual and recognition with the delight of surprise and novelty" (173). Hutcheon insists on the pragmatic relationship the author succeeds in establishing with his faithful readers, who have now become viewers, in terms of the culmination of a creative process involving two distinct stages—first on paper, then on film. For the filmmaker, fidelity to the source in adaptations is one approach among many; it only becomes a criterion from the moment the viewer is aware of the origin of the spectacle.

Miller's comics bear a striking resemblance to the work of Argentine authors Alberto Breccia and Carlos Trillo, published during the 1980s. Black is so pervasive in their stories that the drawings turn into negatives (cf. *Buscavidas, Versiones, Obras Completas,* 1981–82). Miller's work expresses a similar aesthetic. For instance, Miho's murderous jump in *The Big Fat Kill* is shown on the left page against a black background, with only a few white lines tracing the silhouette, clothes, and weapons (48–49); on the page to the right, the same character brandishes her swords against the panel's white background, with only her shadow, part of her hair, and the thick folds of her kimono rendered in black lines. Just before, Miho had thrown a swastika-shaped razor, a black shape against a white background, rendered in negative in the following frame (47). In the film, the fortuitous lightning storm provokes the same effect [57:53], which thus becomes an unrealistic, diegetic excuse for the negative image of the severed hand lying in a pool of blood next to the realistic shadow of the blade stuck in the ground. The ambiguous use of black-and-white images in negative is most pronounced when Dwight sinks in a pool of oil (*The Big Fat Kill*, 119) [72:53–73:22]. The bodies and hands (in close-ups) are but white flecks, paradoxical shadows against the black backdrop of the panels and screen; the black refers to the oil and the night, but the white lacks a stable referent. The lack of consistency between the color and the object or person represented establishes a certain distance. The explicit reminder that these are just images keeps the viewer aware of the artificiality of the situation (Lefèvre 2), while enabling the readers to relate to the characters. We are immersed in the fiction, a situation the fiction self-consciously underscores in its play with black-and-white.

Moreover, a number of shots in the film explicitly refer to the source material: the title *Booze, Broads and Bullets* appears at regular intervals throughout the film—for instance, on the matchbox Hartigan finds which enables him to find Nancy [93:35], or in the background at the club Hartigan goes to [18:23].

The actors and stars face the double challenge of faithfully respecting the graphic, profilmic existence of their characters and resisting the impact of the digital process on their physical integrity, if not their ego. While some of them physically resemble their characters, others, including Bruce Willis, Mickey Rourke, Benicio Del Toro, and Nick Stahl, resorted to prostheses and/or makeup to approximate the appearance of Miller's characters. One may wonder about the accuracy of Clive Owen's interpretation of Dwight, but the fact that he did not use any artifice may constitute an explanation. Overall, the hybridity of the actors' appearances and the ensuing ambiguities of their personalities are exacerbated from the opening credits onwards [3:18–4:02]. Their names appear alongside the faces of the characters taken straight from the *graphic novels*, and not from images showing what they look like in the movie.

Taking this into account, one should assess what part of themselves the actors project into the digitally created diegetic world and the nature of the pragmatic relationships they establish—or fail to establish—with the audience. Have the characters preserved the psychological identity and fictional dimension that Miller had bestowed upon them? Or have the actors imposed their physicality and emotional aura beyond the layers of makeup and digital filters? In *Sin City*, computer-aided design, special effects, and live film create new filmic material. Deleuze contends that

> [t]he cinema can, with impunity, bring us close to things or take us away from them and revolve around them, it suppresses both the anchoring of the subject and the horizon of the world. Hence it substitutes an implicit

> knowledge and a second intentionality for the conditions of natural perception. It is not the same as the other arts, which aim rather at something unreal through the world, but makes the world itself something unreal or a tale. (57)

Sin City offers an extreme version of this by confronting the viewer with an aesthetic alternative that ignores the traditional genre boundaries. The very existence of the actor is called into question, just as it was in the work of Tex Avery in his time.[6] If cinema truly transforms the world into "something unreal," while simultaneously often making it into the mirror of its own deceptions, then *Sin City* really drives the point home by overemphasizing—through staging—certain devices and digital processes, which the use of black-and-white, made conspicuous through a few touches of color, exacerbates even further. Thus, the completely black background of the sequence where Hartigan is shown in his cell, or rather, in his cage as if dizzyingly suspended in emptiness, draws attention to the use of the green screen [88:38] (fig. 35), thus further intensifying the effect produced in the graphic novel's images (*That Yellow Bastard* 94); only the head and yellow feet of his visitor disrupt the harmony of the nightmarish prison environment. The color of the character, which contrasts with the film's overall aesthetics, in combination with his unlikely diegetic presence, amount, each in their own way, to intrusions in the cinematic sequence. Such a distancing effect reverberates as a reflexive viewpoint on cinematic *monstration*.

And yet we are still watching real actors. In such an environment, they personify their iconographic characters, their bodies standing out against the digital screen in such a way that they quite literally "animate" them. If the film manages to convey meaning and emotion in spite of its aesthetic strategy, I would suggest that it succeeds thanks to the resilience of the actors' humanity underneath the hybrid creatures they embody. Gesture and speech are instrumental in this respect. Their appearance may be altered for the sake of the narrative, but at least the integrity of their voices persists. For example, a frame from the first *Sin City* comic shows a left profile view of Marv, whose features and scars are illuminated by the flame of his lighter, while the rest of the image is filled with text (13). One shot in the film repeats this aesthetic scheme: Rourke appears in profile, his face cut off by improbable lighting, with a cigarette between his fingers held up to his mouth, while the surrounding penumbra is inhabited by the deep, groggy, and threatening grain of the actor's voice [13:55]. This endows the character with an outspokenly carnal dimension, breathing life into the written text of the panel that inspired the shot. The impact of the actors' personality thus shines through in their words,

Fig. 35: *Sin City* (Miller and Rodriguez, 2005): Hartigan meets Roark Jr. / the Yellow Bastard in his prison cell.

even though *Sin City* is paradoxically not a "wordy" film. Incidentally, such strategies also further the gap between the virtuality of the environment and the reality of the actor.

Miller's graphic novels offer a veritable choreography, a total spectacle that mixes movements, dialogues, monologues, and voice-over narrations. The images sometimes illustrate the words, which to a certain extent puts the cinematic act of movement and a narrative function approximating the writing of the graphic novel on an equal footing. In addition, we rarely hear the actors' voices in *Sin City*. But when they do speak, they often do so to themselves, and thus, ontologically speaking, to the spectators as well, following the usual pragmatic function of the voice-over. Their words are rare, making the silences—or "intervals," according to Michel Chion[7]—all the more expressive.[8] The words are, therefore, not necessarily in sync with the action; the characters' commentary on their actions and feelings are like punctuations in the diegesis. To some extent, they perform a function similar to that of the placards in silent films.

Finally, the voice-overs provide the film adaptation with an immediacy that cannot be achieved in comics. Indeed, they relate what is being said to what is being shown, as image and sound are perceived simultaneously by audiences. By contrast, a reader must decide on the order with which to tackle the contents of the page: the graphics on the one hand, the texts and other writing on the other (Eisner 43).

Indeed, the harsh use of a crude black-and-white, the boldness of the makeup, and the scarcity and tone of dialogue distance the actors from reality, placing them in a violent and mysterious no man's land, a fictional, liminal space where Rourke, Willis, and the others are at the same time the narrative tools of a graphic animation and masters of a performance. Moreover, these narrative and aesthetic choices, together with framing, lighting, and cinematography, are reminiscent of the great, dark classics of the 1920s such as *Dr. Jekyll and Mr. Hyde* (Robertson, 1920) and *Nosferatu* (Murnau, 1922). They also evoke film noirs such as *Double Indemnity* (Wilder, 1944) and *The Killers* (Siodmak, 1946).[9] The, at times, almost stroboscopic succession of images reworked in postproduction aims at producing a hypnotic effect on the viewer that goes beyond the images' strictly plastic density. This recalls what Marc Vernet writes about film noir: "The image, reduced to black spots and white dots, becomes a trap for the gaze which ceaselessly shifts from black to white and back again" (228). In *Sin City*, the legacy of film noir is both a challenge and a burden for the actors. Their performances, however, can be explained thanks to the writings of Paul Wells, one of the main theorists of animated film: "Animation legitimised the social and political ambivalence of narratives by simultaneously approximating some of the conditions of real existence whilst distancing itself from them by recourse to the unique aspects of its own vocabulary" (21). It is precisely this ambivalence that the actors in *Sin City* embody. In doing so, *Sin City* proclaims the specificity of film as a medium: the images relate to reality while questioning its essence, which may even involve relativizing their own reality and iconographic virtuality.

Unlike the first installment of *Final Fantasy: The Spirits Within* (Hironoby Sakaguchi and Motonori Sakakibara, 2001), one of the first 3D animated films, in which the digital characters struggle to approximate the grittiness and reality of human appearance; unlike the technical and aesthetic achievements in the pursuit of realism that movies such as *Avatar* (James Cameron, 2009), *A Christmas Carol* (Zemeckis, 2009), and, more recently, *Iron Man 3* offer, the all-too-human actors in *Sin City* are to some extent made "less real" than life. Their makeup, but also their confrontation with the iconographic environment which remains faithful to the original drawings, bind them to the specific and overdetermined universe of the adaptation. As such, they are excluded from any extra-filmic existence, which they nonetheless preserve in the mind of the viewer. According to Sylvie Bauer, "[e]very representation of the body seems intent on stripping it of its substance and presence to the benefit of scriptural, pictorial or sonic signs that point to the body's absence and lability" (4). Thus, in addition to showcasing a resolutely innovative artistic approach, the aesthetic stance embodied by the actors of *Sin City* can also be seen as the film's tribute to its precursors and influences.

■ ■ ■

Some might take this blurring of the boundaries between real and animated films as a sign of the end of animation, and celebrate the death of an outdated medium (the second death of Winsor McKay's Gertie, so to speak) as the inevitable consequence of digitization. Instead, one should see this blurring—especially in *Sin City*—as a creative phenomenon where both actor and character originate from the drawn character of the graphic novel; the otherness of these three beings is founded on the expression of a hybrid digital entity. Should we read this as a manifestly innovative aesthetic or instead as a respectful return, in the form of a measured tribute, to the pioneers of cinema such as Méliès and his painted decors, or to Emile Cohl's works, which already mixed live actors with animation processes?

Through Rodriguez and Miller, the viewer is not only forced to face intertextual labyrinths, but also the maze of alternative representations at the heart of fictional nightmares in this twenty-first-century freak show. Whether silent or screaming at the top of their lungs, the creatures in *Sin City* simultaneously embody and express this hybridity, the "monstrous" result of the interweaving of all of the resources of film narration.

In this respect, Chekhov's reflections on the actor can be applied quite literally: "Art is not like life. Art cannot be like life, because in life most people do not know what they want. But the actor must always know what the character wants. The character must always have clear-cut objectives!"[10] (161). In *Sin City*, filmed movement is given consistency by virtue of its close link with the original drawings. They make the gap between photographic and drawn fully visible, while constructing a "space-movement" between digital stills and comic panels, thereby putting into practice Norman McLaren's famous thesis:

> Animation is not the art of drawings that move, but the art of movements that are drawn. What happens between each frame is more important than what exists on each frame. Animation is therefore the art of manipulating the invisible interstices that lie between frames. The interstices are the bones, flesh, and blood of the movie, what is on each frame, merely the clothing. (Inge, *Concise* 19)

Lastly, non-dubbed versions released in non-English-speaking countries add an extra dimension to this blurring of genre boundaries in a kind of mirror effect of the creative process, perhaps as an allusion to that other hybrid: the transition from one voice to another, from one language to another, and from one medium to another. Like modern versions of silent film intertitles, the subtitles take on the narrative function of the speech balloons, since they are not appropriated into the iconic space of the screen the way the texts in the original graphic novel are. Thus, subtitles create an incongruous space that is nonetheless completely in tune with Rodriguez and Miller's artistic approach: a reflexive cinematic device to the second degree!

▪ ▪ ▪

Sin City highlights the directors' readiness to take into account the preexistence of a narrative in a different medium. The faithful transposition of the panels recalls the original medium while offering an animated representation. Adaptation requires the transfer from page layout to cinematic staging, transforming the pages into a scene. Moreover, the hybridity of the artistic process is complexified by the fact that the adaptation uses real actors, two different media (animation and film), as well as the hybridization of the real image through digital processing and the actors' makeup. Paradoxically, the multiplicity of deformations does justice to the atmosphere of the graphic novels authored by Miller. The drawn, animated, filmed, and digitized all become relevant tools for Rodriguez and his co-director. Without resorting to spectacular special effects, they remain attached to the "reality" of comics and invent a specific aesthetic coherence. However, originality and efficaciousness in adaptations seem to be the exception, in this case probably owing much to Miller's involvement. Indeed, neither the adaptation of his graphic novel *300* (Snyder, 2006), nor his attempt to use the same techniques in his own film adaptation of *The Spirit* (2008, based on the comics by Will Eisner), met with the same success as *Sin City*. The second installment in the adaptation of the Sin City series, *A Dame to Kill For* (Miller and Rodriguez, 2015), will perhaps answer the question whether these aesthetics have not become too formulaic to last.

Notes

1. See, for example, *Iron Man 3: The Liberation of Tony Stark* by Christopher Orr.

2. Ray Harryhausen is famous for his stop-motion animation technique known as "Dynamation."

3. Everyone keeps strong images of various, highly eclectic representations of mythological scenes, each interpretation often feeding on a previous one, and so on.

4. In 1999, *Antz* was nominated, among others, for four Annie Awards and a BAFTA Award for special effects and animation, but only won the prize for best soundtrack.

5. See *The Illusion of Life: Disney Animation* by Franck Thomas and Ollie Johnston.

6. See "Y a-t-il un acteur dans le cartoon ?" by Pierre Floquet.

7. During the fourteenth SERCIA conference at the University Paris Ouest Nanterre in 2009, Michel Chion stressed the need to study not just speech, but also the "intervals" between speech by showing an excerpt from *Lost Highway* (David Lynch, 1997).

8. Interestingly, the French words for "word" (*mot*) and "mute" (*muet*) both come from the Latin "*mutus*."

9. The first sequence of the execution of the young woman harks back to the murder of Phyllis Dietrichson by Walter Neff in Wilder's film, even though the staging more closely resembles the movie poster than the scene in the femme fatale's living room. The sequence of the cage/jail cell invokes, through the play of light and shadow on the bars, as well as the high angle, the shot of the jail cells in *The Killers*.

10. The pun in French—"well-drawn objectives (objectifs bien *dessinés*)"—is lost in the official translation.

Works Cited

Bauer, Sylvie. "Poétiques du corps dans la littérature américaine." *RFEA* 132 (2012): 3–8.

Bellour, Raymond. "The Double Helix." *Electronic Culture: Technology and Visual Representation*. Ed. Timothy Druckrey. New York: Aperture, 1996. 173–200.

Breccia, Alberto, and Carlos Trillo. *Buscavidas Versiones, Obras Completas, 1981–1982*. Buenos Aires: Doedytores, 1994.

Cardinal, Serge. "Les « convulsions paroxystiques » de l'acteur : La synchronisation de l'image et du son sur le corps de Jerry Lewis." *Synchroniser / Synchronizing*. Eds. Philippe Despoix and Nicolas Donin. Montréal: Université de Montréal, 2012. 65–83.

Chekhov, Michael. *On the Technique of Acting*. Ed. Mel Gordon. New York: HarperCollins, 1991.

Cholodenko, Alan, ed. *The Illusion of Life: Essays on Animation*. Staten Island, NY: Power Publications, 1991.

Cugier, Alphonse. "Réalité(s) du corps et fiction de l'image en cinémas exposés." *Cinéma(s) et nouvelles technologies*. Eds. Patrick Louguet and Fabien Maheu. Paris: L'Harmattan, 2011. 181–97.

Deleuze, Gilles. *Cinema 1: The Movement-Image*. Trans. Hugh Tomlinson and Barbara Habberjam. London: Athlone Press, 1986.

Eisner, Will. *Expressive Anatomy for Comics and Narrative: Principles and Practices from the Legendary Cartoonist*. New York: W. W. Norton, 2008.

Floquet, Pierre. *Le Langage comique de Tex Avery*. Paris: L'Harmattan, 2009.

Floquet, Pierre. "Would Computer Generated Images Conceal Genuine Emotions? Or CGIs vs 'CGEs.'" *Selected Writings from the UTS: Sydney International Animation Festival 2010 Symposium*. Sydney, Australia: UTS, 2010–11. www.dab.uts.edu.au/research/conferences/siaf/SIAF-SYMPOSIUM-WRITINGS-2011.pdf. Accessed on June 10, 2013.

Floquet, Pierre. "Y a-t-il un acteur dans le cartoon ?" *Bulletin du Ciclaho* 2 (2000): 49–55.

Hutcheon, Linda. *A Theory of Adaptation*. 2nd ed. London: Routledge, 2013 [2006].

Inge, Thomas. *Anything Can Happen in a Comic Strip: Centennial Reflections on an American Art Form*. Jackson: University Press of Mississippi, 1995.

Inge, Thomas. *Concise Histories of American Popular Culture*. Westport, CT: Greenwood Press, 1982.

Kral, Petr. *Le Burlesque, ou morale de la tarte à la crème*. Paris: Ramsay, 2007 [1984].

Lefèvre, Pascal. "Incompatible Visual Ontologies? The Problematic Adaptation of Drawn Images." *Film and Comic Books*. Eds. Ian Gordon, Mark Jancovich, and Matthew McAllister. Jackson: University Press of Mississippi, 2007. 1–12.

Miller, Frank. *The Big Fat Kill*. Milwaukie, OR: Dark Horse Comics, 1995. [1994].

Miller, Frank. *Sin City*. Milwaukie, OR: Dark Horse Comics, 1992 [1991–92].

Miller, Frank. *Sin City: Booze, Broads, and Bullets.* Milwaukie, OR: Dark Horse Comics, 1998.

Miller, Frank. *That Yellow Bastard.* Milwaukie, OR: Dark Horse Comics, 1997 [1996].

Orr, Christopher. "*Iron Man 3*: The Liberation of Tony Stark." *The Atlantic*, May 3, 2013: http://www.theatlantic.com/entertainment/archive/2013/05/-i-iron-man-3-i-the-liberation-of-tony-stark/275524. Accessed on June 10, 2013.

Rancière, Jacques. *Film Fables.* Trans. Emiliano Battista. Oxford: Berg, 2006 [2001].

Renouard, Caroline. "*Le Corps hybride : la chair et le virtuel.*" *Cinéma(s) et nouvelles technologies.* Eds. Patrick Louguet and Fabien Maheu. Paris: L'Harmattan, 2011. 249–65.

Sin City. Directed by Robert Rodriguez and Frank Miller (with Quentin Tarantino), based on Miller's graphic novels. With Jessica Alba (Nancy Callahan), Rosario Dawson (Gail), Benicio Del Toro (Jackie Boy), Clive Owen (Dwight), Mickey Rourke (Marv), Nick Stahl (Yellow Bastard), Bruce Willis (Hartigan), and Elijah Wood (Kevin). Dimension Films / Troublemaker Studios, 2005. DVD. Metropolitain Vidéo, 2015.

Thomas, Franck, and Ollie Johnston. *The Illusion of Life: Disney Animation.* New York: Disney Editions, 2001 [1981].

Vernet, Marc. "Clignotements du noir-et-blanc." *La Théorie du film.* Eds. Jacques Aumont and Jean-Louis Leutrat. Paris: Albatros, 1980. 3–33.

Wells, Paul. *Understanding Animation.* London: Routledge, 2002.

From Screen to Page? *Castle* (ABC, 2009–2016) and *Richard Castle's Deadly Storm*

SHANNON WELLS-LASSAGNE

Richard Castle's Deadly Storm's[1] incipit is voluntarily hackneyed, beginning with the traditional preface by the source text's author, conferring legitimacy on the adaptation:

> Adaptation. It's a word most authors hate. It conjures up images in their minds of their beloved perfect prose being hacked to pieces by literary infidels. I'm sure it happens, but if it does, this graphic novel stands as a startling exception. Seeing my book *Deadly Storm* be translated into comic form has been a remarkable joy.[2]

The author's unmitigated satisfaction with the comics adaptation of his book seems rather banal, fodder for an interview in any newspaper, except for two details: neither the book *Deadly Storm*, nor its author Richard Castle, actually exist. The comic is actually a spinoff from the television series *Castle*, and Richard Castle is its (fictional) main character.

At first glance, *Castle* appears to be a run-of-the-mill procedural, conforming to all of our expectations. Thus, for example, it features a tense relationship between Castle and the series' heroine, Detective Kate Beckett, which eventually evolves into the traditional *will they, won't they* banter typical of mainstream films and series. Likewise, its episodic structure, in which every week features a new investigation resolved by the end of the episode, is contrary to the current vogue for serial narratives in what is commonly referred to as "quality television." Instead, it adheres to the classic narrative structure favored by the major networks (ABC, NBC, CBS), because it allows them to rerun episodes regardless of their initial broadcast order. However, upon closer analysis, the series reveals original elements that merit further examination. Foremost among these is the status of the titular character, a writer of uninspired, popular detective novels, who, with the help of the mayor (one of his personal friends), decides to accompany a beautiful young detective

Fig. 36: S3E24 of *Castle* (ABC, 2009–2016): cover mock-up of *Richard Castle's Deadly Storm*.

on her cases. This will eventually inspire him to write a new series of novels starring detective Kate Beckett's fictional twin, Nikki Heat.

Throughout the television series, the writing and publication of four of these novels are mentioned—and, as they were announced in the show, those same books actually appeared in bookstores. They were published by Hyperion Books, "written" by "Richard Castle" (complete with an author's photo of Nathan Fillion, the actor who plays the title role, on the back cover), without any overt indication giving away its unique nature. In the final episode of season three, Castle reveals that one of his earliest novels, *Deadly Storm*, is going to be adapted into a graphic novel—and, once again, the comic in question was just about to be published by Marvel Comics. When the graphic novel actually did appear, during the beginning of the following season, a thematic episode of *Castle* entitled "Heroes and Villains"[3] aired, in which the murderer appears to be dressed up in superhero costumes. The Castle/ Beckett duo investigates the case in a shop specializing in comics, where a display filled with copies of *Deadly Storm* occupies the entire screen at a certain point (fig. 36). The character's enthusiasm for the adaptation of his work essentially works to reinforce some of his traits in the series, namely, his vanity and refusal to grow up (his "Peter Pan complex"), as mirrored through his teenage passion for comics.

The idea of adapting the imaginary work of a fictional author in a TV series into a real graphic novel is quite unusual, if not unique. As such, it is of particular interest for both the theory and practice of adaptation. Indeed, the graphic novel *Deadly Storm* seems to be a deliberate attempt to problematize the nature of adaptation. Fittingly, the comic starts with a close-up of Derrick Storm, the protagonist, who is holding the camera he uses to get video evidence of one of his clients' infidelity, a choice that reminds the reader of the audiovisual nature of the source text; in the pages that follow, the focus is on the text, most notably through the protagonist's inner monologue. Interestingly, the text of the graphic novel's version of a "voice-over" is printed in a font reminiscent of an old Smith Corona typewriter, invoking the virtual source text, i.e., the Derrick Storm novel series which made Richard Castle a bestselling author in the world of the television series.

From a theoretical point of view, the graphic novel undermines the question that has tormented adaptation scholars from the beginning, a question they cannot escape: "Is the book better?" *Deadly Storm* is, indeed, an adaptation. (Its full title is *Castle: Richard Castle's Deadly Storm*, and the logo of the broadcasting company and production house, ABC, figure on the cover of the American version, in case the potential readers have not yet grasped the connection with the series.) But what exactly has been adapted? The fictitious source text, the novel *Deadly Storm*, does not exist, and unlike the novels featuring the protagonist Nikki Heat, which were the first spinoffs of the *Castle* series, the *Derrick Storm* books are supposed to have been written before the stories in the television series. The books starring Nikki Heat may refer to the events of the series and help to better understand the relationship between the protagonist and the other characters: Detective Nikki Heat is assisted by Jameson Rook, a journalist who follows the investigations to write articles about them, and who later becomes her lover. The parallel between Nikki Heat and Jameson Rook, on the one hand, and between Richard Castle and Kate Beckett, on the other, is clear (the rook, of course, being a reference to the chess piece that can be "castled" in a strategic move). The graphic novel *Deadly Storm*, however, has only the protagonist as a possible referent, and the association between Castle and Storm is deeply problematic, as the series begins when Castle, the author, despite the advice of his agent and his peers, kills off his character because he finds he has nothing left to teach him. What, then, is being adapted in the comic?

A first answer would no doubt be that *Deadly Storm* adapts the expectations of the comic book aficionado. Indeed, one could see the complex relationship between the source text (series) and the graphic novel itself as a reference to the very medium into which it is being adapted. After all, American comic books are well known for traditionally being only loosely connected to one another, often foreswearing continuity or coherence for the sake of a good story. Similar to the series, the graphic novel seems to favor an episodic form. Like *Castle*, *Deadly Storm* also tells a tale that begins and ends within a single issue, unlike the unbearable suspense of the cliffhanger that often characterizes classic comic books in the American tradition. The fact that the graphic novel is presented twice in the series, first simply as cover art in the last episode of season three, and then in an episode that deals with comics culture and superheroes in season four, suggests that the series is cross-promoting its tie-in; the fact that the second episode addresses comics culture explicitly also testifies to an intention to highlight the medium. Indeed, while at the beginning of the series a number of police officers express their distrust of the writer—asking whether his novels were available as audiobooks, teasing Beckett who is a fan and wrote her name in the books (1.1, "Flowers for Your Grave")—these same officers are impressed when they learn that *Deadly Storm* has been deemed worthy of being transformed into a comic (3.24, "Knockout").

The episode "Heroes and Villains" (4.2) provides an opportunity to remind the viewer of the prevalence of comics in popular culture, in that it shows the influence of various comic book characters on the killer who disguises himself as a superhero and kills his victims with a samurai sword. The focus on the superhero may also be an allusion to the career of Nathan Fillion. Fillion, who plays the role of Richard Castle in the series, died very memorably in his role as a demented preacher in episode 7.22 ("Chosen") of *Buffy the Vampire Slayer* (WB, 1997–2003) by being literally sliced in two—and the same outlandish death is the fate of the victim in the "Heroes and Villains" episode. Fillion has also lent his voice to legendary comics figures like the Green Lantern (Chris Berkeley, Lauren Montgomery and Jay Olivia, 2011) and Steve Trevor in *Wonder Woman* (Lauren Montgomery, 2009), as well as short film collections, and as Vigilante in *The Justice League Unlimited* (2004–2006); he even parodied a superhero as Captain Hammer in *Dr. Horrible's Sing-Along Blog* (Joss Whedon, 2008).

Of course, this raises a number of questions: why this emphasis on superheroes while the graphic novel being promoted has a plot supposedly lifted from a detective novel? Perhaps the answer is to be found in the image of the series: *Deadly Storm* effects a fusion between two traditions: the police procedural as presented in *Castle*, and the comics, especially their adaptation to the screen, be it small or silver. This hybridity is evident in the visual elements of the graphic novel, with graphics reminiscent of comics, but a depiction of lighting and angles that cannot fail to remind the reader of film noir.

In a sense, it is as much an adaptation of a genre as of the fictional universe to which *Castle* belongs. The graphic novel clearly positions itself as an adaptation of the quintessential *noir* novel (or hard-boiled novel in the purely literary tradition), with the protagonist a private detective/CIA operative whose relationship with a mysterious and experienced *femme fatale* on a case leads to excessive first-person narration and plotlines reminiscent of Raymond Chandler's novels (or rather, a second-rate imitation). The stereotypical aspects of the narrative (indeed, the very names of the characters, Derrick Storm and Clara Strike) make it obvious that the book is a tongue-in-cheek adaptation of the *noir* genre; though the character Richard Castle is a best-selling author, he has no qualms in admitting that he is not a particularly talented one, to the extent that he actually makes fun of Beckett for reading some of his lesser-known works, including a novel called *Hell Hath no Fury* with "witches thirsting for vengeance" (1.1), and Beckett mocks his purple prose at a reading of his latest Derrick Storm novel (1.3).

Moreover, upon closer inspection, it becomes clear that the plot is a reworking of a famous neo-noir film, *Chinatown* (Roman Polanski, 1974). The complexity of the film's plot, so typical of film noir, makes it almost impossible to summarize, so I will limit myself to a comparison of the most compelling similarities. Early on in the film, the private detective, Jake, who was hired to investigate a husband's faithfulness, takes compromising photos. He discovers that his client is in no way the wife of the man in question. He then meets the actual wife, Evelyn, with whom he will examine the case to try and understand her husband's adultery and his subsequent murder. After a brief affair with Jake, Evelyn eventually dies while protecting her sister Catherine, who was born out of an incestuous relationship and is therefore also her daughter. The comic also opens with a detective spying on a man suspected of adultery, Jefferson Grout/Daniel Sanchez, for his supposedly beleaguered spouse. Said spouse, it turns out, is actually a spy, while the supposed adulteress is actually his wife, whom he is trying to protect by keeping her in hiding. The graphic novel ends with the death of Clara Strike, who dragged our hero into the world of espionage and sacrificed herself to save her protégé. These allusions to *Chinatown*, a New Hollywood version of the classical film noir, heighten the adaptive aspect of the graphic novel as the textual transposition of a visual source, and link it back to screen versions of classic *noir* plots like *Chinatown*, and in a much more derivative fashion, a procedural that emphasizes detective stories like *Castle* itself.

Of course, it is also an adaptation of fiction to the multimedia platforms that are so ubiquitous today. In keeping with the tendency to flood audiences with behind the scenes bonuses, cast interviews, novelizations, companion volumes, etc. (whether on the DVD or in the mass media), *Castle* creators chose to take merchandising one step further. By creating these novels, whether the *Nikki Heat* novels or the *Derrick Storm* graphic novels, the creators are able to "fill in the gaps" in a way that is much subtler and ultimately more satisfying than a simple novelization.

We are thus dealing with a transmedia work *par excellence* that takes advantage of the vertical and horizontal concentration of media: Disney Studios is the parent company of not only ABC, the broadcasting and production company of the series, but also Hyperion Books, which publishes the *Nikki Heat* novels, as well as Marvel Entertainment, which creates the graphic novels. It also addresses two different audiences. Fans of the series, of course, are likely to buy the novels that have established the renown of Richard Castle as he appears in the fictional television universe (in this case, the "back story" is literal rather than figurative). On the other hand, Marvel Comics seems to have chosen an author who is sure to appeal to comic book fans: Brian Michael Bendis is one of the most popular contemporary comic book writers, having written many episodes of *The Avengers* and *Spider-Man*, thus helming the renaissance of both franchises. By using Bendis, the graphic novel *Deadly Storm* takes its place within the lineage of Marvel's most respected authors (including Stan Lee, whose name is used as a pseudonym for a comic book author in "Heroes and Villains"), adding an additional title to the staple of crossovers[4] that secured Marvel's success. Targeting this double audience for the comics is based on a perceptive analysis of the television series' audience; although produced with the general public in mind, a niche of viewers watches out of devotion to Nathan Fillion, a recurring actor in the work of Joss Whedon, and a veritable "Geek God" in his own right, especially given his enthusiasm for comics.

Lastly, this graphic novel adapts the series that inspired it, and especially the episode in which it appears. The preface of the comic, which first speaks of adaptation, then goes on to reflect on the influence of Marvel comics on the (virtual) oeuvre of Richard Castle:

> From a young age, I aspired to be one of those complicated, hard-charging heroes driven by circumstance and fate to do what was right, no matter the personal cost. [. . .] I don't think it's an exaggeration to say that my early love of these comic characters had a huge influence on me during the creation of Derrick Storm. There's no doubt that Derrick, my rugged and morally complicated Private Investigator turned CIA spy who fights the forces of darkness and conspiracy at every turn, owes much to those rainy days I spent buried beneath an avalanche of dog-eared comics, living out adventures far beyond my imagination.

It is hardly a coincidence that the episode in which *Deadly Storm* is presented focuses on the origin stories of superheroes and the traumatic events that led to their career choice. Just like Spider-Man, Batman, and Iron Man, the woman who inspires Castle, Kate Beckett, also experienced a defining moment that changed her life forever. It was the death of her mother that made her choose a career as police detective, just like the superhero in that episode (who is actually a girl, thereby both subverting gender stereotypes in comics and reinforcing the parallel with Beckett), who chose the path of "vigilantism" to exact revenge for her father's death. It seems that origin myths are essential to understanding the nature of what makes people who they are, as Castle puts it himself in the episode. Clearly, the writers of the show want to highlight the relationship between the protagonist and the comics, suggesting that in order to understand the character of Castle in the series, one must also grasp the character of Storm. When we learn that the superheroine and the creator of the comics who recounts her adventures are in love, but that the woman—also a police officer—hesitates between her quest for vengeance and committing herself to a relationship, the series becomes almost theatrical in a scene where each of the two protagonists confronts his or her double—the cop/superhero for Beckett, the comics creator for Castle—in order to express their views on this relationship. In episode 4.2, the character of the series can be seen in the foreground, while the camera focuses on the member of the couple in the background [38:40–40:22]. In the grand tradition of American comics, the viewer can see the hero very clearly behind his alter ego.

In more general terms, *Castle* is a series that interrogates the idea of adaptation (in the broad sense) and its stakes from the very outset. Castle gets to meet Beckett and follows the investigation because someone is imitating the murders described in his books. The deep-seated *raison d'être* of adaptation—the willingness of the audience to remain within the fictional world of the artist—is part of the conflict that animates the whole series, namely, the relationship between fiction and reality.

The duo of the writer and the tough female cop (and their resulting conflicts) clearly embodies this relationship between "reality" and "fiction." To return to the episode that showcases the comic, it is thanks to the rereading of comics, and the album that inspires the acts of the heroine in particular, that the puzzle is solved by reading between the lines, or more precisely outside the panels. Castle realizes that the comics are dated after the incidents they recount, enabling him to determine that the author has somehow taken part in the events. In the same way, we must look beyond the small screen if we are to understand our titular hero and read between the lines. The series is clear in its derision for those who cannot distinguish fiction and reality; it questions the quest for justice on an individual rather than an institutional level, as we see in the ongoing debate between police officers Ryan and Esposito:

> ESPOSITO: He got what was coming to him.
> RYAN: Dude, that's for the criminal justice system to decide.
> ESPOSITO: Well, maybe a sword is a justice system.
> RYAN: Yeah, if you're Quentin Tarantino, maybe. [4.2, 5:19–5:26]

The series has always entertained a complex relationship with fiction. A fictional work itself, it highlights its ability to transport us to an enthralling world where justice is spectacular and, in the case of the series, where it only takes one hour to resolve crime cases with determination and humor, all the while insisting that on its fictional nature.

What is so fascinating about this series and its spinoffs, and what ultimately distinguishes it from others of its ilk, resides in its postmodern self-awareness. It is this aspect of the series that is most clearly adapted from screen to page. The dumbed-down *Chinatown* references, the B-series tropes are each served up with a touch of humor and an awareness of the profoundly generic nature of its narrative. It is not about mere repetition; it is pastiche, which prompts the reader to ask whether film noir is still possible without irony in the postmodern world we inhabit. Similarly, the show's recognition that it is but one amongst the many other police series saturating the screens, that it exploits every cliché that Castle, a hack writer, glories in when solving crimes, makes it a much subtler police series than the host of others on the air. By deciding to not just adapt the series from one medium to another, but to add elements to the fictional world of the source, *Deadly Storm* opens new perspectives on adaptation.

Notes

1. In the French translation the title is rendered as *Richard Castle présente : La Dernière aube, une histoire de Derrick Storm* (*Richard Castle Presents: The Last Dawn, A Story by Derrick Storm*).

2. As the comic is not paginated, the quotes will necessarily omit page numbers.

3. Episode 2 of season 4 of the series; henceforth 4.2.

4. The term means "to cross barriers," and refers, for example, to a story that crosses separate worlds (*The Avengers*, which brings together Marvel superheroes) or passes from one medium to another (from TV to comics).

Works Cited

Bendis, Brian, Michael Deconnick, and Sue Kelly. *Castle: Richard Castle's Deadly Storm*. New York: Marvel Entertainment, 2011.

Bendis, Brian, Michael Deconnick, and Sue Kelly. *Castle: Richard Castle's Storm Season*. New York: Marvel Entertainment, 2012.

Castle. Created by Andrew W. Marlowe. With Nathan Fillion (Richard Castle) and Stana Katic (Kate Beckett). Beacon Pictures / Experimental Pictures / ABC Studios, 2009–2016. DVD. Disney, 2017.

Castle, Richard. *A Bloody Storm*. New York: Hyperion Books, 2012. Kindle edition.

Castle, Richard. *A Brewing Storm*. New York: Hyperion Books, 2012. Kindle edition.

Castle, Richard. *Frozen Heat*. New York: Hyperion Books, 2012.

Castle, Richard. *Heat Rises*. New York: Hyperion Books, 2011.

Castle, Richard. *Heat Wave*. New York: Hyperion Books, 2009.

Castle, Richard. *Naked Heat*. New York: Hyperion Books, 2010.

Castle, Richard. *A Raging Storm*. New York: Hyperion Books, 2012. Kindle edition.

"New York Times Bestseller List: Hardcover Graphic Books." *New York Times*, October 16, 2011. https://www.nytimes.com/books/best-sellers/2011/10/16/hardcover-graphic-books/?_r=0. Accessed on May 7, 2013.

CONTRIBUTORS

Jan Baetens is professor of Cultural Studies at the University of Leuven. He has published widely on contemporary French literature, as well as word-image relations, mainly in so-called minor genres (comics, photo novels, and novelizations). He has recently published *The Graphic Novel: An Introduction* (Cambridge University Press, 2015, with Hugo Frey) and *À Voix haute*, an essay on the public reading of poetry (Les Impressions Nouvelles, 2016). A published poet, he is the author of some fifteen collections of poetry, including the recent *La Lecture* (Les Impressions Nouvelles, 2017, with Milan Chlumsky).

Alain Boillat is professor in the Department of Film History and Aesthetics at Université de Lausanne, Switzerland. His research interests include the history and theory of screenwriting, the role of the voice and orality in audiovisual apparati (*Du bonimenteur à la voix-over*, 2007), technological imaginaries, the relationship between comics and cinema, and, more generally, questions of intermediality associated with adaptation, narration, and fiction in media productions. He is the author of *Cinéma, machine à mondes. Essai sur les films à univers multiples* (2014) and the cofounder of the film studies journal *Décadrages*, of which he has edited several issues. He has recently edited the collected volumes *Dubbing* (2014), *Dialogues avec le cinéma. Approches de l'oralité cinématographique* (2016), *BD-US : les comics vus par l'Europe* (2016), *Case, strip, action!* (2016), and the forthcoming *L'Adaptation. Des livres aux scénarios* (2018).

Philippe Bourdier is associate professor of Film Studies and Education Sciences at the École Supérieure du Professorat et de l'Éducation of the University of Orléans, France. His research focuses on cultural policies of film education and on the training of professions dealing with media education. He has recently published *Formation et éducation par le cinéma : Ufocel informations, la revue professionnelle des instituteurs projectionnistes (1946–1949)* (2017).

Laura Cecilia Caraballo is a curator, researcher, and teacher. After receiving her degree at the Universidad Nacional de La Plata, Argentina, she joined the Chair of History of Media and Contemporary Communication Systems, from 2008 to 2015, at La Plata and spent four years teaching visual communication and cultural industries. Pursuing her research on comics and its visual qualities, and on the interactions between comics and contemporary art, she defended her PhD dissertation in aesthetics at the University Paris Nanterre in 2016. She was in charge of the Heritage Fund at the 9ème Art Gallery in Paris. As a curator, she coauthored the collective exhibition *Briser la glace* in 2016 at the National Contemporary Art Center Le Magasin in Grenoble. She is currently working on a retrospective exhibition of comics artist Alberto Breccia in Toulouse for 2018.

Thomas Faye is associate professor of Spanish at Université de Limoges, France, where he teaches Medieval and Classical Spanish literature and history, as well as translation studies. Having written a PhD dissertation on the semiotics of intralingual translation processes, he is currently exploring (1) the processes of adaptation and rewriting, especially in contemporary Spanish graphic novels; (2) the relationship between text and context, notably storytelling strategies in graphic literature and press illustrations; (3) the treatment of space in graphic novels and press illustrations; and (4) graphic humor. By combining semiotics and linguistics, his work aims to analyze the production of meaning in iconotexts and at the borders of the textual and the literary.

Pierre Floquet is associate professor of English at INP, Bordeaux University. He has written on linguistics applied to cinema, particularly in the cartoons of Tex Avery. Since then, he has organized Tex Avery retrospectives and conferences, and has been a member of the jury at various animation festivals in France and abroad. He has also broadened his research interests to live-action cinema, participating in national and international books and journals. He edited *CinémAnimationS* (2007) and published *Le Langage comique de Tex Avery* in 2009, for which he received the 2011 McLaren-Lambart award for the Best Scholarly Book on animation.

Jean-Paul Gabilliet is professor of American History at Université Bordeaux Montaigne, France. A cultural historian of American comics, he has edited themed issues on comic books in *Transatlantica* (2010) and *Image and Narrative* (2001), and is the author of *R. Crumb* (2012) and *Of Comics and Men: A Culture History of American Comic Books* (2010).

Christophe Gelly is professor of British and American Literature and Film Studies at Université Clermont Auvergne, France. He has worked mainly on film genre, film noir, and adaptation. He has published two book-length studies on Arthur Conan Doyle (Le Chien des Baskerville : *Poétique du roman policier chez Conan Doyle*, 2005) and Raymond Chandler (*Raymond Chandler : Du roman noir au film noir*, 2009), and coedited *Approaches to Film and Reception Theories* (Christophe Gelly and David Roche, 2012). He has also edited the issue of the journal *Écrans* devoted to French literary realism and film adaptation (2016) and coauthored a book-length study of Ang Lee's adaptation of Jane Austen (*Sense and Sensibility*, 2015). He has also written on Alan Moore's adaptation of Lovecraft in *Neonomicon* (in *Lovecraft et l'Illustration*, Christophe Gelly et Gille Ménégaldo, 2017). His main focus is now on general film theory.

Nicolas Labarre is associate professor of American Culture at Université Bordeaux Montaigne, France. His research focuses on North American comics, with an emphasis on issues of genre, legitimacy, and adaptation. He also seeks to approach these issues from a practical angle by creating comics. He maintains a research blog, which can be found at http://picturing.hypotheses.org/. He has recently published *Heavy Metal, l'autre Métal Hurlant* (PUB, 2017), a cultural history of *Heavy Metal* magazine.

Benoît Mitaine is associate professor of Spanish at Université de Bourgogne (Dijon, France). His research interests include Spanish comics and literature. He has edited several books on comics, including *Autobio-graphismes* (2015, with Danielle Corrado and Viviane Alary), *Bande dessinée et adaptation* (2015, with David Roche and Isabelle Schmitt-Pitiot), and *Lignes de front : bande dessinée et totalitarisme* (2012, with Viviane Alary).

David Roche is professor of Film Studies at Université Toulouse Jean Jaurès and vice president of SERCIA (www.sercia.net). He is the author of *Making and Remaking Horror in the 1970s and 2000s* (2014) and *L'Imagination malsaine* (2008), and has edited a themed issue of *Transatlantica* entitled "Exploiting Exploitation Cinema" (2016), as well as the collected volumes *Steven Spielberg: Hollywood Wunderkind and Humanist* (2018), *Bande dessinée et adaptation* (with Benoît Mitaine and Isabelle Schmitt-Pitiot, 2015), *Intimacy in Cinema* (with Isabelle Schmitt-Pitiot, 2014), and *Approaches to Film and Reception Theories* (with Christophe Gelly, 2012). He has published articles on North American and European auteur and horror cinema in *Adaptation*, *E-rea*, *CinémAction*, *Horror Studies*, *Miranda*, *Post-script*, and *Textes & Contextes*. His new book *Quentin Tarantino: Poetics and Politics of Cinematic Metafiction* is forthcoming.

Isabelle Schmitt-Pitiot is assistant professor of English at the Université de Bourgogne (Dijon, France) and secretary of SERCIA. Her research focuses on English-language films and television series, film genres (musicals, Westerns, comedies), and film spectatorship. She has published articles on John Ford, John Huston, Milos Forman, and Woody Allen, as well as *Desperate Housewives* and *Justified*. She is the coeditor of *Intimacy in Cinema* (2014, with David Roche) and of *De l'intime dans le cinéma anglophone* (2015, with David Roche) and *Bande dessinée et adaptation* (2015, with Benoît Mitaine and David Roche).

Dick Tomasovic is professor of Film and Performing Arts Theory at Université de Liège, Belgium. He is also a scientific supervisor at the Bibliothèque des Littératures d'Aventures (BiLA) and often appears on Belgium public radio and television as a cultural commentator. He is the author of several books, including *Le Palimpseste noir* (2002), Freaks, *la monstrueuse parade de Tod Browning* (2006), *Le Corps en abîme, sur la figurine et le cinéma d'animation* (2006), *Kino-Tanz. L'art chorégraphique du cinéma* (2009), and *SHOTS ! Alcool & cinéma* (2015).

Shannon Wells-Lassagne is a professor at Université de Bourgogne (Dijon, France) in television and film adaptation. Her work has appeared in the *Journal of Adaptation in Film and Performance*, *Screen*, and *Critical Studies in Television*. She has coedited special issues of the *Journal of Screenwriting*, *GRAAT Online* and *Interfaces*, as well as a dossier in *Screen*. She has coedited a number of volumes on adaptation, notably *Screening Text* (2013), and recently published a book on adaptation on television (*Television and Serial Adaptation*, 2017).

INDEX

T

U

www.ingramcontent.com/pod-product-compliance
Lightning Source LLC
Chambersburg PA
CBHW031127270326
41929CB00011B/1534

9781496828187